The Sea Dreamer

The Sea Dreamer:

A DEFINITIVE BIOGRAPHY OF

Joseph Conrad

Gérard Jean-Aubry

Translated by Helen Sebba

Doubleday & Company, Inc.
Garden City, New York, 1957

To
André Gide

A man's real life is that accorded him in the thoughts of other men by reason of respect or natural love.

Under Western Eyes. I

Foreword

To THE CHARGE that I have too long withheld from the public this account of the life of a man whose career surpasses the limits of the ordinary, I must reply that, although I was already planning this account during the great novelist's lifetime, his death laid upon me the more urgent duty of enabling French readers to appreciate for themselves the scope, diversity, power, and richness of his work by publishing it in translation. This duty could not be performed except with undivided attention and painstaking care; and no less than twenty years were needed to carry the enterprise to its conclusion.

It was during these years that I gradually succeeded in bringing together the documents that would shed light on the true circumstances of a very checkered life. One glance at the bibliography at the end of this work will show the abundance and variety of its sources, mostly unpublished, and the need for seeking them out, not always without difficulty, in places which were often far apart.

Some time ago I was urged to publish—prematurely—the results of my first inquiries in the form of an introduction to two volumes of Conrad's letters; I agreed, reluctantly, looking upon this as a rough sketch, published in English, preliminary to the precise and detailed account I had in mind; an account called for, not only by so strange a destiny whose motivations I wanted to reveal, but also by my desire to comply with the personal wishes of a man upon whom the exigencies of a seafaring life had left their stamp.

Indeed, it seemed to me impossible to recount the successive phases of a seaman's life except in the precise and detached fashion of a ship's log. Others may perhaps, in time to come, paint portraits in their own style: the first thing needed was to set down the indisputable facts. Their singularity, and the singularity of their inter-

7

play, would in any event hold the attention of the most casual reader.

The reader will also understand why wartime conditions caused a further delay in the publication of this book, which was almost finished when the war broke out.

We have here, then, for the first time, the "Life of Joseph Conrad" as complete as I have been able to make it. Though I have been at pains to conceal the documentary framework of the work itself, nothing has been put forward here that is not supported by proof. Wherever a gap still exists, it has been indicated, so that perhaps some more fortunate student may one day fill it.

As my research went on, it became increasingly clear that the writer's work reproduced the man's experiences during the first part of his life, far more than had been supposed, and as a rule with perfect fidelity. This is why I have at every opportunity used excerpts from his works to show, along with their authenticity, the force and permanence of the impressions that gave birth to them. The story of this life thus casts penetrating light upon the conditions and character of Conrad's artistic creation.

In the course of the twenty and more years spent on this work I have received from many people help, information, suggestions and advice which have been invaluable to me. I should like to set down here the names of these people, uniting today in the same gratitude the living and the dead.

Mrs. Joseph Conrad; Mademoiselle Angèle Zagórska; Madame Luniewska, nèe Rakowska; Mademoiselle Cécile Zoltowska.

M. Zaleski, Minister of Foreign Affairs of the Republic of Poland; M. Skirmunt, Polish Ambassador to the Court of St. James; Mademoiselle Cécile Podoska and M. F.-B. Czarnowski of the Polish Embassy in London; M. Zsuk Skarjewski of Cracow.

M. and Madame Cyprien Godebski; M. Spiridion Kliszczewski. Sir Sidney Colvin; Sir Edmund Goose; Sir Hugh Clifford.

Mr. John Galsworthy; Mr. H. G. Wells; Mr. R. Cunninghame Graham; Mr. Edward Garnett; Mr. Edward Lancelot Sanderson; Mr. Henry James (nephew of the novelist); Mr. T. J. Wise; Mr. Basil Lubbock.

Mr. Eric Pinker.

M. Savinien Mérédac of Curepipe, Mauritius.

M. le Directeur de la Société Anonyme Belge pour le Commerce du Haut-Congo; M. Berthet, Administrateur de la Marine, Le Havre; M. Nègre, Administrateur de la Marine, Marseilles; M. Joseph Colmain, Commis de l'Inscription Maritime, Marseilles.

Captain Nicholson, secretary of The Ship Masters' Association, London; M. Busquet, archivist for the Département Bouches-du-Rhône and M. François Prieur of the "Petit Provençal."

G. J-A.

Contents

The Sea Dreamer

being gifted people, great talkers with sharp tongues, but not very skillful in managing their affairs.

Apollo Nalecz Korzeniowski had started school in Kamieniec and continued his studies in Niemirov and Winnica; he had attended the *Gymnasium* in Jitomir in Volhynia. With this haphazard schooling and with his kind of character, he completed his education there without distinction and without acquiring any sort of solid knowledge. But before his twentieth year, in 1840, the vivacity of his mind and the ardor of his temperament were already assuring his success in Jitomir society.

At this time, wanting to get to know the world, he applied for a passport for Berlin, proposing to go from there to Italy and France. Upon being refused any passport at all, he resigned himself briefly and halfheartedly to taking Oriental Languages at St. Petersburg, but he soon abandoned this in favor of the Faculty of Arts where he felt much more at home.

Uninterested in the curriculum, he turned out to be an avid reader, particularly in French literature. In his teens he had shown a poetic talent which, while never reaching great heights, was well above average. This talent, together with a certain studied elegance in his dress, set him apart from the country squires with whom he associated during his vacations in his Polish province. Although he was not generally considered handsome, he was not without charm. He had a quick and often biting wit despite his basic kindliness, an animated expression and, pervading his whole personality, a kind of flame capable of kindling more hearts than one. He was the spoiled darling of the salons where he dominated his elders by the charm of his light conversation and the fear of his sarcasm, while treating them with the "Old Poland" courtesy that came completely naturally to him. As for the young people, he attracted them by his enthusiasm, his generosity, and his spiteful remarks.

In 1847, while he was staying in Korytna, near Lipwiec, he met Evelina Bobrowska, who was then sixteen and whose brother Thaddeus he had met in St. Petersburg. The girl was beautiful; her education was superior to that of most women of her position; her mind was keen; and a modest, angelic seriousness added to her charms. Apollo Korzeniowski fell in love almost immediately, with a passion that held him spellbound. The girl was not unconscious of the impression she had made, yet she had to fight against her feelings in obedience to the wishes of her father who, despite his liking for the young man, did not see in him the makings of a son-in-law. The father died when she was only nineteen, but Evelina Bobrowska had no wish to be unfaithful to a memory extremely dear to her or to seem to disregard a judgment which she had invariably respected and followed. For five years she led a life of mental stress, torn by conflicting impulses, until her already precarious health broke down.

Her whole family was upset. Madame Bobrowska could not bear the thought of losing her only remaining daughter through obstinacy: besides, she liked the young man, and he was a great friend of her sons, who adored their sister. After six or seven years' delay, the marriage had finally been agreed upon.

At this time, Apollo Korzeniowski, impelled by the need to find a job so that he might marry Evelina Bobrowska, was managing the property of Countess Mélanie Sobanska, at Luczynczyk in Podolia. This little Podolian town, moreover, was not far from Nielmirov, the residence of Stefan Buszczynski, at that time a young writer and philosopher, who consistently encouraged Apollo in his literary labors and who had recommended him to Joseph Kraszewski, the best known Polish novelist of this period.[1]

The young couple spent their first year in this simple but spacious country residence, while awaiting the sale of the Oratov property and the settlement of Joseph Bobrowski's estate. The following year, the sale having gone through and his wife's dowry having been paid (a very modest dowry: eight thousand rubles, some silver, a trousseau, some furniture and a carriage constituted the fortune of the young bride), Apollo Korzeniowski rented the Derebczynka property in the district of Mohilov with the idea of developing it. Toward the end of autumn Madame Korzeniowska spent some time on a neighboring estate which belonged to one of her maternal uncles and it was there, at Terechowa, near Berdichev, on November 21, 1857, that she gave birth to the son who was to be her only child and who was given the Polish names Teodor Józef Konrad.

---

[1] Józef Ignaz Kraszewski (Warsaw 1812–Geneva 1887), one of Poland's most prolific novelists; he has been compared to Alexander Dumas.

The first two names were those of his grandfathers: the name Konrad had been chosen, not, as it might seem, in memory of Byron's *Corsair* and its strange hero, haunted by the constant desire to break with society, but in memory of the Konrad of Mickiewicz, the central figure in his poem on the *Dziady* (*Forefathers' Eve*). That same day Apollo sent an announcement of the birth to the novelist Joseph Kraszewski, then in Jitomir, whom both he and his bride respected and admired, asking his blessing on their son. This Kraszewski hastened to bestow. Literature, one can see, presided over the first moments of this destiny.

Due to the rigor of the winter and the precarious health of the young mother, the infant was baptized privately, without ceremony. He came close to being baptized at St. Joseph's in Berdichev, the church in which, eight years earlier, the marriage of Madame de Hanska, née Rzewuska, to Honoré de Balzac had been solemnized. Wierchownia, Madame de Hanska's estate, was only about ten miles away, and the visits of the French novelist were still a frequent topic of conversation in neighboring houses.

Until the beginning of spring, 1859, the young couple lived almost continuously on the Derebczynka estate, but the failure of the tenancy, which in less than three years had consumed their whole fortune, and even part of Madame Bobrowska's—for she had taken a third share in the lease—determined Apollo Korzeniowski once more to try his luck elsewhere: this time in Jitomir.

He had plenty of connections there, chief among them Joseph Kraszewski, who was approaching fifty and whose personality was the heart and soul of intellectual life in the provincial capital. Apollo Korzeniowski hoped to turn his literary gifts to good account there. His talent had ripened; his reputation was growing. He was offered an executive position in a publishing house called "Publications." He accepted this and set about arranging for the appearance of several of the works he had completed in recent years. He brought out a three-act drama called *A Comedy* and a satirical three-act play in verse *For the Sake of Money,* which was produced very successfully in Jitomir. The Jitomir theater, built by the landowners by subscription, was at that time directed by Kraszewski and had rapidly become the leading provincial stage in Poland.

The year of his son's birth, he had published a translation of De

Vigny's *Chatterton* with an eloquent preface in which he paid homage to the profound humanity of the French poet and to his ideal of noble stoicism. Shortly after his arrival in Jitomir he gave fresh proof of his taste for French poetry by publishing, in collaboration with A. Plug, the translation of the first part of the *Légende des Siècles,* later followed by *Hernani* and *Marion Delorme*—translations held in high esteem to this day.

Yet Apollo Korzeniowski's thoughts were not given over entirely to literary matters. Ardent as he was, he could not have remained deaf to the first appeals of those who were dreaming of liberating Poland from Russian oppression. Right at the beginning of the Crimean War, when a peasants' insurrectionist movement began to emerge in the Ukraine, Apollo Korzeniowski had made contact with the Ukrainian leaders to co-ordinate their action. A representative had been sent to Adam Czartoryski in Paris, but Czartoryski, engaged in a deal with European diplomats from which he expected imminent results, was opposed to Korzeniowski's intentions, particularly since it would not have been easy to get the Poles to accept the idea of a joint rebellion with the Ukrainian peasants, whose crimes of 1846 had not been forgotten and who were regarded as enemies rather than allies.

This had been a great blow to Apollo Korzeniowski, reflected in his poetic output of this period. It had seemed to him that Poland was losing a unique chance in not exploiting Russia's difficulties with the Western powers and Turkey.

Six years had gone by since then: the accession of Czar Alexander II and the political maneuvering of Count Alexander Wielopolski had brought about a mitigation of Russian tyranny in Poland. New hopes arose in those who had never ceased to dream—some of them for more than thirty years—of national liberation; but the opinions of the Polish patriots varied widely as to the best course to follow. The younger men were naturally impatient; they had no liking for Wielopolski's half measures, caution, and shilly-shallying, nor for the hesitations of those who had witnessed the enthusiasm and the debacle of 1831. Two parties had been formed more or less secretly, the Whites and the Reds. Apollo Korzeniowski had friends in both groups, but his whole nature urged him toward the second and he soon became its leading figure. Yet, mindful of the essential interest of his country, he worked for the formation of the "Central Committee," composed of representatives of both wings, whose activities during almost three years prepared the rebellion that was to break out in 1863.

In Volhynia, in Podolia, in the Ukraine, secret bonds were forged and strengthened between patriots. Apollo devoted all his energies to this. Nationalist sentiments began to declare themselves more openly. In Jitomir, in the very church in which the infant Conrad had just been baptized, they sang a hymn with the refrain: "Our fatherland and liberty—give these back to us, O Lord." The Russian police took the names of the demonstrators and threatened to arrest those who, on leaving the church, were explaining the significance of this hymn to the peasants who were not familiar with it. During the services collections were taken up for the nationalist movement. Meetings, more or less clandestine, were held at the houses of Kraszewski, the poet and critic Prusinowski, and Apollo Korzeniowski.

Early in 1861 Korzeniowski received an offer to come to Warsaw and take over the direction of a literary periodical, *The Fortnightly,* which was about to be founded. He accepted the more readily because he had had differences of opinion with the board of "Publications" and because he thought his presence in Warsaw could better serve the activity of the Central Committee.

He arrived there at the beginning of May. His wife and son were to spend some time in the Polish Ukraine, at Nowofastov, between Berdichev and Kiev, on an estate recently acquired by the child's maternal uncle, Thaddeus Bobrowski.

Discontent was rife in the capital. In April Russian troops had, without provocation, fired on a religious procession. In July, after a High Mass celebrated for the death of Adam Czartoryski,[2] the crowd had marched in procession to the Archbishop's palace, to kneel there and receive the prelate's blessing. Everything became a pretext for demonstrations. Defying the laws, women dressed in black as a sign of national mourning; national costume was deliberately worn; little boys caught sparrows and fixed strips of red and white paper to their feet. Yet there were gun emplacements in the squares and Cossacks camping at street intersections. At

[2] Died July 15, 1861.

night pedestrians were arrested and searched, ostensibly for forbidden arms, actually to relieve them of their watches and wallets.

Apollo Korzeniowski had not intended a long separation from his wife and child. The deep affection between them, the closeness of their outlook, their common faith, the ardor of their patriotic convictions—even more intense in the young woman—all this suggests that Evelina Korzeniowska was not ignorant of the real reasons that had impelled her husband to go to Warsaw; she may even have had a hand in it herself.

From Jitomir, at the end of July, the maternal grandmother sent the father some news of his little Conrad:

> There are no words to describe all the shades of goodness in this child. He is very friendly towards the poor, gives them news of the family and asks them to pray for the return of his father from Warsaw. I heard this from the beggars at church.

But two months earlier even, Madame Korzeniowska had written to her husband that Jitomir was no longer a safe place for him to live and that he ran the risk of being arrested there. Korzeniowski thereupon decided to take an apartment at 45 Nowy Swiat, one of the principal streets of Warsaw, in a house quite close to the one where Chopin's family used to live. At the end of the summer the Korzeniowskis were reunited there.

Early in October came the death of the Archbishop of Warsaw, Msgr. Fijalkowski, who had been reproached by the Russians for allowing patriotic hymns to be sung in the churches and whose only answer had been that he was forbidden to interfere in political matters. His last words had been: "Get rid of the Russians!" All Warsaw came to the funeral; even rabbis and Greek Orthodox priests were seen paying tribute at the coffin. This unanimity did not fail to alarm the Russians. On October 14 a state of siege was proclaimed and the cavalry made charges in the streets. On October 15 a Mass was said at St. John's for the anniversary of Kosciuszko's death. Troops surrounded the church and entered it, dealing blows with their rifle butts. Those that refused to disperse and went on singing hymns were taken to the Citadel. An order was issued closing all the churches.

In the house on Nowy Swiat secret meetings were held: an atmosphere of conspiracy reigned, a habit of whispering. Little Conrad watched the coming and going of shadows which seemed to him beyond the usual stature of mankind and which went down an extremely high corridor to a white drawing room with crimson hangings: secret meetings of the Central Committee.

During the night of November 1 the police raided the house, searched the apartment from top to bottom, terrifying the child, and took Apollo Korzeniowski to the Citadel.

Immediately upon hearing of the arrest of her son-in-law, Madame Bobrowska came hurriedly to Warsaw from the Ukraine to be with her daughter and grandson and to mobilize all her connections. It was in vain.

The accused waited more than a fortnight for his first interrogation; the second did not take place until February; the two concluding ones were in March. The main charge was based on his wife's correspondence during the early days of their separation. Apollo Korzeniowski was accused of connections with Count Wielopolski, whom he denied knowing; he was accused of being the author of an anonymous pamphlet entitled *The Union of Lithuania and Poland,* which he had probably edited; he was accused of having incited the workers who, on August 3, the birthday of the Empress, had sung "God Save Poland" and prevented the singing of the official "Te Deum"; in addition he was accused of having planned to escape and of having transmitted to his wife a map showing the location of his cell. Madame Korzeniowska had tried repeatedly to speak to the prisoner, and much later Conrad retained the impression of a visit to the Citadel with her. He remembered himself standing beside his mother in a big prison yard from where he had glimpsed his father's face watching them from behind a barred window.

On the last day of March, 1862, the prisoner addressed to the Commission a handwritten statement denouncing proceedings arising out of the evidence of private letters to which secret meanings had been attributed. The inquiry was completed in mid-April. The Commission, *while admitting that it had no absolute proof* of the charges brought against him, ruled that the accused was a politically dangerous person, according to the report of Colonel

Jalobow who, in Jitomir, considered him as such, and decided to place him under the jurisdiction of the military tribunal, in view of the state of siege existing in the "kingdom." Ten days later the military governor of Warsaw proposed to the lieutenant general of the kingdom that Korzeniowski be deported to Perm, where he was to be kept under police surveillance.

Through a lucky chance, the president of the military commission, Colonel Roznoff, had been a friend of his brother-in-law, Stanislas Bobrowski, in the Grodno Hussars, and these bonds of friendship were probably the reason for the relatively light sentence, which condemned Korzeniowski to be deported to a distant province but not to Siberia.

Governor Laszkareff in Perm was an old university friend of his. From him Apollo Korzeniowski might expect some relaxation of the rules governing political prisoners. Did Laszkareff refuse to accept a relationship that might compromise him? Did higher authorities get wind of this friendship? In any case the convoy was already en route to Perm when the prisoner was informed that he was to proceed, not to the Urals, but to Vologda in northern Russia.

He did not go there alone. His young wife, not wanting to abandon him, had requested the favor of being allowed to accompany him. Permission was granted by the Russian authorities only on condition that she, too, was to be considered a political prisoner, subject to the same rules. Beneath her frail exterior, this thirty-year-old woman had an inflexible will. As her son was to write later: "Meeting with calm fortitude the cruel trials of a life reflecting all the national and social misfortunes of the community, she realized the highest conceptions of duty as a wife, a mother, and a patriot, sharing the exile of her husband and representing nobly the ideal of Polish womanhood." [3]

On the last stage of the journey before Moscow, little Conrad was taken seriously ill. The police escort absolutely refused to interrupt the journey, although the desperate parents declared that nothing but force would induce them to continue. By great good fortune a traveler, moved to pity by what he saw, went on ahead to fetch a professor at the University of Moscow, Dr. Mlodzianowski, whom

[3] *A Personal Record.*

Korzeniowski had known in Winnica. This compatriot came immediately, saved the child, and managed to have the prisoners' departure postponed for a few days until the little invalid was fit to
continue the journey without risk.

A little later, when they were just outside Nijni-Novgorod,
Madame Korzeniowska fell so ill that the escort had to carry
her, but they obstinately refused to break the journey. At one halt,
a passing officer, revolted by the guards' brutality toward the
prisoners and by the insolence with which they replied to his remarks, turned his horse and galloped off toward the town, where
he succeeded in having the guards reprimanded and the young
woman taken to an inn for a few days' convalescence. The convoy
finally reached Vologda in early summer, 1862.

Fortunately the governor of this town, Chominsky, was not
entirely devoid of humanity. He treated the Poles with forbearance.
The little colony of exiles consisted, besides the three Korzeniowskis,
of twenty-one people, mostly priests from the kingdom or from
Lithuania. When winter came, the Vologda climate proved extremely severe. Nearly all the men contracted scurvy, and although
the Korzeniowski family was spared that, they did not escape
anemia.

From this exile in Vologda, there survives a particularly touching
document containing some of the first words penned by the great
writer-to-be, whose hand on this occasion had obviously been
guided by his father's. It is a photograph, printed on the back:
Polish photograph—Stanislas Kraƙow—Vologda, with this inscription in the writing of little Conrad: *To my dear grandmother who
helped me to send caƙe to my poor father in prison—Pole, Catholic,
gentleman. July 6, 1863. Konrad.*

At this time life became even harder for the exiles. To the de-
pressing effects of the rigorous climate were added grievous blows
to their nationalist sentiments and their family affections. The
rebellion prepared by the Central Committee had failed, and bitter
reprisals were being taken. Apollo's brothers were among the
victims. One, Robert, who had hitherto shown no devotion to anything except gambling, had been killed in action; the other, Hilary,
had been arrested by the Russian authorities before the rising and
deported to Tomsk in Siberia, where he was to die ten years later.

Madame Korzeniowska, for her part, had just lost her youngest and most brilliant brother, Stefan Bobrowski, a remarkably gifted young man, a member of the provisional government of 1862, who had met his death, shortly before the rebellion, in a duel with Count Grabowski, one of the leaders of the Whites.

Moreover, hardships began to be felt in Vologda. His arrest had taken Apollo Korzeniowski by surprise: the family was almost without resources and owed its survival only to the generosity of one of the young woman's brothers, Casimir Bobrowski, who, without telling his family or even his sister, sent his brother-in-law all the money he could raise, one or two thousand rubles.

From the moment he arrived in Vologda, Apollo Korzeniowski had established his leadership among the other exiles and had become, so to speak, the soul of the band of Polish prisoners. Helped by his wife, he managed to keep up their morale, alleviate the sadness of their exile, foster their patriotic convictions. One of his companions in exile later reported that, through his inspiration, the band of Polish exiles won not only the respect of the Russians but even their friendship. Governor Chominsky and the colonel of the gendarmes often came to visit the Korzeniowskis socially.

Meanwhile, Madame Korzeniowska's health, never robust, was deteriorating visibly, while Apollo had aged ten years under the misfortunes visited upon his country and his family in the past six months. Toward the end of July, 1863, at the governor's request, the exiles were allowed to leave Vologda and were transferred to Chernikov, in a more southerly region—comparatively—closer to their home province, about a hundred and twenty miles northeast of Kiev.

Thanks to connections once made by Stanislas Bobrowski in St. Petersburg society, an influential person obtained for Madame Korzeniowski a three months' leave from exile. In August, 1863, leaving her husband in Chernikov (for it goes without saying that the Russian authorities had not granted him a similar favor), Madame Korzeniowska left for her brother's estate at Nowofastov, taking her little six-year-old boy with her.

That summer relatives and friends came from far and near to show their affection and admiration for this courageous young woman who kept her patriotic faith despite recent disasters. They were the more anxious to come since some of them were probably not unaware that Evelina's state of health was hopeless. The severe climate of Vologda, the privations, the national tragedies, had broken down a constitution long since undermined by personal grief. Her only chance would have been a long stay in a more favorable climate and in the affectionate atmosphere of her brother's home. Thaddeus Bobrowski applied for an extension of his sister's visit, but in vain. The only answer was a refusal. A month before the expiration of her leave she was suddenly taken so ill that it seemed impossible that she should ever be fit to go back to exile. The governor general of Kiev was asked to grant the invalid a fortnight's delay. No reply came. A few days later at dusk the captain of the local *gendarmerie* came to talk to Thaddeus Bobrowski and, without any preliminaries, handed him an official form.

"There. Pray read this. I have no business to show this paper to you. It is wrong of me. But I can't either eat or sleep with such a job hanging over me."

That police captain, a native of Great Russia, had been for many years serving in the district.

Thaddeus Bobrowski unfolded the document. It was a service order from Governor General Bezak to disregard all remonstrances and explanations in regard to the condition of the sick woman, either from medical men or others. "And if she has not left her brother's house," the document went on to say, "on the morning of the day specified on her permit, you are to despatch her at once under escort, direct" (underlined) "to the prison-hospital in Kiev, where she will be treated as her case demands."[4]

Conrad, a little boy of six at the time, was unaware of all this. With the carefree confidence of early childhood, he did not realize the seriousness of his mother's condition, or that the doctors had already given her up. He had found a playmate: his uncle's little girl, Josefina, a charming, lively little cousin, a few months younger than himself, destined to die at thirteen. There were also neighboring children to play with. Little Conrad, who had never since his birth had any company but that of adults, in an atmosphere of anxiety, worry, and mourning, was at last having a happy life. It lasted only three months.

[4] Ibid.

Among the members of the family who came to see the young exile, one in particular made a deep impression on the child. He was a thin man with white hair and a curved nose: a figure always buttoned up to his chin in a military overcoat—none other than his maternal great-uncle, Nicholas Bobrowski, former lieutenant in the French Army from 1811 to 1814 and aide-de-camp to Marmont, then captain in the Second Light Cavalry Regiment of the Polish Army, Chevalier de la Légion d'Honneur, and holder of the Military Cross for Valor. These distinctions aroused in the child a great respect for the taciturn old man; but one exploit in this heroic existence had filled him with a crowning wonder, both attracting and repelling him. Great-Uncle Nicholas always remained for him the unfortunate being who once upon a time had eaten a dog: a ghastly extremity into which he had been forced by the hardships of the retreat from Russia.

"I could not have eaten that dog," said the shuddering child.

"Perhaps you don't know what it is to be hungry," replied his grandmother with a smile.

And to get rid of this feeling of horror the child ran to the stables, where Joseph, his grandmother's groom, a young man in a dark blue cap and wide Cossack's trousers, would throw him up on a pony and take him on the leading rein, followed by the anxious eyes of his mother. Those were happy days.

Yet however carefree childhood might be, it could not remain untouched by such impressions as the day when mother and son, driven out by the heartlessness of the Russian authorities, had to tear themselves away from the loving arms of grandmother, uncles, and friends to set out on their return to exile. These memories remained forever etched on Conrad's heart. Forty-five years later, in *A Personal Record*, he brought them to life again with restrained emotion:

> The elongated, *bizarre*, shabby travelling-carriage with four post-horses, standing before the long front of the house with its eight columns, four on each side of the broad flight of stairs. On the steps, groups of servants, a few relatives, one or two friends from the nearest neighborhood, a perfect silence; on all the faces an air of sober concentration; my

grandmother, all in black, gazing stoically; my uncle giving his arm to my mother down to the carriage in which I had been placed already; at the top of the flight my little cousin in a short skirt of a tartan pattern with a deal of red in it, and like a small princess attended by the women of her own household; the head *gouvernante,* our dear, corpulent Francesca (who had been for thirty years in the service of the B[obrowski] family), the former nurse, now outdoor attendant, a handsome peasant face wearing a compassionate expression, and the good, ugly Mlle. Durand, the governess, with her black eyebrows meeting over a short thick nose, and a complexion like pale brown paper. Of all the eyes turned towards the carriage, her good-natured eyes only were dropping tears, and it was her sobbing voice alone that broke the silence with an appeal to me: *"N'oublie pas ton français, mon chéri."* In three months, simply by playing with us, she had taught me not only to speak French but to read it as well. She was indeed an excellent playmate.

In the distance, half way down to the great gates, a light, open trap, harnessed with three horses in Russian fashion, stood drawn up on one side with the police captain of the district sitting in it, the vizor of his flat cap with a red band pulled down over his eyes.

All this time, in a little house in a suburb of Chernikov, Apollo Nalecz Korzeniowski was fighting his loneliness by translating Victor Hugo, his favorite writer. He had published, in the Polish Library edition, a new comedy entitled *What Shall I Do With It?*. He had tried his hand at translating some English authors and that summer was finishing a version of Dickens' *Hard Times.* At the same time, still obsessed with the nationalist problem, he was writing a study on *Poland and Moscow.*

Back in Chernikov, Madame Korzeniowska began to sink fast. During the summer of 1864 her mother, growing more and more worried, came to help her take care of little Conrad, for, despite all her motherly love, the invalid could not longer attend to him properly. Apollo Korzeniowski, grieving over the ruin of his political dreams and in his daily anxiety about his wife's health, was stricken by a new blow: the sudden death of his father at Dubno, where he had gone to keep an eye on the lawsuit of his son Hilary.

At New Year, 1865, it was Thaddeus Bobrowski's turn to visit the exiles. Appalled at his sister's condition, he forced her to consult Dr. Romanski, whom he had brought with him from Jitomir and who held out a slim chance of saving her. Thaddeus Bobrowski came back to see his sister again in February: the consumption had made frightful gains and the doctor told him that Madame Korzeniowska was doomed. Apollo Korzeniowski himself was not unaware of his wife's condition, as can be seen from a passage in a letter he wrote to his friend Casimir Kaszewski [5] on February 26, 1865:

> For several years my poor wife has been dying of homesickness and of the series of blows that have fallen on members of our families. For four months she has been cruelly and very gravely ill. The lack of everything here that might sustain her heart and body, the lack of a doctor and medical treatment is the cause of her plight. For several months I have had to be both master and servant in our house; I don't complain except that so often I cannot manage to satisfy or comfort her. Of course, our little Conrad is sadly neglected in the midst of all this.

In this gloomy atmosphere the child was growing up in silence. At home, a mother who grew weaker every day; a father bowed down by grief, steeling himself against the anxieties of a hopeless situation; outside, people whom the Poles could only consider enemies and who were deeply suspicious of them.

Two days later the father once more opened his despairing heart to his friend:

> Homesickness, like rust, has slowly eaten away my poor wife's constitution. For the last year and a half she put it all down to nerves. Very worried, I did something I could never have done for myself: I begged, entreated that our place of residence be changed. Having been refused again and again,

---

[5] Kasimierz Kaszewski (1813–90). An outstanding critic and translator of classical writers and a man of great philosophical learning, then living in Warsaw.

I have lost all hope. For several months now there has been fever, consumption, and an internal tumor caused by bad circulation, which calls for an operation. . . . Only her mind remains untouched. Doesn't she realize her condition or is she accepting it with courage? Who could read it in her eyes, if I, for whom they were an open book, can decipher nothing? Only, sometimes, a squeeze of her hand in mine or in little Conrad's gives proof of her valiance. We are indeed wretched and unhappy now, but we thank God for at least allowing us to bear everything together.

A few days later, at the beginning of March, Madame Bobrowska and her son Thaddeus, summoned by Apollo to his wife's bedside, arrived back in Chernikov and stayed until the death of Evelina Korzeniowska, who passed away on April 6, 1865, in her thirty-fourth year. She was buried in her place of exile, in the cemetery at Chernikov.

With the wife he adored, Apollo Korzeniowski seemed to lose not only a cherished being, but his very reason for living. The hopes he had fed on for so long had foundered: the crushing shadow of the Russian Empire weighed more heavily than ever upon his country. This death was the final blow to a soul devoid of earthly hope, to a heart that owed its life to her flame and that held nothing but ashes. Apollo Korzeniowski was under no illusions as to his own state: he thought of little but his own approaching end, and his religious faith enabled him to await it calmly. It came less quickly than he expected. He lingered on for another four years, putting his last strength into literary work from which he expected neither profit nor glory. The very day after his wife's death, he was making plans to entrust his son's future to hands more durable than his. To this same friend to whom he had opened his inconsolable heart, he wrote two months later:

Do you remember saying to me in the sadness of our parting, looking at our little Conrad: "If you can't come back soon, send him to me and I will take care of him as my own son"? And now she will never come back and perhaps I, too, will not come back, and little Conrad who is now growing up here with me will have to finish growing up without me. Keep your promise. I want all that remains of her on this earth to be a worthy memorial to all that she was: and who could pass on her moral qualities to him better than you?

Her heart and soul were so wrapped up in this child that if I were to leave him without this certainty or part from him without this hope, I should feel I had been false to that heart and soul. I am arranging for Conrad to have a small legacy, enough to cover his education and leave something over. Now I have made all the necessary sacrifices to provide for his future. He may be a heavy material responsibility for you, but at least not a burden. Tell me, my dear friend, if you will do this for me, so that I may know what instructions I should leave for those who, when the time comes, will take care of little orphaned Conrad.

Deprived of his mother's love, in the company of a sick father who was generaly sunk in speechless grief and whose only distraction lay in reading and the pursuit of letters, an exile among foreigners, Conrad was growing up without playmates in this atmosphere of heartache and sadness that had been his almost without interruption since the first days of his life but which had now become even more oppressive. Repressing his hereditary enthusiasm, in daily touch with the most profound forces: death, faith, patriotism, liberty: brought up in an unswerving secret loyalty to practically unattainable ideals, the child had one single doorway to the world, one single escape for his lively imagination— reading. Shut up with his father, who was now approaching fifty and physically almost worn out and yet, among the ruin of his hopes, still passionately devoted to the greatest monuments of human thought, the child read, indiscriminately and practically unsupervised, books that were generally too heavy for his age. Eager to escape from the atmosphere of despair imposed on him by the special circumstances of his birth, little Korzeniowski, his elbows on his knees, his forehead in his hands, spent long hours reading in the small, sad, silent house on the outskirts of Chernikov. The child reveled in books telling of far-off countries where one could breathe freely, run, shout, act, fight, in the open air instead of whispering beneath this heavy lid which confined them everywhere.

How he would have loved to set out for those remarkable countries where a man could be free, could imagine being free!

Book after book the child read, in two languages, Polish and French: mainly French, because the control of the Russian authorities was less strict there. His father's library in this place of exile was not very extensive; often, finding nothing new to read, nothing to play, nothing to do, he had to open the same old books at the same page and go into long daydreams, conjuring up actions, people, scenes, as if they were real. Gifted from the outset with a vivid imagination, extremely nervous, especially after the series of disasters in his home life, living so intimately with a father touched by the finger of death, for whom this earth no longer held any attraction or hope, little Conrad, now eight years old, with all the strength of his dream, imagined the world.

Life went on in its sadness. Apollo Korzeniowski's health grew worse every day; he was forbidden any kind of activity. He wrote his memoirs of the preparations for the insurrection and read them to his mother-in-law, but he must have destroyed them shortly before his death, for no trace of them was found. He spent his time writing other things, translating favorite works. Sometimes, in his absence, little Conrad would steal into the room where he used to write. One day he found the child perched on a chair, kneeling, his elbows on the table, absorbed in reading his father's translation—still in manuscript—of Shakespeare's *Two Gentlemen of Verona:* his first contact with English literature.

Apollo Korzeniowski hesitated a moment in the doorway, looking at the child, who was expecting to be scolded.

"Read the page aloud," he said.

When the child reached the end of the page, Apollo Korzeniowski nodded. That was all. He had already discerned a feeling for literature in his son, not long ago, when, being ill, he had asked the boy to read aloud from beginning to end the proofs of his translation of *Les Travailleurs de la Mer*—Conrad's first encounter with the ocean.

In this unbroken contact in which both of them choked back their emotions for fear of breaking down, the father had a suspicion, not, to be sure, of his son's future genius, but of the seriousness, melancholy, and desperate restlessness which the unusual conditions of his young life might have developed in him. For the present he busied himself with laying the groundwork—so far as that was possible—of his child's schooling. On September 18, 1865, he wrote to his friend Kaszewski:

> Let me thank you for your kindness to my poor orphan. What you promise him was our dream in days of despair and our stand-by in difficult times. I am overjoyed by your promise to send me textbooks and outlines. I impatiently await its fulfillment. Sell my writing desk to pay for these books. It was her favorite piece of furniture, but she will never again see me working at it. . . . Poor child, he does not know what it is to have a playmate of his own age. All he sees is my sad old age, and, who knows, this outlook may be withering his young heart and freezing his young, awakening soul. That is one of the main reasons that induce me to send this child away from my widowed heart.

In his extreme isolation the father could not resign himself to parting with his son, his only visible link with the past and the future, with the woman he had lost and with his country, so near and yet so unattainable. Some time later he wrote again to this friend—a letter from which the following passage shows that in their daily and, for the most part, wordless contact, he had divined the deep nature of his child and distinguished the singular products of his heredity on both sides.

> I remind you of your promise to send books and a school syllabus for my little Conrad. I would like to prepare him in accordance with requirements. . . . Since autumn my health has been much worse and my darling child has to take care of me. I have no fears for him. As far as his heart goes, he has his mother's qualities; but his head—poor chap—he got from me.

A lengthier document gives a still better idea of the extent of the noble grief, the mystical resignation, of this father who, absorbed in the memory of the woman he had lost and in the assurance of his religious convictions, hardly dared even to think of a future in which, as he could see, he would soon have no part. In a letter he wrote to his cousins, Jan and Gabriella Zagórski, on New Year's Eve, 1866, the following lines occur:

> The little orphan is always at my side and I can never get rid of my anxiety about him. . . . My whole life is centered in my little Conrad. I am teaching him what I know, but that, unfortunately, is not much. I shield him from the atmosphere of this place, and the child grows up as though in a monk's cell. As a monastic *memento mori* we have the grave of our loved one, and every letter we receive from one of the cardinal points is for us a day of fasting, a hair shirt, a chastisement.
>
> If I were to describe my place of exile, I should say that on one side it is bounded by locked doors behind which my beloved breathed her last, while I was not even able to wipe the sweat of death from her brow. The other door is open and, while I may not cross the threshold, I may nonetheless look out beyond it at what Dante *did not* describe, for in his soul, so Christian in spite of the terror that assailed it, there was no room for inhuman visions. Such is our life!

Other extracts from letters from Apollo Korzeniowski to his friend Kaszewski give, in the directness and sincerity of their confessions, far better than any commentary the feel of the atmosphere in which little Conrad, who had just had his eighth birthday, was living:

> When your letter arrived I was in such a state of prostration that I had to ask Conrad to write to you that your letter was the only drop of balm in this useless, worn-out life I lead. (January 31, 1866.)

> I mapped out the French course myself on the pattern of Robertson's English course and I am proud of the excellent result I have obtained with my little boy. But, my friend, I simply must have a geometry book. Apart from that I have everything I need, for the time being, for Conrad's education.
>
> It is not good to be so old; the soul cannot exist in a broken machine, and if I could with my own hands put Conrad in good hands I should have nothing more to wish for. (February 1, 1866.)

My little boy is well and we are working, although many, many hands have a strangle hold on both our throats. Oh, if I could describe those hands what a strange study that would be! Why do you talk to me of my satirical talent? An acquaintance once told me that I write best when I am in a bad mood. (February 11, 1866.)

Only literature still offers the sick, dejected exile a slight personal interest in life:

Did I write to you that for a long time now Victor Hugo and his function as poet and citizen have been the subject of a major work of mine? I am sending you the translation of the introduction and the conclusion of the *Chansons des Rues et des Bois*.[6] They show admirably the scope of the mind of this poet whose hair has grown white; his views on the destiny of inspiration and on the responsibilities that weigh upon the poet. This Victor Hugo is a very learned gentleman. Note how in these songs everything is tastefully arranged, with supreme mastery. (March 4, 1866.)

In May, a year after losing his wife, Apollo Korzeniowski finally decided to part from his son and to entrust him to his brother-in-law. From May to September Conrad lived in the country, at Nowofastov in the Ukraine, in the home of his uncle Thaddeus Bobrowski, building up his health and leading the normal life of a child of nine, in the company of his girl cousin and other neighboring children.

Thaddeus Bobrowski, who had lost his wife when his little girl was born, was then thirty-seven. His character was the exact opposite of Apollo Korzeniowski's. Yet he was a subtle, witty man, very honest and very clear-sighted, but his sane warmheartedness had nothing to do with the romantic spirit. He had refused to take part in the insurrection of 1863, having no confidence in its success.

He had studied law at St. Petersburg and intended to become a professor of international law when, in his twenty-second year, the death of his father caused him to abandon this plan and called him

---

[6] This apparently refers to the poems *Le Cheval* and *Au Cheval* which form the opening and the close of the *Chansons des Rues et des Bois* which had just appeared at the end of 1865.

back to the Ukraine to manage his mother's big estate. He was a quiet man, of great scholarship in legal matters, always ready to use his prestige with the Russian authorities on behalf of compatriots in danger. Although he recognized in his nephew more than one alarming Korzeniowski trait, Uncle Thaddeus extended to Conrad the particular love he had always felt for his own sister.

At the end of the summer Madame Bobrowska took her grandson back to Chernikov, but soon afterward the child's state of health became so alarming that he had to be hastily taken to Kiev to consult a doctor. He spent the whole winter there and returned in spring to complete his recovery at his uncle's.

The father had had the greatest difficulty in deciding to let his son go; the child, for his part, seems to have felt a sort of homesickness for that atmosphere of sad exaltation. This kind of homesickness marks, perhaps, not only a certain affinity of character between father and son, but the early symptoms of that deep-rooted nostalgia which was to permeate the work of the writer.

Stifling his emotions under a superficial irony—an attitude which his son often adopted later, Apollo Korzeniowski spoke of Conrad to his friend Kaszewski in these words:

> Conrad has gone to his uncle in the country. Both of us are unhappy. This child is so foolish that he misses our loneliness and his orphan's existence when he had nothing to look at but my gloomy face, and when education was the only diversion of a nine-year-old. He is pining for me, in spite of the fresh country air and in spite of being able to play with his cousin, just his age. He is pining under the doting wing of his grandmother and the indulgence of his uncle who has transferred to him all the love he bore his sister; and since he considered the unforgotten one a superior being, he surrounds her child with a kind of affectionate respect. He is pining because he is foolish, and I am afraid he may stay that way all his life. He has grown; his face has changed; he is beginning to resemble his mother. May God bless him, for I, alas, can do nothing for him and never shall be able to!

During this visit, which lasted all summer, little Conrad inevitably saw a number of visitors coming to his uncle's house. Thaddeus Bobrowski's reliable judgment brought people from all over the province to ask his advice and to take their problems to him. The integrity of his character, together with his broad culture and distinguished manners, made friends for him in all classes. Of all these visitors he saw, one in particular impressed the child. The previous evening he had heard that a prince was coming to visit his uncle. Just as he was being taken off to bed, by flattening his nose against the drawing-room window, he had managed to catch a brief glimpse, in the glare of the footmen's torches, of a traveling carriage on sleigh runners, harnessed with six black horses, standing before the great snow-covered lawn. But he had not been able to see the prince—surely a fairy-tale prince, young and handsome, dressed in brilliant colors and covered with gold braid.

The next day, having slipped into the billiard room, he was surprised there by the unexpected approach of his uncle and the guest. The prince! How disappointing was the first sight of this old gentleman with a white mustache, this spare and stiff old gentleman in his frock coat of military cut! This visitor seemed to him prodigiously old; but what struck him still more was to see this strange prince ask Uncle Thaddeus a question and then hand him a writing tablet and pencil; his uncle took them and scribbled a few words as though this were the most natural thing in the world. What was this strange ceremony? Was this personage too great to be spoken to directly?

Forty-three years later, Joseph Conrad was to remember the encounter and evoke the figure of Prince Roman Sanguszko,[7] hero of the insurrection of 1831, who had been deported to Siberia, had served as a private in the Caucasus, finally returning to Poland, completely deaf. But at the time it happened, little Conrad had felt only great astonishment to find that a prince could be deaf, bald, thin, and also prodigiously old.

Conrad's long stay of almost eight months in the Ukraine was to be his last for a quarter of a century. During the autumn he spent some time with his grandmother in Jitomir. Meanwhile, the health of the Chernikov exile was dangerously deteriorating. He lived now entirely on the letters he received from his son and from a few relatives and friends. His health was so obviously broken that the Russian authorities were no longer afraid of him. After six years of exile, in December, 1867, as a result of steps taken by Madame

---

[7] See "Prince Roman" in *Tales of Hearsay*. (Tr.)

Bobrowska without her son-in-law's knowledge, the Minister of the
Interior in the name of Czar Alexander II granted a passport, valid
for one year, to "Apollo Korzeniowski Esquire, accompanied by his
son, Conrad, aged ten, to proceed to Algeria and the Island of
Madeira." This passport, signed by Prince Galitzine, governor of
Chernikov, was not handed to the prisoner until early January.

The two travelers were never to reach the faraway destinations
named in this passport. In any case, Apollo Korzeniowski's health
was already too bad for him to go there directly. After receiving
permission to spend three weeks in Volhynia and Podolia to visit
relatives and friends, he decided instead to go to the Austrian part of
Poland and, stopping in Lwow, he installed himself there in two
rather gloomy rooms in the suburb of Zotkiewcki. There Conrad
attended the *Gymnasium,* "although," Apollo wrote, "the teaching
is not to my taste and the faculty, apart from two or three, cannot
have any useful influence on the children."

Since 1866 the Russian and Prussian governments had redoubled
their persecution of the Poles, while Austria, after the severe defeat
of Sadowa, had realized the necessity of securing some support
within her own frontiers by granting more liberal conditions to her
Slav subjects. Significant concessions were made to the Polish minor-
ities at this time. Shortly after Apollo Korzeniowski's arrival in
Galicia, that province was given relative autonomy and a "minister
for Galicia," a Pole, was appointed in Vienna. Finding himself back
in a Polish province where one had almost the illusion of political
independence and, at the very least, freedom to speak one's own
language openly, the prisoner had regained some strength and heart.
He even began to take care of his health, though he was worried
about Conrad's. He wrote to his friend Kaszewski:

I am entirely absorbed in taking care of my own health
and worrying about Conrad's. I am deep in the mountains at
Topolnia. I am drinking sheep's milk with such conviction
that when the Imperial Royal Police came to ask me what I
was doing in Galicia, I was able to answer in good faith that
I was drinking sheep's milk. My little boy has had another
attack of the illness that causes him painful cramps in the
stomach. It is difficult to teach him anything at all with his

health in this state. He is already eleven and for almost two years he has learned nothing. He is still a nice fellow.

And to another friend he writes about his son again:

My main aim is not to make Conrad a democrat or an aristocrat, a demagogue, a republican or a monarchist, nor a servant or a lackey of these parties, but a good Pole.

When school reopened in October Conrad was still too ill to attend, and his father decided to keep him at home and supervise his studies himself. Another reason for this decision was, in his own words, "the terrible Polish spoken in Galicia," which Conrad heard from the school children and which his purist father could not bear. In his letters he frequently goes into this subject.

On Christmas Eve he writes to his usual correspondent that Conrad is much better and that he is especially glad of this because the child has been very nervous and tense. As for himself, he has been thinking of devoting himself to journalism; he has managed to finish a study on Shakespeare, which has just appeared in the *Warsaw Library,* but since autumn his health has been very bad; he can no longer leave his room; he has even had to give up studying with his son and turn him over to a tutor from the *Gymnasium.* Only he is watchful that during the lessons "the Polish language does not turn into Galician."

He has revised and decided to publish in Lwow a drama in verse *Akt Pierwszy (First Act),* the preface to which is dated "Lwow, December 1, 1868" and which was performed in the Polish theater in that town.

According to some reports, Conrad showed during this period an interest in dramatic literature and, emulating his father, even wrote two or three plays which he and his friends performed, among others a drama entitled *The Eyes of Jan Sobieski.*

Was the Lwow accent too unbearable for his father's ears? Was he afraid that his son would acquire habits of speech that were too provincial, or was it pure coincidence? In any case, at the end of January, 1869, Apollo Korzeniowski and his son went to live in Cracow, in Poselska Street. The exile had received an offer to join the editorial staff of the paper *Cjaz* (the *Times*).

Almost immediately after their arrival Conrad was enrolled as a day student in a preparatory school, the dim memory of which he called up long afterward while he was depicting the atmosphere of that period of his life:

At eight o'clock of every morning that God made, sleet or shine, I walked up Florian Street. But of the school, I remember very little. I believe that one of my co-sufferers there has become a much appreciated editor of historical documents. But I didn't suffer much from the varous imperfections of my first school. I was rather indifferent to school troubles. I had a private gnawing worm of my own. This was the time of my father's last illness. Every evening at seven, turning my back on the Florian Gate, I walked all the way to a big old house in a quiet narrow street a good distance beyond the Great Square. There, in a large drawing-room, panelled and bare, with heavy cornices and a lofty ceiling, in a little oasis of light made by two candles in a desert of dusk I sat at a little table to worry and ink myself all over till the task of my preparation was done.

The table of my toil faced a tall white door, which was kept closed; now and then it would come ajar and a nun in a white coif would squeeze herself through the crack, glide across the room, and disappear. There were two of these noiseless nursing nuns. Their voices were seldom heard. For, indeed, what could they have had to say? When they did speak to me it was with their lips hardly moving, in a claustral clear whisper. Our domestic matters were ordered by the elderly housekeeper of our neighbour on the second floor, a Canon of the Cathedral, lent for the emergency. She, too, spoke but seldom. She wore a black dress with a cross hanging by a chain on her ample bosom. And though when she spoke she moved her lips more than the nuns, she never let her voice rise above a peacefully murmuring note. The air around me was all piety, resignation, and silence.

I don't know what would have become of me if I had not been a reading boy. My prep finished I would have had nothing to do but sit and watch the awful stillness of the sick room flow out through the closed door and coldly enfold my scared heart. I suppose that in a futile childish way I would have gone crazy. But I was a reading boy. There were many books about, lying on consoles, on tables, and even on the floor, for we had not had time to settle down. I read! What did I not read! Sometimes the elder nun, gliding up and casting a mistrustful look on the open pages, would lay her hand lightly on my head and suggest in a doubtful whisper, "Perhaps it is not very good for you to read these books." I would raise my eyes to her face mutely, and with a vague gesture of giving it up she would glide away.

Later in the evening, but not always, I would be permitted to tip-toe into the sick room to say good-night to the figure prone on the bed, which often could not acknowledge my presence but by a slow movement of the eyes, put my lips dutifully to the nerveless hand lying on the coverlet, and tip-toe out again. Then I would go to bed, in a room at the end of the corridor, and often, not always, cry myself into a good sound sleep.[8]

Apollo Korzeniowski's strength was waning fast. One evening in May, sitting in an armchair propped up with cushions, he asked his nurse to burn all his remaining manuscripts that he had not sent to his friend Stefan Buszczynski. In the doorway little Conrad, silent and aghast, watched this final act of renunciation on the part of his father, who seemed to him not so much desperately ill as mortally weary, a vanquished man.

The next day Apollo took to his bed and a fortnight later, on May 23, 1869, the Polish patriot breathed his last.

Although he had not lived long in Cracow and had been seen by very few people, his own role and that of his family in furthering the Polish cause were generally known. His death did not go unnoticed. His funeral was the occasion for a silent, reverent demonstration in which all classes of society joined, from the delegations of the trade guilds to the school children and the senate of the university.

The long procession moved out of the narrow street in which

[8] *Notes on Life and Letters,* "Poland Revisited."

the house was situated, past the Gothic front of St. Mary's and through the Florian Gate. Half the town had turned out on that fine spring afternoon. All these people had not come to honor a great achievement or even some splendid failure. The dead and they were victims alike of an unrelenting destiny which cut them off from every path of merit and glory. They had come only to render homage to the ardent fidelity of the man whose life had been a fearless confession in word and deed of a creed which the simplest heart in that crowd could feel and understand. Walking alone, in a space kept clear, conscious of this enormous procession behind him, a twelve-year-old child who had shed all his tears followed the hearse to the grave on which a headstone was soon to bear this inscription:[9]

> TO APOLLO NALECZ KORZENIOWSKI
> VICTIM OF MUSCOVITE TYRANNY
> Born   Feb. 21, 1820
> Died   May 23, 1869
> TO THE MAN WHO LOVED HIS COUNTRY
> WORKED FOR IT AND DIED FOR IT
> HIS COMPATRIOTS

Apollo Korzeniowski's literary work did not altogether die with him. Although it attained no wide reputation among the general public, critics later agreed that it was too good to fall into oblivion. In his Memoirs, Thaddeus Bobrowski, his brother-in-law, who was by no means prejudiced in his favor, wrote that Apollo Korzeniowski may be considered one of the best of the writers influenced by Krasinski, and that his dramatic works, the *Comedy* and *For the Sake of Money,* are perfect in style even though the depiction of the various classes of society is sometimes lacking in simplicity and clarity. He adds that Korzeniowski was unrivaled as a translator of Victor Hugo, whose style he admirably rendered, and of Heinrich Heine, with whose lyrical bitterness he was in deep sympathy.

Joseph Conrad Nalecz Korzeniowski, as we can see, came of good stock. Nature seems to have made two separate efforts to bring gifts of artistic genius to their full flowering. Though forgotten or

[9] See Ibid., "Poland Revisited" (Tr.)

neglected for almost twenty years, the grounding in literary discipline that he underwent in childhood certainly had its influence on the unexpected work of his maturity.

At the age of eleven, after a five months' stay in a strange town, Joseph Conrad found himself an orphan. Stefan Buszczynski took charge of the child the day after his bereavement and, in accordance with the dead man's wishes, he was placed in the pension of a certain Mr. Georgeon, while attending classes at St. Anne's *Gymnasium*. He had not studied German or Latin and was behind his school-mates—the result of a schooling interrupted by frequent changes of residence and of his delicate health. However, he set to work with a will.

Three weeks after the death of the father, Madame Bobrowska, the child's maternal grandmother, wrote to Casimir Kaszewski:

> We hope that next year he will be promoted to the fourth class, for the principal and teachers speak highly of his diligence and intelligence. May God protect his health, to which he devotes any time left over from his studies. His tutor says he knows no child easier to deal with or more generous by nature. He lavished such loving care on his father right to the very end . . .

Stefan Buszczynski carried out his duties as temporary guardian with affection. He lived on Florian Street, a short distance from Mr. Georgeon's pension, which was moved soon afterward to the Street of the Franciscans, opposite the Franciscan church, on the third floor of a big building, part of which was inhabited by the Taube family with whom the orphan soon became very friendly.

Despite his name, Mr. Georgeon spoke almost no French, and it was with a Polish refugee named Czapski that Conrad continued to study and practice this language, particularly since this Czapski, the son of an 1831 emigrant, spoke hardly any Polish and had come to Poland from France solely to take part in the insurrection of 1863. In this way the pupil's pro-French sympathies were strengthened.

At that time he suffered from very painful headaches which made work impossible while they lasted, and when summer came his grandmother took him to Wartenberg in Bohemia to take the cure.

When school reopened, she decided to come to live in Cracow to keep an eye on the child's health. The following year, a family council decided that his legal guardians should be his grandmother, Madame Teofila Bobrowska, and Count Ladislas Mnizek, a cousin of the George Mnizek who, ten years earlier, had been Balzac's son-in-law. A friend of his father's, Dr. Isidor Kopernicki, university professor, served as a sort of "substitute parent" for him at school.

From the beginning of 1870, Conrad, still at Mr. Georgeon's pension, attended classes at St. Anne's *Gymnasium*. Thaddeus Bobrowski, very worried about his daughter's health, took her to Montreux for several weeks in June and appointed a young philosophy student at the University of Cracow, Adam Pulmann, to supervise and encourage Conrad in his studies. Pulmann, who was to be his tutor for several years, took him three times to the spa of Krynica in the summer.

Conrad's memories of St. Anne's school were not particularly pleasant. He studied there for four years and was, he tells us, a good student in mathematics and history but not in grammar. To a child with such a rich imagination, who had until then been left entirely to himself, school routine and discipline, even though not harsh, were inevitably distasteful. His appetite for adventure and daydreams, fed on avid reading, did not do him much good, while the routine subjects which formed the major part of the curriculum were, on the whole, not among his favorites. On the other hand, he showed even then a special liking for geography. Fifty years later he was to refer in the following words to this childhood enthusiasm and the scant encouragement it received from the teachers:

Unfortunately, the marks awarded for that subject were almost as few as the hours apportioned to it in the school curriculum by persons of no romantic sense for the real, ignorant of the great possibilities of active life; with no desire for struggle, no notion of the wide spaces of the world—mere bored professors, in fact, who were not only middle-aged but looked to me as if they had never been young. And their geography was very much like themselves, a bloodless thing with a dry skin covering a repulsive armature of uninteresting bones.

I would be ashamed of my warmth in digging up a hatchet which has been buried now for nearly fifty years if those fellows had not tried so often to take my scalp at the yearly examinations. There are things that one does not forget. And besides, the geography which I had discovered for myself was the geography of open spaces and wide horizons built up on men's devoted work in the open air, the geography still militant but already conscious of its approaching end with the death of the last great explorer. The antagonism was radical.[10]

In homage to the memory of Apollo Korzeniowski and to the services he had striven to render the cause of Poland, the municipal council, at its meetings of December 28, 1872, conferred the freedom of the city upon young Conrad, exempting him from taxes. This award entitled the recipient to Austrian nationality upon attaining his majority, and, in fact, Thaddeus Bobrowski's accounts for the years 1873 and 1874 do record applications for Conrad's Austrian naturalization—applications which never came to anything. Possibly mutual agreements between the two empires concerning Poles prohibited the exchange of citizens, particularly of those who had not done their military service. In any case there is definite proof that neither his relatives nor he himself expected that he would remain what he was in effect, for administrative purposes: a subject of the Russian Empire. Moreover, this determination shows that his relatives had accepted the prospect of his not returning to the Russian provinces—at any rate not in the near future—but, instead, of continuing his life and education in Cracow and later perhaps in Vienna. They had no inkling of what was already quietly brewing in the imagination of this young mind.

Since his father's death Conrad had associated solely with reasonable adults and with school friends who were probably no less reasonable. The atmosphere of the old university city of Cracow was quite different from that of Jitomir, or Warsaw before the insurrection, or of the years of exile. Just when the prisoner's son was beginning to lead a conscious life in Cracow, and more particularly after the French defeat at Sedan, a new tendency had arisen

[10] *Last Essays,* "Geography and Some Explorers."

in Galicia to rule out all emotion in studying the nationalist problem. The history of Poland was now regarded as a series not of misfortunes but of mistakes, and her reverses as a punishment from God. This was what has been called the "Historical School" of Cracow whose mouthpiece was the *Polish Review*. Thanks to the relatively liberal treatment of the Poles in Galicia, there was a tendency to come to terms with reality and to put aside dreams of emancipation—a reasonable attitude perhaps, particularly in the circumstances then prevailing in European politics, but one which makes it easy to understand that Conrad should have found the air of Cracow in the '70s unbreathable.

Reasons of the heart may also have influenced the course of his ideas at this period. After an unsuccessful first love a young man of exalted temperament may want to get away at all costs from its scene and cause. We shall find an example of this later in Conrad's own life. Twice he has discreetly raised the veil covering his early emotions. Once, quite openly, in the preface to his novel *Nostromo,* speaking of the town that is the setting of the story, he says:

If anything could induce me to revisit Sulaco (I should hate to see all these changes) it would be Antonia—and the true reason for that—why not be frank about it?—the true reason is that I have modelled her on my first love.

How we, a band of tallish schoolboys, the chums of her two brothers, how we used to look up to that girl just out of the schoolroom herself, as the standard-bearer of a faith to which we were all born, but which she alone knew how to hold aloft, with an unflinching hope! She had perhaps more glow and less serenity in her soul than Antonia, but she was an uncompromising Puritan of patriotism with no taint of the slightest worldliness in her thoughts. I was not the only one in love with her; but it was I who had to hear oftenest her scathing criticism of my levities—very much like poor Decoud—or stand the brunt of her austere, unanswerable invective. She did not quite understand—but never mind. That afternoon when I came in, a shrinking yet defiant sinner, to say the final good-bye, I received a hand-squeeze that made my heart leap and saw a tear that took my breath away. She

was softened at the last as though she had suddenly per-
ceived (we were such children still!) that I was really going
away for good, going very far away—even as far as Sulaco,
lying unknown, hidden from our eyes, in the darkness of
the Placid Gulf.

He makes another more complex allusion in a deleted passage in
The Arrow of Gold.[11] Given the clearly autobiographical nature of
this novel, the deleted pages may be regarded as a confession, the
main points of which fit in with the preface to *Nostromo*. Factors of
this kind, without actually having been decisive, may have intensified a feeling of uneasiness in this fifteen-year-old boy and a desire to
get away, without quite knowing where he was going, to far-off
lands endowed with all the glamor of the unknown.

It was during the year 1872 that he first spoke of a project he had
been harboring secretly for some time. Coming of a family whose
loyalty was all for the soil, a military career, or the pursuit of the
arts, this young boy, born in a country with no seacoast, suddenly
announced that he wished to go to sea.

This desire, nourished by avid reading (including Fenimore
Cooper and Captain Marryat in translation), springing forth from the
troubled depths of his consciousness, long cherished in silence, un-
willingly repressed and thereby strengthened, now made bold to
show itself.

Everywhere—in the family and among his friends—it was received
with amazement, then with protests; some people were even indig-
nant. The Korzeniowskis were known to be a bit eccentric, but up
until then their eccentricity had never taken this form. Summoned by
his mother, Uncle Thaddeus, still grieving bitterly over the loss of
his only daughter the previous year, hastened to Cracow from the
depths of the Ukraine to try to get at the roots of this extraordinary
whim. At first he saw in it nothing more than a childish fancy
which would evaporate at its first contact with life, but, not wanting
to give it a firmer hold on a character that was already showing signs
of a patient obstinacy, he did not formally forbid it, but tried
gently to wean Conrad away from it by showing him the para-

[11] See Appendix.

mount necessity of finishing his studies, which could not fail to
be useful to him in the strange career he was proposing to follow.

The end of the school year arrived; Conrad's marks were good.
Mr. Pulmann, the young tutor, who had gained his pupil's friendship
and confidence, was instructed to dissuade him tactfully from his
plan. In May, 1873, on doctors' advice, it was decided to send
Conrad with his tutor on a six weeks' tour of southern Germany
and Switzerland, but shortly after their departure cholera broke
out in Cracow and the uncle sent the two young travelers orders
to prolong their trip, which in the end lasted three months.

Conrad and his tutor went first to Vienna, then up the Danube
valley to Linz and Passau. Then on to Munich and Schaffhausen
and from there, after a detour to Lake Constance, they reached
Zurich, then Lucerne, climbed up to the Righi, crossed the Lake of
the Four Cantons to Flüelen and then made their way up the
valley of the Reuss, on foot, in slow, easy stages, by way of Ander-
matt and Hospenthal. It was the time when the Saint Gotthard
Tunnel was being built. They climbed up to the Furca Pass, toward
the Rhône glacier and the Häsli valley.

Between Hospenthal and the Furca Conrad and his tutor had
their last argument about his career, as he reported later in *A
Personal Record*:

> We sat down by the side of the road to continue the
> argument begun half a mile or so before. I am certain it was
> an argument because I remember perfectly how my tutor
> argued and how without the power of a reply I listened with
> my eyes fixed obstinately on the ground. . . . He argued in
> railway trains, in lake steamboats, he had argued away for
> me the obligatory sunrise on the Rigi, by Jove! . . . When
> he started to argue on the top of the Furca Pass he was
> perhaps nearer a success than either he or I imagined. I listened
> to him in despairing silence, feeling that ghostly, unrealized
> and desired sea of my dreams escape from the unnerved grip
> of my will. . . . What reward could I expect from such a life
> at the end of my years, either in ambition, honour or con-
> science? An unanswerable question. . . . Then our eyes met

and a genuine emotion was visible in his as well as in mine. The end came all at once. He picked up the knapsack suddenly and got on to his feet.

"You are an incorrigible, hopeless Don Quixote. That's what you are."

I was surprised. I was only fifteen and did not know what he meant exactly. But I felt vaguely flattered at the name of the immortal knight turning up in connection with my own folly, as some people would call it to my face. . . . I walked behind him for full five minutes; then without looking back he stopped. The shadows of distant peaks were lengthening over the Furca Pass. When I came up to him he turned to me and in full view of the Finster-Aarhorn, with his band of giant brothers rearing their monstrous heads against a brilliant sky, put his hand on my shoulder affectionately.

"Well! That's enough. We will have no more of it."

And indeed there was no more question of my mysterious vocation between us. There was to be no more question of it at all, nowhere or with any one.

This maritime career decided upon in the heart of Switzerland is by no means the least singular incident in a life so extraordinary in many ways.

Receiving instructions to continue their journey, the two young men came down into Italy, reached Milan, where the future writer stored up the memory of the cathedral by moonlight, then Venice, where the future sailor got his first glimpse of the sea and ships and made the first sea voyage of his life, from Venice to Trieste. By the end of July they were back in Cracow.[12]

Since his grandmother, Madame Bobrowska, had decided to live from now on in Warsaw with her son Casimir, Conrad was put in the charge of a distant relative, Antoine Syroczynski, with whom

[12] In an article entitled "Conradiana" appearing in *Epoka,* March 19, 1929, Mr. Stanislas Czosnowski quotes a letter from Mme. Tekla Wojakowska, née Syroczynska; third cousin of Conrad, according to which Conrad spent two months at the seaside near Odessa in 1866 or 1867. This seems clearly contradicted by Conrad's own phrase: ". . . Neither he nor I had ever had a single glimpse of the sea in our lives. That was to come by and by for both of us in Venice, from the outer shore of Lido." (*A Personal Record.*)

he spent the month of September in Lwow, in a home where most of the conversation was in French.

The efforts of the tutor, the affectionate objections of his uncle, the entreaties of his grandmother, the astonishment, teasing, and indignation of relatives and friends who went so far as to accuse him of having no common sense, no heart, and no patriotism—none of these had any effect on this adolescent obstinacy—an obstinacy so self-sustaining that its compulsiveness always remained a mystery to him.

When one knows the events that dominated his childhood and bears in mind that there burned in him a hereditary ardor, a family exaltation, that his great hopes and far-reaching desires were confronted by barred doors simply because he was a Pole at a moment when to be a Pole meant the end of all hope, is it so surprising that this child, brought up on travel books and imbued with the adventurous spirit that had for so long inspired his race and nation— that this sixteen-year-old boy who had felt upon his childhood the tragic, crushing weight of tyranny and mourning and who saw himself imprisoned, smothered, fettered forevermore by a prudent bourgeois way of life, should want to escape, cost what it might?

It could not really be the sea that drew him, for he did not know the sea. It was an adventurous life in the open air, far from oppression, prudence, rules. These lungs, which had hardly ever since the day he was born been able to breathe freely, this soul, which had almost always felt smothered, craved open spaces—open like those of his native Podolia, but free.

Perhaps, too, he had caught, through his father's enthusiasm for Byron, a whiff of the salty tang of *The Corsair* or *Childe Harold,* in which the sea figures as that element that most strongly resists men, and therefore tyrants too, and as the eminent domain of freedom.

> Man marks the earth with ruin,—his control
> Stops with the shore . . .
> *Childe Harold.* Ch. IV, CLXXIX

There was nothing for it but to yield to the reasoning of an obstinacy which did not seem to be reasonable. Uncle Thaddeus, with his affectionate liberal wisdom, did not want his nephew to be able to accuse him some day of having ruined his life. The decision was made, in the secret hope of a speedy return of the prodigal. Again Conrad spent the month of September in Lwow with his relatives Antoine and Léon Syroczynski. His grandmother and uncle joined him there in the middle of October and took him to Cracow and there, on October 14, 1874, amid tears and blessings, Joseph Conrad Korzeniowski, supplied with a small amount of luggage, a few introductions and the promise of a modest income, got into the train that was to take him, by way of Vienna, Zurich, Geneva, and Lyons, to Marseilles and the unknown.

Standing at the train window, watching the two uneven towers of St. Mary's disappear, he could have no idea that the day would come when the house in Poselska Street, in which he lived for a few months with his father, would bear a plaque in English and Polish with these words, which he was to write forty years later:

> It was in that old royal and academical city that I ceased to be a child, became a boy, had known the friendships, the admirations, the thoughts and the indignations of that age.[13]

He left feeling liberated and at the same time sad at heart, desperately committed to his desire, without suspecting that this day, the eve of his seventeenth birthday, was to mark the end of the Polish life, that as many years would go by again before he set foot on his native soil or walked once more among the streets and fields that had seen the passing of the ardent melancholy faces of his ancestors and had been the first witnesses of his sorrows, his impatience, and his dreams.

[13] *Notes on Life and Letters.* "Poland Revisited."

II

French Days

(1874-1878)

For me the Cannebière has been a street
leading to the unknown.
                      The Arrow of Gold

In Marseilles, society is no use at all to a
young man. All he would feel is its
shackles.
            STENDHAL. *Mémoires d'un Touriste*

SINCE THIS YOUNG Pole wanted to be a seaman, it was quite natural
that both his relatives and he himself should think first of France.
To serve in the Russian or German Navy, or even in their merchant
fleet, was out of the question, considering a Pole's attitude to those
two countries. On the other hand, he would have had no difficulty at
all in entering the Austrian Navy, for this was just the time when
Poles were beginning to attain the highest positions in the dual
monarchy. His family had thought seriously of sending him to the
naval academy at Pola, but Conrad himself had never taken this
seriously. Up to then his mind had never entertained the idea of a
career. What he wanted above all, whatever the cost, was to escape
from a certain atmosphere, a certain stifling sensation: to reach
what at this time vaguely represented to him salvation, liberation,
hope, life itself—the sea.

The simplest, most natural way for him to reach it was, of

course, via France. For centuries France and Poland had been linked by ties of friendship. From 1831 to 1863, more than a quarter of a century, Poland's true capital had been Paris. There was hardly a good Polish family that did not have relatives or friends there, or even members who had become French citizens. In France, too, it would be possible to keep an eye on this peculiar boy for a while. Besides, hadn't Conrad spoken French fluently since his early childhood?

From Cracow and Lwow all available strings were pulled leading to France or points en route. Conrad himself noted forty years later that he spent a day in Switzerland, at Pfaftikon on Lake Zurich, with a Mr. Orzechowski, a former representative of the Polish Government at Constantinople (in 1863), who must have been connected with either the Korzeniowskis or the Bobrowskis.[1] The first connecting link between Conrad and the sea was a former compatriot, now French, who had himself joined the French merchant navy at Marseilles and who belonged to a well-known Polish family: Victor Chodzko. Chodzko, who did not expect to be in Marseilles at the end of October when the young traveler was to arrive, had recommended him to a very fine young man, Baptistin Solari, who had promised to see about finding a decent ship for Conrad "if he really wanted a taste of *ce métier de chien.*"

He kept his promise, and in *A Personal Record* Conrad has noted his impressions on first waking up in Marseilles:

> This Solary (Baptistin), when I beheld him in the flesh, turned out a quite young man, very good-looking, with a fine black, short beard, a fresh complexion, and soft, merry black eyes. He was as jovial and good-natured as any boy could desire. I was still asleep in my room in a modest hotel near the quays of the old port, after the fatigues of the journey *via* Vienna, Zurich, Lyons, when he burst in, flinging the shutters open to the sun of Provence and chiding me boisterously for lying abed. How pleasantly he startled me by his noisy objurgations to be up and off instantly for a "three years' campaign in the South Seas." O magic words!

[1] M. Dombrowski, "Interview with Joseph Conrad," *Tygodnik Illustrowany,* No. 16, April 18, 1914.

"Une campagne de trois ans dans les mers du sud"—that is the French for a three years' deep-water voyage.

He gave me a delightful waking, and his friendliness was unwearied; but I fear he did not enter upon the quest for a ship for me in a very solemn spirit.

This Solari had been to sea himself but he had given it up as soon as possible in favor of earning his living more comfortably on land, so he regarded this young foreigner's enthusiasm with a slightly disillusioned benevolence. Yet he was not too old to understand such youthful ardor and to sympathize with it, and even if he was in no great hurry to find Conrad a ship, at least he promptly introduced him to various members of his family: ship brokers, marine-store dealers, stevedores, calkers, and pilots. Conrad soon made friends with all of them, for southern Frenchmen are hospitable people and he had the inborn democratic spirit of the Poles. He deliberately spent most of his time with the men who could best help him to get to know the sea as quickly as possible— the pilots. If it was at the Lido that the future writer of sea stories first saw the sea, it was at Marseilles that he had his first intimate contact with it; it was there that he first spent a day on salt water. In *A Personal Record* he has left this account of his early life at Marseilles:

The very first whole day I ever spent on salt water was by invitation, in a big half-decked pilot-boat, cruising under close reefs on the lookout, in misty, blowing weather, for the sails of ships and the smoke of steamers rising out there, beyond the slim and tall Planier lighthouse cutting the line of the wind-swept horizon with a white perpendicular stroke. They were hospitable souls, these sturdy Provençal seamen. Under the general designation of *le petit ami de Baptistin* I was made the guest of the Corporation of Pilots, and had the freedom of their boats night or day. And many a day and night too did I spend cruising with these rough, kindly men, under whose auspices my intimacy with the sea began. Many a time "the little friend of Baptistin" had the hooded cloak of the Mediterranean sailor thrown over him by their honest hands while dodging at night under the lee of Château d'If on the watch for the lights of ships. Their sea-tanned faces, whiskered or shaved, lean or full, with the intent wrinkled sea-eyes of the pilot breed, and here and there a thin gold loop at the lobe of a hairy ear, bent over my sea-infancy. The first operation of seamanship I had an opportunity of observing was the boarding of ships at sea, at all times, in all states of the weather. They gave it to me to the full. And I have been invited to sit in more than one tall, dark house of the old town at their hospitable board, had the *bouillabaisse* ladled out into a thick plate by their high-voiced, broad browed wives, talked to their daughters—thick-set girls, with pure profiles, glorious masses of black hair arranged with complicated art, dark eyes, and dazzling white teeth.

Conrad retained a lively and grateful memory of the inhabitants of the Vieux-Port, as can be seen from these tributes he paid them many years later, but the world of pilots and their families was not the only one young Korzeniowski frequented. From time to time he moved in very different society, if not with the same pleasure, at least with the same ease.

At this time, just after his seventeenth birthday, he was rather shorter than average in height; his regular, oval face, with slightly prominent cheekbones, protruding lips, and very dark, lively, piercing eyes, was crowned by a shock of brown hair combed back from his forehead and reaching to the nape of his neck. Meticulous in his dress, completely natural in his behavior, notwithstanding the great courtesy of his manners, reserved in spite of his vivacity and enthusiasm, he seems never to have felt lost in France and to have become popular immediately with all kinds of people.

Soon after his arrival he had been recommended to a banker and shipowner, head of the firm C. Delestang & Son, whose quiet, impressive office was situated on the ground floor of No. 3 Rue d'Arcole. This M. Delestang belonged to the Royalist party. In 1875 the Republican government was still shaky enough to keep Monarchist hopes alive. A large section of the elegant society of Marseilles could, without being anachronistic, dream of re-establishing the old order. Punctilious, his pale bony face clamped together, as it were, by short side whiskers, M. Delestang was, in Conrad's

words, such a frozen-up, mummified Royalist that he used in
current conversation turns of speech contemporary with the good
Henri Quatre and reckoned money in *écus* as they did in the reign
of Louis Quatorze. The excellent and worthy M. Delestang was
accompanied by his wife, *"la belle Madame Delestang,"* whose
imperious bearing and haughty weariness reminded Conrad of
Lady Dedlock in Dickens' *Bleak House*. Her aristocratic appearance and distant manner, however, sometimes softened enough
for her to show her liking for the young man by way of a question
or a friendly phrase, or even an invitation to go for a drive with
them to the Prado at the fashionable hour in the front seat of
their carriage, or to come to one of her afternoon teas where the
triumph of the Monarchist movement was promoted over cups of
tea and little cakes.[2]

During the time Conrad spent at Marseilles before embarking
and in between voyages, he used to visit his friends in the Vieux-
Port more often and with more enjoyment than the ones in the
Monarchist drawing rooms or in the Rue d'Arcole offices, where
his uncle had arranged for him to draw his little income. Yet, by an
irony of fate of which we shall see several more examples in his
life, the decisive influence on the double course of Conrad's "French
period" was that of the Delestangs far more than that of his friends
in the Vieux-Port. It was, in fact, M. Delestang who found him his
first berths, and it was in the drawing room of *"la belle Madame
Delestang"* that he made the connections whose strange interplay
was to precipitate him for a time into an utterly romantic adventure.

Delestang & Son at that time owned two ships—sailing ships,
of course—one four-hundred-ton bark, built more than twenty
years earlier, the *Mont-Blanc,* the other, the *Saint-Antoine,*
brand-new, a most handsome schooner of approximately the same
tonnage. Conrad eventually became a crew member of both these
ships.

Before this he seems to have made a short trial run in another
ship, at least according to this passage in *The Mirror of the Sea:*

> The very first Christmas night I ever spent away from
> land was employed in running before a Gulf of Lyons gale,

[2] See *A Personal Record,* (Tr.)

which made the old ship groan in every timber as she skipped
before it over the short seas until we brought her to, battered
and out of breath, under the lee of Majorca. . . .

We—or, rather, they, for I had hardly had two glimpses of
salt water in my life till then—kept her standing off and on
all that day, while I listened for the first time with the curiosity of my tender years to the song of the wind in a ship's
rigging. . . .

The thing (I will not call her a ship twice in the same
half-hour) leaked. She leaked fully, generously, overflowingly,
all over—like a basket. I took an enthusiastic part in the
excitement caused by that last infirmity of noble ships, without concerning myself much with the why or the wherefore.

But his first real voyage was aboard the *Mont-Blanc,* in the
second half of 1875. The crew muster records his presence: "Conrad
Korrcuiwski (sic), apprentice, age 17 1/2, born Dec. 3, 1857 at
Jitomir (Russia)." Leaving Marseilles on June 23, the ship reached
Saint-Pierre in Martinique on July 31, spent almost two months
there, called at St. Thomas on September 27 and sailed from there
the same day for Cap-Haïtien, where she arrived on October 2,
leaving again on November 1 with a cargo of logwood for Le
Havre.

Here Conrad went ashore the day before Christmas Eve, after
a voyage which had lasted six months almost to the day since
his departure from Marseilles. While it had shown him some
West Indian scenery somewhat different from that of his native
Poland, the voyage had by no means been a pleasure trip. Besides
the regular work of handling a sailing ship, the greenhorn had
become acquainted with the sensations and thoughts inspired in a
young man by a spell of stormy weather. Almost the whole of the
last month of the return voyage had been particularly rough and
the ship reached Le Havre quite badly damaged, as can be seen
from the captain's own report:

As she pitched, the upper bobstay broke and also the jib-
boom. It brought the topgallant mast down with it, which
broke too at the truck. The jib-boom, hanging by its rigging,
became a battering ram crashing against the bows. Impossible

to make anything fast. We decided to cut the rigging and let the jib-boom go. At least we saved the topgallant yard and sail.

From Nov. 24 to Nov. 29 wind high and from the E., shifting on Nov. 29 to squalls from the S., then dying down and shifting to S.-E., gale force. Back to S., lasting until Dec. 18 when I sighted the Calf light (Ireland). That same day lightning in the N.-E. and a shift of wind which enabled me to set a course and enter the Channel blind. On the 21st the wind veered to S.-E., gale force, lasting to the afternoon of the 22nd, when I recognized Barfleur. Hove to. Midnight: under way. Sighted La Hève 5 A.M. Dec. 23. Took on the Pilot from Boat 9 who brought me into Le Havre on the evening tide.

In Poland they had held high hopes that an experience of this kind—or even milder—would be enough to satisfy young Conrad's taste for adventure and that he would return to the fold disheartened, his tail between his legs. The family's expectations were totally disappointed. Far from being weary or discouraged, he wanted only to set out again.

Since the *Mont-Blanc* needed substantial repairs at Le Havre, Conrad did not wait and, not even bothering to take along his trunk, reported back to Marseilles after a few days in Paris. When he arrived, the other Delestang ship, the *Saint-Antoine,* was in Martinique and there was nothing he could do but await the return of one or other of these ships in which he was sure of finding a berth. So he spent six consecutive months in Marseilles, from the beginning of January to July, 1876. What he did during these six months is not exactly clear: but one document does shed some light on this period and indicates definitely that the young man was sowing some wild oats. Here is what Thaddeus Bobrowski wrote that year in the notes he kept concerning his nephew:

In 1876 a letter from M. Victor Chodzko of Apr. 5 informed me that, having drawn your income for the next eight months (1,200 francs) in one go, you lent the money to someone (or lost it) and were penniless. Subsequently, in May, you wrote to me about this yourself, apologizing, but not explaining it. On May 21 you sent me a telegram asking me to send you 700 francs, which I did. On July 2, after another telegram, I sent you 400 francs.

On your departure from Marseilles you asked me to pay M. Bonnard, an acquaintance of yours, 165 francs which he had lent you; this I did. So in three months you have spent 1,265 francs in excess of your income. Since it is only fair that everyone should pay for his own foolishness, particularly as regards money, and not possessing any special fund myself to take care of the special expenses of my nephew, I used for this purpose 500 florins of your own money—a gift from Mademoiselle Korzeniowska.

In the depths of the Ukraine Uncle Thaddeus, that exact, parsimonious, rather timid man, must have thought that his nephew was indulging in the wildest extravagances and that it was high time for the Bobrowski sense of proportion to curb his hotheaded Korzeniowski impulsiveness. In any case Conrad must have spent a few weeks enjoying himself and in fact he retained a special affection for Marseilles all his life.

Many hours were spent with young men from all classes, discussing everything under the sun, in one of the sidewalk cafés, more numerous then than now, lining both sides of the Cannebière, or in the café on the Rue Saint-Ferréol, now vanished, whose name Conrad would still pronounce lovingly as his life neared its end: the Café Bodoul, the place of which Stendhal said in the *Mémoires d'un Touriste:* "There you could meet all the upper middle class of the region." The café was small in size but had a very fashionable reputation around 1875 and extremely well-cooked meals were served on the first floor. There the apprentice seaman found a change from sea biscuit and *la vache enragée*. Polish money subsidized French cooking.

The Café Bodoul was frequented at that time by a preponderantly Royalist clientele. Possibly Conrad was first taken there by the Delestangs or acquaintances of theirs. Conrad mentions it twice in his books:

I was the one to speak first, proposing that my companions should sup with me, not across the way, which would be riotous with more than one "infernal" supper, but in another much more select establishment in a side street away from the Cannebière. It flattered my vanity a little to be able to say that I had a corner always reserved in the Salon des Palmiers, otherwise Salon Blanc, where the atmosphere was legitimist and extremely decorous.[3]

For lunch I had the choice of two places, one Bohemian, the other select, even aristocratic, where I had still my reserved table in the *petit salon,* up the white staircase.[4]

Unfortunately the identity of these young men whom Conrad used to meet at this period in these two cafés is not known, except for one whom he knew only very slightly and who later made a name for himself in French letters and politics both as a poet and as a progressive member of Parliament: Clovis Hugues, who had recently been released after being sentenced for his role in the Communist movement. Obviously he was not one of the habitués of the Café Bodoul, which indicates the range of Conrad's social life during his stay in Marseilles. He also knew a sculptor named Frétigny who appears in his novel about Marseilles, *The Arrow of Gold,* under the name Prax. There were others who were connected with Conrad, if not more intimately, at least more secretly, in an adventure to be related later.

After having given six months' play to an exuberance which had been too long repressed, Conrad re-embarked on July 10, 1876, this time in the *Saint-Antoine.* He was listed on the crew muster not this time as "apprentice" but under the unexpected heading "steward," a position he did not actually fill (another steward is listed on the same muster) but which placed him in a rather special position between officers and crew and which paid thirty-five francs a month. On August 18, after a voyage of thirty-nine days, Conrad arrived in Saint-Pierre in Martinique, where the ship stayed a month before setting sail for St. Thomas, where it arrived at the end of September.

The ship had four officers and a crew of thirteen. In addition to Captain Antoine Escaras, of whom Conrad had very pleasant recol-

[3] *The Arrow of Gold,* Vol. I, Ch. I.
[4] Ibid., Vol. IV, Ch. I.

lections, and the third mate, Pierre Defaucompret, who may have been a descendant of the translator of Walter Scott and Fenimore Cooper, there was a first mate on board who was destined to play a unique role in Conrad's thought and work.

He was called Dominic Cervoni and was born at Luri in Corsica. He was forty-two at that time, with more than twenty-five years of seagoing behind him. His personality was definitely formed. Later, in *The Mirror of the Sea,* Conrad drew a physical portrait of him under his own name:

> His thick black moustaches, curled every morning with hot tongs by the barber at the corner of the quay, seemed to hide a perpetual smile. But nobody, I believe, had ever seen the true shape of his lips. From the slow, imperturbable gravity of that broad-chested man you would think he had never smiled in his life. In his eyes lurked a look of perfectly remorseless irony, as though he had been provided with an extremely experienced soul; and the slightest distension of his nostrils would give to his bronzed face a look of extraordinary boldness. This was the only play of feature of which he seemed capable, being a Southerner of a concentrated, deliberate type. His ebony hair curled slightly on the temples. He may have been forty years old, and he was a great voyager on the inland sea. . . .
>
> For want of more exalted adversaries Dominic turned his audacity fertile in impious stratagems against the powers of the earth, as represented by the institution of Custom-houses and every mortal belonging thereto—scribes, officers, and guardacostas afloat and ashore.

Some of the physical and moral traits of this man can be found in *The Arrow of Gold,* again under his own name, but aspects of his personality crop up under different names and in various lands and circumstances in several other places in Conrad's works.

Dominic Cervoni was Conrad's real initiator into the art of the sea. His long experience, the sureness of his eye, the controlled strength of his character, awoke in this young man not only a strong liking but an admiration and affection which were never to be effaced from his heart. Cervoni for his part took an interest in this young foreigner, so enthusiastic and eager to learn. Cervoni's

knowledge was not limited to the sea; he passed on to his avid
disciple his views about the world of men and things—views which
were both humane and yet completely free of illusions. Dominic
made himself the Mentor of this seagoing Telemachus: an unusual
Mentor in his contempt for law, his warm scepticism, and his
cold-blooded taste for dangerous adventures so compatible with the
hot-blooded one in the heart of his impatient disciple. In Dominic
Cervoni Conrad found a man older than himself capable of completely understanding youthful follies, who would try to make them
at least appear reasonable. What more could this young Pole want
or ask just then?

It is not surprising that later, after he became a writer, Conrad
took pleasure not only in recreating Dominic Cervoni in person in
The Mirror of the Sea, in which he summed up his experiences at
sea, and in *The Arrow of Gold,* in which he recounted a major part
of his life in Marseilles, but in incorporating the traits, the character,
the moral attitude—the soul if you will—of Dominic in people as
diverse as Tom Lingard in *The Rescue,* Nostromo in the novel of
that name and, in the very last hours of his life, Jean Peyrol in
The Rover and Attilio in *Suspense,* the latter a reproduction, feature
for feature, of the appearance and role of the then first mate of
the *Saint-Antoine.*

For Dominic and Conrad the voyage of the Marseilles sailing ship
was not limited to the scheduled ports of call nor to the transportation of the cargo listed on the manifests. They—and probably no
one else on board—took part in a ticklish illegal mission which
consisted in convoying to its destination on the Gulf of Mexico a
shipment of arms and munitions destined for a certain political
party in one of the republics of Central America. The trip was
made on a little schooner, probably from St. Thomas. The exact
place of landing is not known; it was probably Puerto Barrios in
Guatemala, or Puerto Cortés in Honduras, but several passages
in Conrad's work prove the reality of this clandestine trip along the
coast of Central America and the west coast of South America:
among others, this passage referring to a character who was to
serve later as the prototype for Ricardo in *Victory:*

It so happened that the very same year Ricardo—the physical
Ricardo—was a fellow passenger of mine on board an ex-

tremely small and extremely dirty little schooner, during a four days' passage between two places in the Gulf of Mexico whose names don't matter.

A clearer allusion is made in *The Arrow of Gold:*

> I had just returned from my second West Indies voyage. My eyes were still full of tropical splendour, my memory of experiences, lawful and lawless, which had their charm and their thrill: for they had startled me a little and had amused me considerably.

Unfortunately Conrad's correspondence gives few hints on this point. In the course of this expedition he had only a few brief contacts with land, but we know he touched Cartagena in Colombia, and we read in one of his letters:

> . . . Puerto Cabello where I was ashore about twelve hours. In Laguayra as I went up the hill and had a distant view of Caracas, I must have been two and a half to three days. It's such a long time ago! And there were a few hours in a few other places on that dreary coast of Venezuela.[5]

This expedition went off without complications during October and November, 1876, and Conrad owed to it, not only the excitement aroused in him by the atmosphere of adventure, but also a story he heard in the course of it about a particularly daring theft of silver bullion which had recently occurred and which, thirty years later, gave him the substance of the plot of *Nostromo.* "That distant time," as he said in the preface to this book, recalling the days of his youth, "when everything was so fresh, so surprising, so venturesome, so interesting; bits of strange coasts under the stars, shadows of hills in the sunshine, men's passions in the dusk. . . ."

In the course of this West Indian voyage Conrad received from his uncle, Thaddeus Bobrowski, the first of those letters written over almost twenty years—in Polish of course—to his adventurous nephew. Even in the first one he draws a distinction which he was always ready to repeat and which seems to have been to a great extent true: when his nephew shows any sign of wildness or

---

[5] Letter to Richard Curle, July 22, 1923.

imprudence it is blamed on his Korzeniowski blood; when he acts with wisdom and restraint the Bobrowski blood gets the credit.

"You are always impatient and scatterbrained," writes Uncle Thaddeus early in October, 1876, while his nephew is sailing the Caribbean Sea. "You remind me much more of the Korzeniowskis than of my beloved sister, your mother. You have lost your trunk and your belongings. Do you need a nurse and do you think I am one? Now you tell me you have lost your family photographs and your Polish books and want me to send you others. . . ."

And after two pages of scolding—though it is affectionate in tone—the uncle declares that he will send him the photographs after all and gives him the name of a Polish bookseller in Paris from whom he can order the books. Nor does he forget to send him the money to pay for them.

Conrad and Dominic Cervoni must have rejoined their ship in Port-au-Prince from where the *Saint-Antoine* sailed on December 5, arriving in Marseilles on February 15, 1877.

Conrad did not abandon his mentor when the crew was discharged. They met in the Café de la Colonne Trajane on the Place Neuve (now the Place Victor-Gelu), a café kept by the beautiful Léonore, nicknamed "la Romaine" who was enamored of Dominic. She was slightly pock-marked but, as someone who knew her said, "it just looked like embroidery." Or else Conrad would take Dominic to the theater, for which the first mate of the *Saint-Antoine* had a weakness, and it must have been this period that left the memories of Rossini, Verdi, and Meyerbeer operas and of Offenbach operettas that Conrad still used to recall with obvious pleasure toward the end of his life.

Aboard the *Saint-Antoine,* where his elegant manners and background which set him slightly apart from the crew had earned him the nickname "The Count," Conrad had made friends with everyone by the energy with which he went to work in spite of a constitution which was still not very robust. Everyone on board tried to prevent him from overtaxing himself. They all hoped he would sign on again—not to mention his uncle who, far away in Poland, was convinced—probably rightly—that it was the interludes in Marseilles that made havoc of his nephew's finances. Everyone expected Conrad to sail in the *Saint-Antoine* when she left Marseilles for the West

Indies and the name "Korrcuiowski Conrad" even appeared on the crew muster; but at the last minute the words *embarquement nul* were written against his name, without further explanation.

A note from his uncle seems to indicate that Conrad had a quarrel with M. Delestang at this time, but the reason for his failure to ship out again is to be sought in an adventure he was engaged in, many aspects of which are still mysterious.

In a letter from Thaddeus Bobrowski to his nephew dated October 14, 1876, there is a reference to Conrad's determination to join the Carlist forces. In the light of this letter, the determination looks very much like a gesture of bad temper on the part of an impecunious young man whose uncle is threatening to cut off his allowance. It is even more inexplicable if one remembers that the Carlist war in the Basque country was almost over by February, 1876, although there were still centers of smoldering activity in other parts of Spain. However, so far as his uncle was concerned, Conrad's determination was not just an empty threat.

In *The Arrow of Gold* Conrad recalled, forty years later, the violent excitement of his eventful life at Marseilles, and, though certain revelations made there are veiled, though the chronology is uncertain, the facts recounted there may be considered true. A hand-written note of the author on a copy of this book does in fact prove that the events and characters are authentic, and there is no reason to doubt it. This is supported by a letter to Sir Sidney Colvin in 1919:

> My dear (as D. Rita would have said), there are some of these 42-year-old episodes of which I cannot think now without a slight tightness of the chest—*un petit serrement de coeur*.

At the Delestangs' house and at the Café Bodoul Conrad had found himself in strongly pro-Carlist surroundings. Royalist circles had enough in common with the aims of the Carlists to support them: weren't they both devoted to the principle of legitimacy? Marseilles had become an important center not only of pro-Carlist feeling but of supplies of money, provisions, and munitions—as the Spanish consul bitterly complained to the authorities of Bouches-du-Rhône.

The adventure in which Conrad had unexpectedly become involved in the Gulf of Mexico had fired his young imagination; now he only wanted to do it again; he was spoiling for a fight.

At the Delestangs' he had been introduced to various people from the legitimist world. This young foreigner of very good family, highly intelligent and wearing the glamorous halo of Poland's so recent misfortunes, who had adventurously plunged into the unknown of life at sea, could hardly fail to please in an environment pervaded by the last flickers of romantic politics and fanatical devotion to almost extinct principles.

The Delestangs' salon was not the only one where they indulged in the secret joys of conspiracy, and it was in another of these salons, if we are to believe the circumstances set forth in *The Mirror of the Sea* and *The Arrow of Gold,* that Conrad one day met an Englishman of about thirty years of age, named Henry C—— whom the sense of adventure had led to take part in a gunrunning expedition in the Gulf of Gascony on behalf of the Carlists. When Conrad met him he had just escaped the fire of a Spanish man-of-war and had had to swim ashore. In the salons of Marseilles he was the hero of the day. The quiet demeanor of this much-lionized hero had deeply impressed Conrad and aroused his sympathy. They became friends and Conrad was introduced by him to an American from North Carolina named J. K. Blunt, a young man of about thirty, very elegant in appearance, whose family had been ruined in the Civil War and who, owning nothing but his sword, had put that at the service of Don Carlos. A young man of Marseilles, Roger P. de la S——, the cousin of a big leather merchant whose wife ran a Royalist salon too, had also become a close friend of Conrad, whose recent adventure, discreetly publicized, gave him a wider reputation than his age would have merited.

None of these young men was really interested in Don Carlos or his claims; for them the attractions of the adventure lay in the risks. For some time they had been looking for someone reliable and with some experience of the sea to run arms and munitions to the east coast of Spain. Conrad was the very man. He was young, full of enthusiasm, had a little experience at sea, a few connections among seamen. There was no possible doubt of his loyalty to the cause. He must have talked to these young men about Dominic Cervoni, about his character, his superb seamanship, his acquaintance with—and scorn for—customs officials of all nationalities. This was the man they needed. Conrad put the matter before him and Dominic let himself be talked into it. It only remained to find the right ship for such expeditions. The four young men formed a sort of syndicate which became the owner of a sixty-ton *balancelle* which Conrad calls the *Tremolino.*

According to *The Arrow of Gold,* the scheme was born about a week after Conrad got back from the West Indies. Fate was playing into the hands of this Pole, so greedy for adventures. Not yet twenty, here he was caught up in the last dynastic venture of nineteenth-century Europe, a venture which still retained its romantic savor.

Dominic Cervoni became the skipper of the *balancelle;* Conrad went with him. How long this series of clandestine voyages between Marseilles and the Spanish coast went on, no one can say exactly: certainly not more than a few months, but it brought Conrad some violent excitement. They had to distract the attention of coast guards, land on dangerous shores, give customs men and carabineers the slip, make contact with muleteers, real or alleged, who were to be at such and such a place on the coast on such and such a day, with no one any the wiser. What bliss! And all this time Dominic continued the education of the "signorino" through talk, aphorisms, and example. As Conrad said:

> He and I were engaged together in a rather absurd adventure, but the absurdity doesn't matter. It is a real satisfaction to think that in my very young days there must, after all, have been something in me worthy to command that man's half-bitter fidelity, his half-ironic devotion.[6]

Several times the adventure almost ended badly under the fire of carabineers who had got wind of what was going on. It finally did finish disastrously when one day Dominic and the "signorino" found themselves with no alternative but to drive the *Tremolino* ashore on the rocky coast of the Gulf of Rosas to escape the persistent curiosity of a Spanish coast guard. Later Conrad turned the death of this little ship into one of the most moving chapters of *The*

[6] *Nostromo,* Author's Note.

Mirror of the Sea, and in *The Arrow of Gold* we find this revealing passage:

> . . . everything slipped out of my grasp. The little vessel, broken and gone like the only toy of a lonely child, the sea itself, which had swallowed it, throwing me on shore after a shipwreck that instead of a fair fight left in me the memory of a suicide. It took away all that there was in me of independent life, but just failed to take me out of the world, which looked then indeed like Another World fit for no one else but unrepentant sinners. Even Dominic failed me, his moral entity destroyed by what to him was a most tragic ending of our common enterprise. . . . And one evening, I found myself weary, heartsore, my brain still dazed and with awe in my heart, entering Marseilles by way of the railway station, after many adventures, one more disagreeable than another, involving privations, great exertions, a lot of difficulties with all sorts of people who looked upon me evidently more as a discreditable vagabond deserving the attentions of gendarmes than a respectable (if crazy) young gentleman attended by a guardian angel of his own.

Looking back on it much later, in 1919, in a letter to a critic, Conrad said:

> All this gun-running was a very dull if dangerous business. As to intrigues, if there were any, I didn't know anything of them. But in truth, the Carlist invasion was a very straightforward adventure conducted with inconceivable stupidity and a foredoomed failure from the first. There was indeed nothing great there worthy of anybody's passionate devotion.[7]

Possibly the end of the *Tremolino* happened immediately before a letter of June, 1877, in which Conrad, who had not breathed a word of this whole exploit to his uncle, offers his intention of sailing for the Indies as the pretext for the advance of four years' income. His uncle's letters reveal also that Conrad was thinking of becoming

[7] Letter to J. C. Squire, August 21, 1919.

a French citizen the following month, to which Uncle Thaddeus replied:

> As to the French naturalization, I am against it because of the compulsory military service, Lord knows for whom or what. I would have preferred Swiss naturalization and I should like you to make some inquiries about that and find out what it would cost. . . . I entreat you to take good care of your documents, your birth certificate and your father's passport, so that you won't run into trouble there. We will make a definite decision on this after you return from the Indies.[8]

On the other hand, a note from his uncle reveals that at the end of 1877 Conrad informed him of his intention of signing on for a year and a half or two years with his former captain in the *Saint-Antoine,* but this was probably nothing but a shrewd pretext to conceal the real reasons for his need of money. The *Tremolino* episode, which had just ended so disastrously, had initiated him into an entirely different domain: that of passion.

Among the supporters of Carlism in Marseilles, one of the most generous had been a young woman who is supposed at one time to have attracted Don Carlos himself and who had inherited a considerable fortune from an amateur painter with whom she had lived for several years in Paris. This painter had died a short time previously, leaving her, among other property, several houses in Marseilles, one of them on the Prado, where she used to take refuge from time to time from the too persistent advances of her admirers, a good many of whom found her fortune an additional attraction.

The young woman herself was extremely attractive. The seclusion in which she lived, her reserved manner, the rumors about her liaison with "El Rey," had created an atmosphere of mystery around her. In the legitimist salons, where her position prevented her being received even if she had wanted to be, she was spoken of in hushed but sympathetic tones.

She had contributed to the purchase of the *Tremolino,* probably

[8] Letter of August 8, 1877.

through J. K. Blunt, the American turned Carlist, and this was the beginning of Conrad's connection with her. Much later, on the eve of his old age, he drew a bewitching, strange portrait of her under the name of Rita de Lastaola, in *The Arrow of Gold*. This name "Lastaola" is that of a pass in the Basque country near La Bidassoa, where the Carlists had set up a customs post and which figured frequently in the papers and in conversation in the early part of 1875. What was the real name of this young woman? It has never been discovered.

In any case, Rita and Conrad were just about the same age: they were in similar situations, having no real roots in society. Conrad's devotion to an enterprise in which his political convictions were not engaged in any way and whose risks he had accepted at first solely out of a craving for adventure and subsequently out of attachment to her, could not fail to touch the young woman. She fought against her feelings for several months. From her experience of life she had acquired a more mature attitude to people and things than this young Pole, but after the loss of the *Tremolino* and the utter ruin of Carlist hopes, when Conrad, haggard and beaten, abandoned even by Dominic, had returned to Marseilles, Rita no longer had the strength to fight against her infatuation with this young man who was suddenly left without anything.

The affair was brief; its setting was probably a quiet village in the Alpes Maritimes, like that of the affair of M. Georges described at the end of *The Arrow of Gold*. It probably occupied the last two weeks of 1877 and the first two months of 1878.

However hard one tries to keep out of the way of a spiteful world, chance sometimes takes a disturbing hand. Conrad had to go to Marseilles if only to draw his income in the office on the Rue d'Arcole. He intended to stay in town only briefly and return immediately to his retreat, but a young man he knew stopped him, glad to see him again, and in the course of the conversation told him of the excitement aroused in a certain circle by the sudden disappearance of "Madame de Lastaola." He thought he ought to tell him that Captain J. K. Blunt (of the extinct Carlist army) was spreading it abroad that she had fallen into the hands of an unscrupulous young adventurer whom she was keeping.

Conrad's blood rose. He had known for a long time that J. K.

Blunt's attitude was not exactly disinterested. He had not forgotten a certain interview he had had a few months earlier with Mrs. Blunt, the mother of the "captain," an extremely distinguished lady, who had advised him to stay away from Madame de Lastaola, since she saw no obstacle to a marriage between her remarkable and unlucky son and the young lady's millions—in a spirit of pure chivalry, of course! The tone and subject of the conversation had amused Conrad, for he was already beyond the age of complete naïveté. Now the situation had become impossible: and Conrad, hiding the real reason for another trip to Marseilles, sent his seconds to Captain J. K. Blunt, "American, Catholic and gentleman," as he used to describe himself, and fought a duel with him. Both adversaries were wounded. "Je lui ai fracassé la patte," Conrad declared to one of his relatives a long time after the event.

The duel must have taken place late in February, 1878, for at the beginning of March Uncle Thaddeus received a telegram from a friend of Conrad in Marseilles, Richard Fecht, telling him that his nephew had just received a bullet wound.

In a house she owned on the Rue Sylvabelle the young woman nursed Conrad tenderly as long as his condition demanded it. Once she was sure he was out of danger, the woman we know only as Rita, determined not to compromise the young man's future any longer, decided to disappear forever from his life, if not from his memory, as suddenly as she had entered it.

Thaddeus Bobrowski, who had hurriedly left Kiev, where he was staying, for Marseilles, arrived to find his nephew on his feet again but in a very precarious position financially and it did not take him long to suspect, perhaps even to recognize, the real reasons. He spent a fortnight in Marseilles and, after paying debts amounting to almost four thousand francs, giving his nephew a serious lecture and informing him that he could from now on count on nothing beyond an income of twenty-four hundred francs a year, he left again for the Ukraine without too much confidence in the future of this nephew in whose veins, it was all too obvious, ran the wild blood of the Korzeniowskis.

Left alone, the sad end of his combined amorous and maritime adventure understandably made Marseilles absolutely unbearable to Conrad. He could not help comparing the emptiness of his existence with the richness it had offered his mind and senses a few months earlier. After three and a half years of independence it never occurred to him to return to his homeland. This would have looked like failure. The only certainty he had to cling to was that of his vocation, and that had been developed and strengthened in him. The sea was his only haven. An opportunity arose for him to leave Marseilles almost without spending a penny. He did not hesitate.

On April 24, 1878, he took passage on an English freighter, the *Mavis,* which had called at Marseilles en route to Constantinople, carrying coal. The Russo-Turkish war had just ended: the preliminary peace treaties had been signed on the preceding March 3, and Conrad could still catch a distant glimpse of the tents of the camp of San Stefano. The steamer was bound for the port of Yeisk at the tip of the Sea of Azov, where she was to pick up a cargo of linseed in the middle of May. On May 21 she again passed through the Dardanelles and on June 18, 1878, entered Lowestoft on the east coast of England.

And that is how, abruptly and yet indirectly, Joseph Conrad ended three years of adventurous life between Marseilles and the West Indies and left France for England for good, and how, in his twenty-first year, he set foot on the soil of this new country for the first time, hardly knowing a word of English.

III

Youth

(1878-1883)

> It is indeed hard upon a man to find him-
> self a lost stranger, helpless, incomprehen-
> sible, and of a mysterious origin, in some
> obscure corner of the earth.
>
> "Amy Foster"
>
> O youth! The strength of it, the imagina-
> tion of it!
>
> "Youth"

WHEN HE STEPPED ashore from the *Mavis* at Lowestoft, Conrad
found himself utterly isolated. In the six weeks' voyage aboard this
Scottish ship he could at best have learned a few words of this new
language. He knew no one at all in England and his very meager
resources had no prospect of improvement in the near future. He
knew that his uncle was too displeased by his unseemly escapades
in Marseilles to be expected to give him anything extra.

About the middle of July a letter from Thaddeus Bobrowski told
him what a young man in this situation is usually told: "to work,
and live within his income, otherwise his uncle will be obliged to
cut off his allowance. After all, plenty of young men his age go to
work to help their families instead of being a burden to their
relatives, etc. etc. His uncle has sacrificed his cure at Marienbad this
year to pay for his nephew's follies." He adds:

You wanted to be a sailor and now you must take the consequences. You have lost my confidence. Work now to regain it. And you will regain it if you apply yourself steadily and settle down.[1]

This letter reveals that Conrad had been—and was still—thinking of joining the French Navy, so he had not yet made up his mind not to return to France. His uncle raised no objection. In spite of his threats, he was an excellent man who was by no means out for blood. Nonetheless he continued to scold his nephew:

If you cannot find a ship at present, do something else. Be a clerk or anything at all, but work. I am having 600 francs sent to you. Live on this money as best you can. Sign on as an ordinary seaman. If you know what poverty is, that will teach you to respect other people's money. . . . If you would rather wait and enlist in the Navy, find yourself a job in the meantime, because even if you were to assure me that you would some day be a vice-admiral, you wouldn't get a penny. I repeat: if you don't find a position before the completion of your twenty-fourth year, you will get nothing from me. I do not wish to work for an idler.

But his nephew had already gone bravely to work. The most urgent thing was to find a job that would give him a chance to learn English without making too big a hole in his modest savings. On July 11, 1878, he embarked as an ordinary seaman aboard a ship with the magnificent name *The Skimmer of the Sea,* although she was only a little two-hundred-ton coaster plying between Lowestoft and Newcastle. By September 25 Conrad had made six voyages between those two ports in this ship.

That is how he learned English: from those fine "East coast chaps. Tan and pink-gold hair and blue eyes, each built as though to last for ever, and coloured like a Christmas card." He also learned it from reading the *Standard.* He tried painfully and not always successfully to guess the pronunciation of many of the words he read which were outside the limited vocabularies of the seamen, fishermen, or ship's chandlers who were his companions

[1] Letter of July 8, 1878.

for those two months. With his first pay he bought a complete Shakespeare in one big volume bound in green, which he read eagerly, supplementing it with John Stuart Mill's *Political Economy* which, he confessed later, always had a soporific effect on him.

He never intended to stay in coastal shipping for good, only just long enough to learn the ropes of the trade and acquire enough knowledge of the everyday and technical language. He wanted to see countries, sail the deep seas, but how was he to manage it without connections or help?

In the *Standard* he had come upon the advertisement of a shipping agent in London who sounded as though he might be able to smooth his way. He wrote him a letter—his very first composition in English—telling him what he wanted and that he would come and see him. Toward the end of his life he recalled that first visit to London:

> . . . After a period of probation and training I had imposed upon myself as ordinary seaman on board a North Sea coaster, I had come up from Lowestoft—my first long railway journey in England—to "sign on" for an Antipodean voyage in a deep-water ship. Straight from a railway carriage I had walked into the great city with something of the feeling of a traveller penetrating into a vast and unexplored wilderness. No explorer could have been more lonely. I did not know a single soul of all these millions that all around me peopled the mysterious distances of the streets. I cannot say I was free from a little youthful awe, but at that age one's feelings are simple. I was elated. I was pursuing a clear aim, I was carrying out a deliberate plan of making out of myself, in the first place, a seaman worthy of the service, good enough to work by the side of the men with whom I was to live; and in the second place, I had to justify my existence to myself, to redeem a tacit moral pledge. Both these aims were to be attained by the same effort. How simple seemed the problem of life then, on that hazy day of early September in the year 1878, when I entered London for the first time.

> From that point of view—Youth and a straightforward scheme of conduct—it was certainly a year of grace. All the

help I had to get in touch with the world I was invading
was a piece of paper not much bigger than the palm of my
hand—in which I held it—torn out of a larger plan of London
for the greater facility of reference. It had been the object of
careful study for some days past. The fact that I could take
a conveyance at the station never occurred to my mind, no,
not even when I got out into the street, and stood, taking
my anxious bearings, in the midst, so to speak, of twenty
thousand hansoms. A strange absence of mind or unconscious conviction that one cannot approach an important
moment of one's life by means of a hired carriage? Yes, it
would have been a preposterous proceeding. And indeed I
was to make an Australian voyage and encircle the globe
before ever entering a London hansom.

Another document, a cutting from a newspaper, containing
the address of an obscure shipping agent, was in my pocket.
And I needed not to take it out. That address was as if graven
deep in my brain. I muttered its words to myself as I walked
on, navigating the sea of London by the chart concealed in the
palm of my hand; for I had vowed to myself not to inquire
my way from any one. Youth is the time of rash pledges.
Had I taken a wrong turning I would have been lost; and
if faithful to my pledge I might have remained lost for days,
for weeks, have left perhaps my bones to be discovered bleach-
ing in some blind alley of the Whitechapel district, as it has
happened to lonely travellers lost in the bush. But I walked
on to my destination without hesitation or mistake, showing
there, for the first time, some of that faculty to absorb and
make my own the imaged topography of a chart, which in
later years was to help me in regions of intricate navigation
to keep the ships entrusted to me off the ground.[2]

The place was not easy to find in the maze of the City. It was a
tiny office, its windows still covered with the dust of 1815, so dark
that a gas jet was burning, although it was one o'clock in the
afternoon. It was occupied by a man with a long white beard, a
big nose, thick lips, and heavy shoulders. His curly white hair

[2] *Notes on Life and Letters.*

made him look like an Italian baroque apostle. Silver-rimmed spectacles on his nose, he was engaged in eating a mutton chop brought in from the eating house round the corner.

The visitor slowly produced a series of sounds which must have borne sufficient resemblance to the phonetics of English speech for the "baroque apostle" to get their drift. Without ceasing to eat he explained that his business certainly was finding ships, but for young gentlemen who wanted to go to sea as premium apprentices with a view to becoming officers. This was not what Conrad wanted at all. He had no money to pay any sort of "premium." He wanted a berth before the mast, but this man could be of no help to him there, for an act of Parliament made it a penal offence to procure ships for sailors. "An act—of—Parliament. A law. You understand?" repeated the "baroque apostle" to this bewildered young foreign gentleman. He had not been an hour in London and he already run his head against an act of Parliament![3]

Noticing the foreigner's obvious distress, the man with the white beard took it upon himself to get around the law as best they could and found him a berth as able seaman aboard the *Duke of Sutherland,* a fine big sailing ship of a thousand tons. She sailed regularly to Australia in the wool trade and, according to her first mate, "knew the road to the Antipodes better than her own skipper."

Conrad embarked at London on October 15, 1878, for Sydney, where he arrived at the end of January, not reaching London again, on board the same ship, until October 19, 1879, just over a year after his departure.

In all of Conrad's work we have only one reference to this voyage—the recollection of a rather unpleasant experience:

> One wintry, blustering, dark night in July, as I stood sleepily out of the rain under the break of the poop something resembling an ostrich dashed up the gangway. I say ostrich because the creature, though it ran on two legs, appeared to help its progress by working a pair of short wings; it was a man, however, only his coat, ripped up the back and flapping in two halves above his shoulders, gave him

[3] See Ibid. (Tr.)

that weird and fowl-like appearance. At least, I suppose it was his coat, for it was impossible to make him out distinctly. How he managed to come so straight upon me, at speed and without a stumble over a strange deck, I cannot imagine. He must have been able to see in the dark better than any cat. He overwhelmed me with panting entreaties to let him take shelter till morning in our forecastle. Following my strict orders, I refused his request, mildly at first, in a sterner tone as he insisted with growing impudence.

"For God's sake let me, matey! Some of 'em are after me—and I've got hold of a ticker here."

"You clear out of this!" I said.

"Don't be hard on a chap, old man!" he whined pitifully.

"Now, then, get ashore at once. Do you hear?"

Silence. He appeared to cringe, mute, as if words had failed him through grief; then—bang! came a concussion and a great flash of light in which he vanished, leaving me prone on my back with the most abominable black eye that anybody ever got in the faithful discharge of duty. Shadows! Shadows! I hope he escaped the enemies he was fleeing from to live and flourish to this day. But his fist was uncommonly hard and his aim miraculously true in the dark.[4]

This first voyage to the East must have left him some less unpleasant memories as well, although on the whole it does not seem to have been particularly agreeable. His still-rudimentary knowledge of English, the fact that he was an ordinary seaman, always having sailed in a more privileged capacity before, the necessity of relying on his pride alone for the nervous strength he needed to help his still-delicate constitution to stand the often exhausting work—all this probably combined to make a pretty discouraging first impression.

He did not sign on again in the *Duke of Sutherland;* moreover, a letter from his uncle shows that on his return to London he was seized with a desire to go back to the Mediterranean. It is uncertain

---

[4] *The Mirror of the Sea.* It was during this stay in Sydney that he met the Frenchman with no hands who kept a tobacco shop not far from the Circular Quay and who served much later as a model for a character in the story "Because of the Dollars."

just what called him: the spell of the old classic sea, the hope of seeing Dominic Cervoni again, some stirring of his emotions, or perhaps a wish to immerse himself again in an atmosphere less foreign to him.

Obviously Conrad had not yet made up his mind. He plans to go to Odessa the following year and meet his uncle there, but the latter replies significantly:

> I should not like you to come to Russia before becoming a British subject.[5]

This explains the persistence with which Thaddeus Bobrowski pursued the question of naturalization over the next seven years. Conrad repeatedly proposed coming to see his uncle in the Ukraine and every time the latter dissuaded him. He was afraid—with some justification, for he had seen such cases—that the imperial government might be inclined to interfere with the liberty of this Pole, son of a political prisoner, who for the last ten years had in fact been in an irregular position as regards the Russian authorities. We see Thaddeus Bobrowski urging his nephew to become first an Austrian then a Swiss citizen. Conrad, for his part, had often thought of becoming French. Since he couldn't legally be what he was, a Pole, the best thing was to get rid as quickly as possible of the label "Russian subject" which the accidents of Polish history had attached to him. There is no doubt that not being able to return to his fatherland was more than once a great grief to Conrad; combined with the memory of the treatment accorded the victims in his own family, this was enough to maintain in him an enduring hatred of Russia, which the generosity of his character never overcame and which seems to have found new food in the reflections of his mature years.

Though he was not making any attempt to become a British subject, he was even then thinking of turning his service in the French merchant navy to account, and toward the end of 1879 he asked his uncle to approach M. Delestang, from whom he had parted on rather bad terms, for a certificate of service. And in fact the Marseilles shipowner lost no time in sending it to Mr. Bobrowski, even extending the dates a little in Conrad's favor.

[5] Letter of October 26, 1879.

Without further delay—and somewhat hastily for a young sailor whose great love, now and forevermore, was sailing ships—Conrad embarked on December 12, 1879, in the *Europa,* a London steamship, aboard which he called at Genoa, Leghorn, Naples, Patras, Cephalonia, Messina, and Palermo, returning to London on January 30. He seems to have come across an unusually unpleasant captain and this experience certainly did nothing to diminish his dislike of steamships.

He got back to London quite ill, feverish, with a bad cough and no money, at a moment when his uncle, who was in difficulties himself, could not come to his help. He spent several weeks, very depressed, in a furnished room at 6 Dynevor Road, Stoke Newington, where he was to stay while he was ashore during the next five years. But his nature was not one to remain downcast long, to look to other people for help, to complain without doing anything; he had great pride. The mere sight of his uncle's letters kept reminding him of the relatives and friends in Poland who predicted that he would never amount to anything, that he was a scatterbrain. His mastery of English and of his trade had grown with such amazing speed that he was already thinking of taking his third mate's examination, scarcely eighteen months after first setting foot on English soil.

During his stay in London after his Mediterranean voyage he wrote letter after letter to his uncle. Only the replies survive but they reveal the doubts tormenting the young man. It is even clear that he thought for a time of leaving the merchant navy and becoming the secretary of a Canadian involved in railways and politics, and his uncle replies:

I thoroughly sympathize with your unfortunate experience with that madman, Captain Monroe. He ought to be deprived of his certificate. On the other hand, if he is not legally mad, his certificate is valid. I don't understand the logic of the English very well, but they can't be changed and we have to adapt ourselves in our dealings with them. I suppose the *Europa* is back now and that you have the certificate from your first mate who is now a captain and that you have taken or are about to take your examination. Remember that I send you my blessing and all best wishes. Françoise[6] prays for you morning and night.

I said all I had to say about your naturalization in my last letter. You can't live forever like a bird on a twig. Sometime or other you have to have some legal standing. You should think about it, and it is better to do so with a clear head than under the stress of circumstances. You wouldn't be a "Nalecz," my dear boy, if you didn't change your mind. I say this on account of what you wrote me about Mr. Lascelle's offer to make you his secretary in charge of his railroad interests. I shouldn't be your uncle nor the man I am, if I failed to say outright that it's no good jumping from one trade to another like this. Changes like that produce misfits who, as we say in this country, gather no moss. . . . Ask yourself if it is sensible to stake your future on one man, whoever he may be, however great and noble, when that man is an American businessman and politician. It is nobler and more sensible to stake your future on a trade you have mastered by hard work. You have chosen to be a sailor; you can branch out into commerce, and I am sure you will manage all right without constantly changing professions. That's my advice. Do as you think best, for as far as your career goes I give you a completely free hand, since I don't know how you are situated. There has never been anything of the adventurer in my make-up and that is why I should like to see you in a steady job.[7]

These temptations to give up the sea are only very short-lived—slight depressions born of his strong ambition. Early in June, 1880, he passes his examination—and with distinction, for Captain Rankin, his examiner, was a hard man to satisfy.

The first of all, tall, spare with a perfectly white head and moustache, a quiet, kindly manner, and an air of benign intelligence, must, I am forced to conclude, have been unfavourably impressed by something in my appearance. His old thin

[6] A family servant.
[7] Letter of May 30, 1880.

hands loosely clasped resting on his crossed legs, he began by an elementary question in a mild voice, and went on, went on. . . . It lasted for hours, for hours. Had I been a strange microbe with potentialities of deadly mischief to the Merchant Service I could not have been submitted to a more microscopic examination. Greatly reassured by his apparent benevolence, I had been at first very alert in my answers. But at length the feeling of my brain getting addled crept upon me. And still the passionless process went on, with a sense of untold ages having been spent already on mere preliminaries. Then I got frightened. I was not frightened of being plucked; that eventuality did not even present itself to my mind. It was something much more serious, and weird. "This ancient person," I said to myself, terrified, "is so near his grave that he must have lost all notion of time. He is considering this examination in terms of eternity. It is all very well for him. His race is run. But I may find myself coming out of this room into the world of men a stranger, friendless, forgotten by my very landlady, even were I able after this endless experience to remember the way to my hired home." This statement is not so much of a verbal exaggeration as may be supposed. Some very queer thoughts passed through my head while I was considering my answers; thoughts which had nothing to do with seamanship, nor yet with anything reasonable known to this earth. I verily believe that at times I was lightheaded in a sort of languid way. At last there fell a silence, and that, too, seemed to last for ages, while, bending over his desk, the examiner wrote out my pass-slip slowly with a noiseless pen. He extended the scrap of paper to me without a word, inclined his white head gravely to my parting bow. . . .

When I got out of the room I felt limply flat, like a squeezed lemon, and the doorkeeper in his glass cage, where I stopped to get my hat and tip him a shilling, said:

"Well! I thought you were never coming out."

"How long have I been in there?" I asked faintly.

He pulled out his watch.

"He kept you, sir, just under three hours. I don't think this ever happened with any of the gentlemen before." [8]

The new-fledged officer found himself at the foot of the stairs without ever consciously descending them. When he came out of St. Katherine's House on Tower Hill and mechanically looked at the Gardens to his left, the front of the Mint to the right, the two policemen stalking up and down the pavement with a superior air outside the Black Horse, he wouldn't have called the King his cousin. It was one of the finest days of his life.

But the finest day of your life is only one day, after all, and this certificate was nothing but a scrap of blue paper. He had to find a berth as third mate, and there is nothing more wearying, more discouraging, than to spend your days "looking for a ship." Fortunately, the search and the wait were not as long as they seemed to his impatient temperament. Less than three months later he was listed in a ship's company as an officer.

Meanwhile, as evidence of his uncle's satisfaction, he received a letter from Poland which sheds a great deal of light on both uncle and nephew:

June 5, 1880, Kazimierowka

My dear Boy and Officer,
I received both your letters two days ago telling me the happy outcome of your examination. You have given me great joy. The sheet of paper on which the Gentlemen of the Board of Trade have written so many terrible threats in the event of your not fulfilling your duties, has been my recompense, and I owe it to you. I fully share your joy, which derives from two sources: 1. you have proved to your uncle and everyone else that you have not been living on other people for the last four years; 2. you have managed to overcome the handicaps of being a foreigner with no influence behind him. You are also indebted to Capt. Wyndham, Prof. Newton [9] and all your comrades who rejoice at your success.

[8] *A Personal Record.*
[9] Tutors who had coached Conrad in the preceding months.

There are honest folk everywhere—just think of Solary and Richard—you only have to find them. You have come across them at the very start and you are bound to love them and to help others who need it. After all, you see, there are far more good folk than bad. I congratulate you, *Monsieur l'officier de second rang de la Marine de Commerce de la Grande-Bretagne!*

Now, sir, you have taken your first step. All you need to get on is hard work and perseverance. You are approaching twenty-four: you have one more year to find a steady position, independent of your uncle. He will continue to watch over your affairs with the same love and interest, but you will have no more claims on his purse, as there are others coming up, your young cousins.

I am grateful to you for taking me into your confidence about your plans and interests, but I repeat: do as you think best, for I have no idea of your situation; you know much better than I what you should do. I give you a free hand, even if it involves becoming a Yankee. In my last letter I told you that it seems to me better to remain a sailor than to plunge into American politics. On the other hand, I shall raise no objection if you do otherwise, on two conditions: that you remember that you will have to take the consequences of your actions and that in the stormy life of America you never forget what you owe to the nobility of your nation and your family. . . . I embrace you and bless you.[10]

By the end of June Conrad was definitely abandoning forever the idea of giving up the sea. It was his last—and very temporary—hesitation.

His uncle is the first to rejoice at his nephew's decision and, as he always does in such cases, he ascribes the young officer's perseverance to his Bobrowski side. He writes jokingly:

I note with pleasure that your "Nalecz" character is being modified by the influence of the "Bobruszczuki" [11] as your

[10] Letter of June 28, 1880.

[11] "Bobruszczuki." A pun on the name Bobrowski and the word "Bobrusz" meaning "beaver."

incomparable mother used to call her own family before she flew away to the Nalecz nest. This time I rejoice over the influence of my own family, though not without acknowledging in the Nalecz an initiative and enterprise superior to that which run in our veins. From the crossing of these two famous strains new blood should emerge, so persevering and so scholarly that it will astonish the whole world.

He did not know how truly he spoke.

From now on Conrad's vocation is fixed. His uncle's letters no longer show the least doubt in the boy's spirit and good will. The experiences of his years in Marseilles, his year's service between England and Australia, the strict and pressing demands of the profession, not to mention the particular circumstances of his birth and his natural energy—all these have matured this young man of twenty-two beyond his years. With inflexible single-mindedness, in the face of disappointments, dangers, and the lack of material gain, he will from now on heed only the unconquerable attraction which the perpetual struggle of the ship and its company against the treacherous or angry sea holds for him. As his responsibilities grow he feels more and more strongly the solidarity of a crew sharing a common life in a common struggle, while every day strengthens in him his feeling of liberty, of individual action in the solitude of the great oceans, of the satisfaction of being able to breathe freely, far from political or social conventions or tyranny. After a childhood so steeped in unhappiness this was more precious to him than to other men and it was later to furnish the very substance of a work where so many people, cut off and separated from social groups and their conventional views, are yet at the same time strongly, irresistibly impelled by a few profoundly simple human convictions and obligations.

On August 21, 1880, he embarked at London for Sydney in the *Loch Etive,* an iron steamship of twelve hundred tons, recently built, belonging to the famous Loch Line of Glasgow and commanded by Captain William Stuart of Peterhead, who for fifteen years had been famous as commander of the *Tweed,* one of the fastest clippers ever known. From a chapter in *The Mirror of the Sea* we know that Conrad was the youngest officer on board and that this was a rather harsh but profitable first training in exercising his initiative and responsibility as an officer under a captain like Stuart who was renowned for his seamanship and under a first mate who "had the reputation of being the very devil of a fellow for carrying sail on a ship."

Captain Stuart was fifty years old and his temper was not always the mildest, owing to his inability to equal in his new ship the record runs that had made him famous when he was master of the *Tweed*. As Conrad wrote later:

> There was something pathetic in it, as in the endeavour of an artist in his old age to equal the masterpieces of his youth. . . . It was pathetic and perhaps just the least bit dangerous.[12]

The young officer's responsibility was increased by an illness of the second mate, which did not make his relations with the captain any easier, seeing that the latter's orders were generally laconic and usually consisted in forbidding his officers to "take any sail off her."

Having arrived in Sydney sometime in November, he left again the following month to return to Europe round the Horn and he landed at London on April 25, 1881, after an absence of eight months. It was in the course of this return voyage that he was to acquire the conviction that "the most amazing wonder of the deep is its unfathomable cruelty," the day that they rescued in mid-Atlantic the crew of a Danish brig who had been working desperately at the pumps for days to keep her hull afloat. The sea was ideally calm: the day exquisite. The crew was saved in the nick of time. Conrad took part in the rescue and, once back in his own ship, looked with other eyes upon the sea after this "initiation" into its treacherous cruelty.[13]

Once more it is the letters of Uncle Thaddeus, more frequent than usual during this period, that tell us what we know of Conrad's life and thoughts during the year 1881. The uncle appears well satisfied with his nephew: he sends him a little money to help him get through his next examinations. Obviously Conrad has shown

---

[12] *The Mirror of the Sea.*
[13] Ibid., "Initiation."

in his letters a very lively enthusiasm for life at sea. His service in the *Loch Etive,* trying though it may have been, the voyage round the Horn—quite an experience for a sailing ship—had given him a sense, still vague but already strong, of the beauty of his lifework.

His uncle would have welcomed a little less enthusiasm and did not want the young officer to set out for Australia again but instead to sign on for a shorter voyage which would bring him back to London in September so that they might meet in Wiesbaden, where he proposed to take the cure. However, by the end of May Conrad has given up hope of meeting his uncle in Wiesbaden or anywhere else. He is anxious to put in without delay the months of active service required for his remaining examinations. His one idea now is to become a captain.

The fire of youth had never burned hotter in him than now. Never had his morale been higher. Never again would his physical health be so robust, so stable.

> The last post [writes his uncle] brought me a letter from you which I appreciate especially because it is full of a spirit of energy and initiative, despite the failure of our plans to meet. Perhaps this disappointment is worse for me than for you—and I don't mean to reproach you in saying that. For when one is young one has much more faith in the future, one is certain of having a favorable balance with fate, while as for me, I've closed the accounts already. You are sure we shall meet again, and I doubt it. I want it to be so and I hope it will be so, but at the same time I see all the uncertainty of my desires. Meantime I assure you that this melancholy tone does not mean any deterioration in my health; it is simply a reasonable judgment upon life.[14]

In this same letter the uncle expressed a wish which has a special significance for us, not only because it is probably the first literary encouragement the future author ever received, but also because it proves that Conrad was already showing literary talent in his native language and that he possessed a sense of style.

This encouragement was not prompted only by family good will;

[14] Letter of June 28, 1881.

it came from a man who, in his letters and in his memoirs, has himself given proof of true literary talent. On June 20, 1881, he wrote:

> Personally I hope you will see new lands and new oceans, for I am sure it is very boring always to see the same things. As you are not forgetting your Polish (God bless you for it—and you have my blessing too!) and as you write very well, I am coming back to a subject I have already mentioned. It would be very good if you would write for the Warsaw *Wedrowiec [Traveler]*. We have very few travelers and even less reporting of this kind. I am sure everyone would be very interested in it and after a while they would pay you for it. It would be a kind of link with your country and a tribute to your father who wanted to serve—and did serve—his country with his pen. Think about it. Put together a few recollections of your voyage to Australia and send them in as a sample. The address of *Wedrowiec* is well known in Warsaw. Six newsletters a year from different parts of the world would not take up much of your time. It would be amusing for you and for others.

This encouragement had no effect at all. Conrad did not yet feel any urge to set down impressions; he was satisfied to receive them. He was quite content to feel young and healthy and to know that the whole world—at least the world of oceans—was open to him with its possible adventures, its probable dangers, its certain risks. This youthful exaltation would perhaps have sought an outlet in writing had it been repressed: being free, it was content with its own freedom. In any case an encouragement to write in Polish, just when he was becoming familiar with English and intending to become an English seaman, could not but deter him a little, and the laziness that comes naturally to sailors ashore got the better of it.

One not very explicit allusion in a letter from Thaddeus Bobrowski indicates that about the middle of 1881 Conrad sailed in a ship, the *Anna Frost* (or *Forst*) which suffered a disaster in August:

> I received your upset letter yesterday. Thank God you escaped alive and got away with a few days' illness and a

stay in hospital which has done you good—which doesn't
often happen. I am sending you the £10 you ask for, and I
am not taking it out of your allowance but sending it to
you as a "seaman in distress." [15]

In this same letter Conrad must have mentioned a commercial
project he had in mind, for his uncle adds:

As you are a Nalecz, beware of risky speculations based
on nothing but hope, for your grandfather lost everything in
speculations and your uncle made debts and bad blood in
the same way.

Although they came a little closer that year—for Thaddeus
Bobrowski spent a month at the Hôtel Suisse in Montreux—the
uncle had to forgo his hope of a reunion with his prodigal son,
with whom he had spent only a fortnight in the last seven years.
After many efforts, the officer in search of a job found one. The
ship, a four-hundred-ton bark, was old; the captain old and bent,
yet it was his first command. The chief mate, too, was a man of
middle age, but Conrad was young and felt sure of success and of
lasting for ever. What did it matter if things didn't look too rosy?
Everything would turn out all right. All the same, when he embarked as second mate on board the *Palestine,* on a dull, rainy day,
September 21, 1881, it was for lack of anything better. This can
be seen from a letter his uncle sent him just before they sailed:

You don't seem to be very pleased with your new position,
first because it's a bark which offends your dignity, and
secondly because it's only £4 a month which offends your
purse. The captain seems to be a poor type whose intelligence
leaves something to be desired, but perhaps this will give
you an opportunity to distinguish yourself as an expert!
Deus te ducat, perducat et reducat, as our ancestors used to
say to those who were going forth to war. I repeat it as I
bid you farewell and embrace you from the bottom of my
heart. [16]

[15] Letter of August 15, 1881.
[16] Letter of September 23, 1881.

In the same letter we see that the officer in the British merchant navy is not uninterested in Polish problems and has been concerned about Poland's hopes from the Pan-Slav movement. His uncle replies with great judgment:

> What you write about the hopes we attach to Pan-Slavism is very fine and quite plausible, but in practice it involves great difficulties. You do not pay enough attention to the effect of numerical strength on world opinion. A more important nation which relies on Pan-Slavism and publicly professes a disinterestedness it does not have, secretly counts on its size to insure its hegemony. You are making the same mistake in attributing qualities to us which are not really ours. By Pan-Slavism Russia understands only the Russification of all other nations and their conversion to the Orthodox Church. She maintains that she is a country of eighty million inhabitants (which is not true) and that our more highly developed culture and longer historical existence represent the culture and life of only one single class claiming to be a whole nation (which is true to a certain extent) and that it is *she,* Russia, who will really develop popular culture.
>
> She tells the Czechs that their nation is too small; that we and they (the Czechs) represent a bastard culture, Slav and Western, while she represents the true Slav-Oriental culture (which is non-existent). She (Russia) tells the other countries that they are too weak, that they, too, are of Oriental extraction and that they should therefore submit to Russia because she is more powerful, or else they will perish. . . . I suppose all this will come to an end some day, but I shall be in my grave before then. In the meantime, we more than anyone else, like the pariahs we are, deprived of political life and of all right to national development, must preserve and defend our individuality today until a turn in historical events, brought about by the efforts of our own minds, produces the deeds that will restore our true existence as a nation.

The bark *Palestine* in which Conrad sailed was none other than the ship later immortalized in the wonderful story "Youth" under

the transparent pseudonym *Judea*. The story is in fact nothing but
an exact transcription of events. Ship, officers, crew, circumstances
—Conrad faithfully preserved them all, even down to the real
name of his captain. The feeling of youth triumphant, which colors
these pages written seventeen years later, was certainly his at that
point in his life, and we see a reflection of it in a letter from his
uncle, written while Conrad was in Falmouth waiting for his ship
to be made seaworthy again:

> I am in despair about your misfortunes of last year. I say
> "of last year" because I sincerely hope that your bad luck will
> end this year. Some of it can be put down to fate, but your
> judgment enters into it too. Yet now, after the wreck,[17] your
> cool judgment seems to have deserted you, since you have
> decided to accept such a wretched ship as the *Palestine*. I can
> well understand that you decided on it so as not to be a bur-
> den to me by staying longer in London and to accumulate
> some service as acting second mate for your final examination.
> But, my dear boy, you haven't considered that if, as a result
> of the mishaps and accidents that are almost bound to happen,
> you fall ill or get hurt, I wouldn't abandon you, and that if
> you are going to be drowned it won't make much difference
> whether you arrive in the Valley of Jehoshaphat as third or
> second officer! I have never claimed any right to interfere
> with you, especially now that you are twenty-four, but all
> the same I do advise you not to embark on such a miserable
> ship as this. Certainly danger is inevitable in a sailor's life,
> but that does not preclude a reasonable attachment to life, nor
> reasonable precautions for preserving it. You and Captain
> Beard seem to me like desperate men looking for trouble and
> the shipowner like a scoundrel risking the life of ten good
> men for his dirty profit.
>
> Think carefully, my dear boy, about what you ought to do.
> I won't object if you go back to London and I will even try
> to help you, because obviously for the sake of 300 to 500
> rubles I don't want to see you at the bottom of the sea or
> ill or hurt, or with rheumatism for the rest of your life. Well,

---

[17] The wreck of the *Anna Frost*.

consider both sides, and the possibility of getting what you want. Curb your abundant ambition and let reason be your guide.[18]

But it was youth that spoke, the spirit of adventure, the thirst for new horizons, the desire for risk. The ship was incredibly old; she leaked, but what did it matter! It was Conrad's first voyage to the Orient, to an Orient bright with all the charms of a far-off unknown, of a legendary past. As he was to say in "Youth":

It was one of the happiest days of my life. Fancy! Second mate for the first time—a really responsible officer! I wouldn't have thrown up my new billet for a fortune. . . . Bankok! I thrilled. I had been six years at sea, but had only seen Melbourne and Sydney, very good places, charming places in their way—but Bankok!

The *Palestine* sailed down the Thames, took more than a week to reach Yarmouth Roads, weathered a gale and did not arrive in Newcastle until three weeks later. Having got there, the ship had missed her turn for loading and could not put to sea until six weeks later, on November 29, 1881, bound for Bangkok with a crew of eight men and two cabin boys and a cargo of five hundred tons of coal. A storm was raging in the Channel: the ship began to leak. Worn out by manning the pumps for several days, the crew refused to continue. They had to put in to Falmouth. At first they thought it was only necessary to unload part of the cargo and calk the hull. The ship was reloaded and left Falmouth, only to return a week later leaking worse than ever. She had to be put in dry dock. This took from January to September, 1882. Conrad spent part of his time in Falmouth reading Shakespeare in a cheap complete edition, to the noisy accompaniment of calkers' mallets driving oakum into the deck seams.

He managed to get a few days' leave and three months' advance in pay and rushed up to London. It took him a day to get there and another to come back, but the three months' pay disappeared. "I don't know what I did with it," he reported. "I went to a music hall, I believe, lunched, dined, and supped in a swell place in Regent

18 Letter of January 20, 1882.

Street and was back to time with nothing but a complete set of Byron's works and a new railway rug to show for three months' work." [19]

The *Palestine* had become a standing joke to the unemployed dockers and harbor men of Falmouth who thought she would never put to sea again. In a characteristic reaction, this strengthened the young officer's loyalty to the old ship and its old captain, whose first command was getting off to such a bad start. Every day he rejected more firmly the idea of looking for another ship. Another extract from one of his uncle's letters gives an idea of the young officer's enthusiasm:

> Your last letter gave me more pleasure than I can tell you because it was full of real energy and conveyed to me your will to work and your excellent health. . . . You are obstinate, my dear boy. Do the honor of the service and the customs of the country really demand that you go off in an old tub and break your neck? Being ignorant of both, I don't understand the problem, and I can only wish you a happy departure and a happy return. I should be very glad if you could be back soon enough for me to see you during the summer. I should like you to come to Cracow or Krynica to breathe a little of your native air. If you get back in time, we could meet in Cracow and go and spend four weeks in Krynica. If you come back in autumn, we could meet in Lwow and spend four weeks there. In any case I take it for granted that we shall meet again next year.

Having wasted a whole year through no fault of his own in order to acquire the months of sea duty required for his second examination, Conrad could not throw up his job, although he was wasting his time and the pay was poor.

At last the *Palestine* really did leave Falmouth, on September 17, 1882. She had a good breeze and a calm sea right to the tropics. She lumbered along at three miles an hour. She lumbered along like this for days without end. She entered the Indian Ocean, still lumbering terribly. The voyage had lasted almost six months when, on March 11, 1883, a strong smell of burning began to be noticeable

---

[19] "Youth."

and the next day smoke appeared. The following day they tried to stifle the combustion. On the fourteenth the deck blew up and the ship had to be abandoned. The boats remained by her until 7:45 A.M. when she was nothing but a furnace.

After the deck blew up Conrad found himself stretched full length on a pile of coal in the midst of a shower of splinters, his hair, eyebrows, and beard singed, but none the less delighted by the exciting unexpectedness of this adventure.

The crew was distributed between three boats. Conrad was in the smallest, with two men, a sack of biscuits, a few cans of meat, and a barrel of fresh water. He had been ordered to stay by the large lifeboat so that in case of bad weather they could be taken aboard her, but the young officer did not want to miss such a fine chance to show his initiative and confidence. He recalls his feelings in "Youth":

> I thought I would part company as soon as I could. I wanted to have my first command all to myself. I wasn't going to sail in a squadron if there were a chance for independent cruising. I would make land by myself. I would beat the other boats. Youth! All youth! The silly, charming, beautiful youth.
>
> . . . We made our way north. A breeze sprang up, and about noon all the boats came together for the last time. I had no mast or sail in mine, but I made a mast out of a spare oar and hoisted a boat-awning for a sail, with a boat-hook for a yard. She was certainly over-masted, but I had the satisfaction of knowing that with the wind aft I could beat the other two.
>
> . . . Next day I sat steering my cockle-shell—my first command—with nothing but water and sky around me. I did sight in the afternoon the upper sails of a ship far away, but said nothing, and my men did not notice her. You see I was afraid she might be homeward bound, and I had no mind to turn back from the portals of the East.

Exactly how long they spent in the boat is uncertain. "I was steering for Java," Conrad wrote later. "I steered many days. I remember nights and days of calm when we pulled, we pulled, and the boat seemed to stand still." What is known is that fifteen days after the disaster he was in Singapore [20] after getting his first glimpse of the Orient off the coast of Java. The impact of his first contact with the East, looked forward to so long throughout this interminable voyage, was never to be effaced from his memory and it impregnates the last pages of "Youth" with an unforgettable beauty.

Conrad spent the greater part of April in Singapore, awaiting the first chance to return to England, for, in spite of the strong attraction the East held for him, he was in a hurry to get back to Europe and take his first mate's examination. At the beginning of May he embarked for Europe as passenger in a steamer. The magnificent and dangerous adventure of the *Palestine* was over.

Eleven years later, in 1894, at a time when Captain Korzeniowski had just broken his connection with the sea for ever, although he did not realize it at the time, he met his old captain from the *Palestine*.

> He was a little grayer, a little more twisted and gnarled. He was very grimy and had a chocolate coloured muffler round his throat. He told me he had piloted a foreigner down the North Sea. His eyes were perfectly angelic. This is not a sentimental exaggeration, but an honest attempt to convey the effect. He was so bent that he was always looking upwards, so to speak. In the poky bar of a little pub, he told me, "Since my wife died I can't rest." He had not been able to snatch her in his arms that time. He said he was glad I "got on" and did not allude to our voyage towards Bangkok. I should think he *can* rest where he is now. [21]

It is unlikely that Captain Beard had really forgotten the unusually desperate circumstances in which he had lost his first command at sea; but when he met his former officer he had no wish to bring back memories which could only be painful to himself. It was different for the former mate. That adventure, despite its dangers and, indeed, because of them, had left in him nothing but a feeling of exaltation. In his memory it remained the most glorious moment of his youth. And that feeling was so vital and passionate

[20] The certificate he received from the captain of the *Palestine* is dated "Singapore, April 3, 1883."

[21] Letter to H. G. Wells, September 6, 1898.

and warm that, when Officer Korzeniowski had become the writer Conrad, it took him only a few days to write that magnificent tale, "Youth," for the thrilling romantic enchantment of his adventurous youth was still fresh—and already regretted—in his memory.

IV

Landfalls and Departures
(1883-1886)

Haven't we, together and upon the immortal seas, wrung out a meaning from our sinful lives?
    The Nigger of the Narcissus

I had elected to be one of them very deliberately, very completely, without any looking back or looking elsewhere. The circumstances were such as to give me the feeling of complete identification, a very vivid comprehension that if I wasn't one of them I was nothing at all.
    Notes on Life & Letters

ON MAY 13, 1883, Second Mate Conrad Korzeniowski landed at Port Said as passenger in a steamship. He had joined the ship, which was bound for Liverpool, at Singapore. Once back in London, early in June, he had two goals in mind: to take his second examination as soon as possible and to go and see his uncle who was impatiently awaiting him and whom he had not seen for more than five years. Again and again the uncle insists that Conrad must become a British subject:

> I would rather see you a little later as a free citizen of a free country than a little earlier as a citizen of the world.

Make your own decision and arrange things as you think best, for, after all, it is your skin that is at stake.[1]

Conrad did, in fact, seem to be treating the question of his naturalization very lightly. As for the meeting, they had at first decided that it should take place in Cracow, but Thaddeus Bobrowski had been ordered by his doctor to take the cure at Marienbad and proposed that they meet there.

At the beginning of July Conrad took the examination that would qualify him as first mate in the ships of the British merchant navy. Of his three seaman's examinations this one stuck in his memory as the worst. The examiner had the reputation of being "simply execrable." Conrad has described the scene in Chapter VI of *A Personal Record,* where he portrays the motionless, remote, enigmatic figure of the old captain who, shading his face in his hands, tries to make the candidate talk all kinds of nonsense and then begins to pile one catastrophe after another upon an imaginary ship, as though for the fun of it:

> It's no use enlarging on these never-ending misfortunes; suffice it to say that long before the end I would have welcomed with gratitude an opportunity to exchange into the *Flying Dutchman.*

And while the disasters descend endlessly upon this unfortunate ship, and the candidate, replying to one of the examiner's questions, says that there is nothing left for him to do but let her go, the examiner asks:

> "Nothing more to do, eh?"
> "No, sir. I could do no more."
> He gave a bitter half-laugh.
> "You could always say your prayers."

Yet after forty minutes of this nightmare and in spite of the handicap of his foreign birth, Conrad once more comes down Tower Hill with his certificate in his pocket and nothing in mind beyond getting ready to leave for Marienbad.

He arrived there on July 24, via Brussels, Frankfurt, and Egger,

[1] Letter of June 5, 1883.

and spent an enjoyable month with his uncle, first at Marienbad, then at Teplitz, near the border of Saxony. There he found himself in a Polish atmosphere, with his cousin, Charles Zagórski, Thaddeus Zaleski, an old friend of his uncle's, and Dr. Kopernicki, with whom he renewed his acquaintance. Uncle and nephew had plenty to say to each other, for it was five years since they had met. All his life Conrad would alternate between long periods of silence and taciturnity and long, copious conversations. A spellbinding story-teller, aside from his other talents, he must have told this Polish audience his reminiscences of five years in the British merchant navy, to which his latest voyage certainly contributed by no means the least startling details.

He returned to London through Dresden and wrote his uncle a letter from that city to which Thaddeus Bobrowski replied:

> Your letter from Dresden gave me real pleasure. I shall keep in mind everything you say. . . . You were right in thinking that back in Teplitz I felt unhappy and depressed when I sat down to table, and lonely over my evening tea when I saw my Admiral's seat empty. . . . As for going to sea again, the sooner the better. About your naturalization: I should like it to take place as soon as possible. Don't let the filthy lucre put aside for it be used for any other purpose.[2]

During their conversations at Marienbad, uncle and nephew had talked about their circumstances and plans. Thaddeus Bobrowski had given Conrad a résumé of his financial situation and, so to speak, shown him his accounts. Thanks to various gifts or legacies from members of his family, Conrad found himself in possession of a small capital of about thirty-six hundred rubles, at that time approximately three hundred pounds. He had met in London—in circumstances of which nothing is known—a man of German descent, Adolf P. Krieger, with whom he had formed a deep friendship. This Krieger was employed by, and probably a stockholder in, a London transport agency, Barr, Moering & Co. Conrad suggested to his uncle that in order to turn his small capital to best account he invest it in this firm. This was actually done and gave rise to some lengthy business discussions in his uncle's letters during the

[2] Letter of August 31, 1883.

following year, besides offering an explanation for some of Conrad's later intentions.

The day after his return from Marienbad, on September 10, he embarked as second mate aboard the *Riversdale,* a fifteen-hundred-ton sailing ship registered at London, bound for Madras.

We have no details about this voyage, certain memories of which are said to have inspired some scenes in the "Ferndale" episode of the novel *Chance,* but we do know beyond the possibility of doubt that Conrad had a rather violent argument with his captain, L. B. McDonald,[3] ending in his throwing up his job and leaving the ship at Madras. From there he went to Bombay in search of another position. He was offered one aboard a mail boat navigating in the Persian Gulf, but he was reluctant to serve in a steamship if he could possibly help it. One evening he was sitting with some other merchant-navy officers on the veranda of the Sailors' Home in Bombay which overlooked the harbor, when he saw a sailing ship approaching, a lovely ship with all the grace of a yacht. It was the *Narcissus,* a ship of thirteen hundred tons built nine years earlier by a sugar refiner of Greenock for a venture in the Brazilian sugar trade. This had failed and he had subsequently decided to employ her in the Orient. Two days later Joseph Conrad Korzeniowski was listed as her second mate. The *Narcissus* put out from Bombay on April 28 and the voyage ended at Dunkirk on October 17. The name of this sailing ship is familiar to everyone who knows the work of Joseph Conrad, and is connected with one of the most authentic stories that have ever dealt with the sea and sailors: *The Nigger of the Narcissus.*

The feeling of real life that pervades it derives not only from the genius of the author, but also from the reliability of his memory, for the pages of *The Nigger of the Narcissus* are actually nothing but the realistic and lyrical record of the actual voyage of the ship.

Conrad himself gave me some details as to the extent to which the novel follows fact, and I write them down exactly as he gave them to me in the course of a personal conversation shortly before his death:

[3] On the back of the certificate he gave Conrad, the captain of the *Riversdale* wrote opposite "Character for ability": "Very good"; opposite "Character for conduct" he wrote the single word "Decline." This is the only instance of an unfavorable comment in the thirteen certificates that cover Conrad's sea life.

The voyage of the *Narcissus* was performed from Bombay to London in the manner I have described. As a matter of fact, the name of the Nigger of the *Narcissus* was not James Wait, which was the name of another nigger we had on board the *Duke of Sutherland,* and I was inspired with the first scene in the book by an episode in the embarkation of the crew at Gravesend on board the same *Duke of Sutherland,* one of the first ships the crew of which I joined. I have forgotten the name of the real Nigger of the *Narcissus.* As you know, I do not write history, but fiction, and I am therefore entitled to choose as I please what is most suitable in regard to characters and particulars to help me in the general impression I wish to produce. Most of the personages I have portrayed actually belonged to the crew of the real *Narcissus,* including the admirable Singleton (whose real name was Sullivan), Archie, Belfast, and Donkin. I got the two Scandinavians from associations with another ship. All this is now old, but it was quite present before my mind when I wrote this book.

I remember, as if it had occurred but yesterday, the last occasion I saw the Nigger. That morning I was quarter officer, and about five o'clock I entered the double-bedded cabin where he was lying full length. On the lower bunk, ropes, fids, and pieces of cloth had been deposited, so as not to have to take them down into the sail room if they should be wanted at once. I asked him how he felt, but he hardly made me any answer. A little later a man brought him some coffee in a cup provided with a hook to suspend it on the edge of the bunk. At about six o'clock the officer in charge came to to tell me that he was dead.

We had just experienced an awful gale in the vicinity of the Needles, south of the cape, of which I have tried to give an impression in my book. . . .

As to the conclusion of the book, it is taken from other voyages which I made under similar circumstances. It was, in fact, at Dunkirk, where I had to unload part of her cargo, that I left the *Narcissus.*

To read *The Nigger of the Narcissus* and *The Mirror of the Sea* is to understand what Conrad's life was like not only during this voyage but for the whole of his twenty years in sailing ships. One can imagine exactly the setting, the atmosphere, the risks, the fatigue, the responsibilities of this existence, as well as the thrilling beauty of the struggle and the enthusiasm it aroused in a character like his, raised since childhood in a consciousness of spiritual values and a climate of unavailing struggle.

Conrad spent the whole winter of 1884–85 in London, mainly in preparing for the theoretical part of his next examination, and it was not until April 24, 1885, that he left for Hull to embark as second mate aboard the *Tilkhurst,* a fifteen-hundred-ton sailing ship registered at London. She went first to Cardiff, where Conrad landed on May 31. Five days later the second mate signed on again, bound for Singapore.

His stay in Cardiff enabled him to deliver a message given him some time previously by a sailor named Komorowski, a fellow Pole. This Komorowski had arrived in Cardiff as a stowaway in a German ship in order to escape Russian military service; he had been helped by another compatriot named Kliszczewski who had set himself up as a watchmaker in that city and who had lent him a little money, which Komorowski had asked Conrad to return. One morning Joseph Conrad presented himself at the watchmaker's shop. Kliszczewski, hearing someone address him in Polish, gave his unexpected visitor a warm welcome. A mutual liking sprang up immediately and was extended to the whole family, and a sincere friendship developed between the officer of the *Tilkhurst* and the watchmaker's son, a young man of about Conrad's age, which lasted until the writer's death.

In the course of this voyage from Hull to Cardiff, Conrad sent his uncle Thaddeus a letter, the reply to which offers further evidence of literary talent in the future writer.

Let us talk first about Barataria, a metaphor you suggested to me in such a witty manner and such a pure Polish style that reading this passage gave me real pleasure. I must defend myself against the suspicion you seem to hold that I don't know the work of Cervantes. Let me tell you that I reread him only last year at Teplitz. And more than one of my generation could tell you the same thing. You have a habit of dropping into metaphor without warning.[4]

This same letter ends with the words:

I am reassured by your explanations about the safety of your voyage to India, considering your well-known sobriety as far as wine and rum are concerned.

The *Tilkhurst* finished loading at Penarth and sailed on June 5. The voyage to Singapore went off without incident, as Conrad indicates in his letters to Spiridion Kliszczewski, son and partner of the Cardiff watchmaker. These letters are doubly precious as they are the only ones in existence written by Conrad before 1890. The complete series of letters he wrote to his uncle between 1874 and 1894 was destroyed in 1918 in the sack of the Kazimierowka house by the Bolsheviks.

The letters to Spiridion Kliszczewski from Singapore and Calcutta from the end of September, 1885, to the beginning of January, 1886, prove how touched this lonely foreigner had been by the friendliness shown him by the watchmaker's family "on the strength of a distant national connection." They prove, too, how strongly Polish he still felt, despite his service in the British merchant navy.

Whatever may be the changes in the fortunes of living nations, for the dead there is no hope and no salvation. We have passed through the gates where *lasciate ogni speranza* is written in letters of blood and fire and nothing remains for us but the darkness of oblivion. In the presence of such national misfortune personal happiness is impossible in its absolute form of general contentment and peace of heart. Yes, I agree with you that in a free and hospitable land even the most persecuted of our race may find relative peace and a certain happiness—materially at least; consequently I understood and readily accepted your reference to "home." When speaking,

[4] Letter of June 15, 1885.

writing or thinking in English, the word "home" always means for me the hospitable shores of Great Britain.[5]

One of these letters reveals an extraordinary project which he has had in mind, he says, for a long time: to take part in a whaling expedition in the Arctic. At the end of November he writes to his new friend from Calcutta that he is brimful with the most exhaustive information upon the subject. He has read, studied, pumped professional men, and imbibed knowledge upon whale fishing and sealing for the last four years. He is acquainted with the practical side of the undertaking and has the assurance of active help from a man brought up in the trade. He even has a vessel in view. He is wondering how to raise the necessary capital and asks his compatriot's advice, adding that it is not so much the desire to make a lot of money that prompts him but that he is "sick and tired of sailing about for little money and less consideration."

It is possible that this plan was of long standing; most likely it had been bolstered the year before aboard the *Narcissus* in conversations with the captain, for in *The Nigger of the Narcissus* this passage occurs, referring to Captain Allistoun (who may well be a replica of the real Captain Archibald Duncan):

> He was born on the shores of the Pentland Firth. In his youth he attained the rank of harpooner in Peterhead whalers. When he spoke of that time his restless grey eyes became still and cold, like the loom of ice. Afterwards he went into the East Indian trade for the sake of change.

Spiridion Kliszczewski dissuaded his compatriot from following up this whaling scheme. He did not consider his fellow Poles good businessmen and, besides, he knew nothing at all about the people Conrad would actually be dealing with. Conrad soon accepted his arguments and never did add the Arctic to the collection of oceans he had seen.

After a month in Singapore (September 25 to October 25), the *Tilkhurst* sailed for Calcutta, where she arrived on November 21 and stayed six weeks. Just at this time, when Conrad was in Cal-

[5] Letter to Spiridion Kliszczewski, Singapore, October 13, 1885.

cutta, a very young man published in the Christmas number of the *Civil and Military Gazette* of Lahore, in collaboration with his father, mother, and sister, a series called "Quartet," his first work. This was Rudyard Kipling, but it is unlikely that at the time the second mate of the *Tilkhurst* came across this first work of the man who, ten years later, was to be his rival.

It was in Calcutta that he heard of the death of his old tutor, Adam Pulmann, who, after taking his degree in philosophy, had decided to study medicine. He had established himself as doctor in a little town in Galicia. The letter that brought him the news told how all the poor people of the district, Christians and Jews alike, had followed the good doctor's funeral procession to the cemetery, weeping and wailing. And on the deck of his ship, in that Eastern town, Conrad saw again the Swiss landscape in which, twelve years ago, his fate had been decided.

At this time Conrad's health was unreliable; and during the following years it caused him considerable anxiety. His constitution, only moderately strong, was often under tremendous strain. He was high-strung by nature and often made demands on himself which were beyond his strength, prompted by his indefatigable pride and strong ambition. In spite of his antecedents and his often sickly childhood, life in the open air and his extreme sobriety had strengthened his constitution, but the unhealthy influence of sometimes exhausting climates, the fatigue, often crushing, of a seaman's life, undermined his reserves, without actually breaking his health.

An echo of this comes to us in a letter his uncle wrote to him on August 14, 1885, which reached him in Singapore:

In exchange for the detailed news I give you, I hope you will give me yours. How is your health in general and your liver in particular? In spite of your assurances that the climate of India is good from September to December, I am not as convinced of it as you are, and I would rather you had sailed for other latitudes. Seeing that your first voyage to India already affected your liver, the second may make the trouble much worse. Even if you become an admiral, at this price your lot won't be a happy one.

The homeward voyage must have been as uneventful as the outward one, for neither the *Tilkhurst* nor her crew figures in any
dramatic adventure in the writer's work. Nevertheless we do find,
at the beginning of *The Mirror of the Sea* a touching reference to
his captain, poor Captain B(lacke), and at the end of his career at
sea he pays homage to this little man, "stout, dignified, perhaps a
little pompous . . . a man of a singularly well-informed mind, the
least sailor-like in outward aspect, but certainly one of the best
seamen whom it has been my good luck to serve under."

The ship unloaded at Dundee in the middle of June and as soon
as he had carried out his duties Conrad, accompanied by Captain
and Mrs. Blacke, went directly to London to take his final examination.

As they said good-by, Captain Blacke paid him an indirect com-
pliment which touched the young officer deeply and which he always
remembered with pride. "If you happen to be in want of employment," he said, "remember that as long as I have a ship you have
a ship, too." But poor Captain Blacke, who had already been ill
during much of the homeward voyage, was never to go to sea again.
One of the most moving passages in Conrad's work is the one
where he tenderly recalls his last visit to his captain in London.[6]

Now he had to see about his examination and his naturalization.
He was very anxious to go to Poland as soon as his examination
was over, or at least somewhere where he could meet his uncle,
but the latter had to tell him of the serious illness of his brother
Casimir (who died a short time later), necessitating his presence,
and of the additional burden of Casimir's invalid wife and six
children who had suddenly become dependent upon his purse.

Thaddeus Bobrowski was a fine man but timid by nature, and
the approach of old age was increasing his desire for a settled life
for himself and security for others, so that he could not contemplate
without misgivings his nephew's appetite for adventure. After all,
his nephew was now thirty, and, though Uncle Thaddeus knew
better than anyone else where he got this appetite, it was less and
less understandable to him. He was approaching sixty; he had lost,
one after another, the sister he adored, his wife, his daughter;
he was about to lose his second brother. His affection for his sister-

[6] See *The Mirror of the Sea.*

in-law and her children was not so deep; Conrad was the dearest of his links with the past and his only projection into the future.

It is easy to understand that this country gentleman, in the depths of his peaceful Ukrainian province, should have wanted the prodigal to come home for good and, even if he could not live in his vicinity —which was out of the question—at least stop roaming the oceans of the world and, tired of risks, adventures, and strange countries, settle down in London to a commonplace existence.

Long ago he had expressed the wish that Conrad would combine the sea with commerce. This idea still lurked in his mind and when he so readily agreed to send Conrad the necessary money to become a stockholder in the firm of Barr, Moering & Co., it was with the secret idea that the need to supervise his interests would keep him in London more. The good man had even thought up a way of establishing a profitable connection between Barr, Moering & Co. and Poland:

> For your guidance, in case you should be thinking of going into business, and for the guidance of your partners, I would recommend a thorough study, on the spot, in London, of two problems: viz. the wheat-flour trade, because in Poland flour milling has been intensively developed lately and wheat is now to be exported in the form of flour. The second would be the granulated-sugar trade. Under my direction you could do a nice business in these two commodities. You would have to know not only the market but also the qualities and defects of the merchandise, as well as conditions at our end, etc., etc., etc.[7]

One can imagine the adventurous spirit in which his nephew must have read these lectures on business, and yet, strange as it may seem, the examination of documents has convinced me that those lectures were not inspired solely by the uncle's fond hopes for his nephew. At that time Conrad really was thinking seriously of giving up the sea and devoting himself to business. Probably, in addition to the advice of Thaddeus Bobrowski, Adolf Krieger was also urging the bright prospects of a life in commerce. True, if Conrad did for a time seem to accept this idea, it was probably nothing but a

[7] Letter of April 5, 1886.

stand-by in case he should fail to get his master's certificate—unlikely as this seemed to him. Another reason, too, may have contributed to his hesitation—his health. His uncle's letters of this period show that the young man was constantly worried about this: and at this time Conrad even hints to his uncle that if he passes his examination he will be content with one single voyage as captain before settling down to business.

The uncle cannot leave the Ukraine and Conrad cannot go there until he is a British subject, so he finally decides to settle this matter, on which his uncle has been prodding him incessantly for almost twelve years.

On August 19, 1886, Joseph Conrad Korzeniowski, "subject of the Russian Empire, of the age of twenty-nine years, mariner, unmarried," was granted a certificate of British naturalization. A few weeks later he received a letter in which Thaddeus Bobrowski said:

> I rejoice from the bottom of my heart that you have settled the matter of your naturalization, and I clasp my Englishman, as well as my nephew, to my breast.[8]

Three months later Conrad gave his uncle another reason for gratification—one that was this time just as satisfying to himself. On November 11, 1886, he was awarded his "Certificate of Competency as Master." This final examination had been as agreeable as the two earlier ones had been disagreeable. It had taken the form of a friendly conversation and a recommendation—which Conrad had no intention of following and never did follow—to "go into steam."

This foreigner who had landed in England knowing hardly one word of the language had taken only eight years to reach the top of the ladder in his irrational career. He had a right to be proud; looking back on the past, recalling the indignation aroused in his family by his incomprehensible ambitions, he might well experience the feelings expressed in this passage of *A Personal Record:*

> It was a fact, I said to myself, that I was now a British master mariner beyond a doubt. It was not that I had an exaggerated sense of that very modest achievement, with which,

---

[8] Letter of September 9, 1886.

however, luck, opportunity, or any extraneous influence could have had nothing to do. That fact, satisfactory and obscure in itself, had for me a certain ideal significance. It was an answer to certain outspoken scepticism and even to some not very kind aspersions. I had vindicated myself from what had been cried upon as a stupid obstinacy or a fantastic caprice.

Someone else, too, could rejoice just as much at his success: the man who had given him the material help necessary to reach this point and whose helpful advice and affectionate moral support had never failed him for twelve years, wherever he might be.

My dear boy,
  Long live the "Master, British Merchant Service." May he live as long as possible and may God grant him health. May he have all possible luck by land and sea. Your news of the *cachet rouge sur ton brevet* really gave me great joy. Since I am not an admiral, I have no right to give orders to the newly promoted captain. . . . As the humble provider of the means to this achievement, it only remains for me to rejoice that my pennies were not thrown away and that they have brought you to the top of the profession you have chosen, although twelve years ago Mr. Antoine [Syroczyncki], inheritor of the Greek and Roman virtues, cast such a discouraging horoscope for the young aspirant to the service of Neptune.[9]

But his naturalization and his certificate as a master mariner are not the only two events that made the year 1886 of particular account in Joseph Conrad's life. It was during this same year that he seems to have made his first attempt at writing in English. Not that he had at the time the least intention of publishing anything, but he had the style, as we have seen from his uncle's letters, and, now that he was master of a new language, a vague need to express himself was seeking an outlet. Uncertain of the subtleties of literary language, if not of everyday English, although as an inveterate and insatiable reader he had devoured many a book in English during his voyages, he began to write, as a kind of exer-

[9] Letter of November 26, 1886.

cise, the tale entitled "The Black Mate" for an open competition being run that year by the magazine *Tit-Bits*.

Although a story by this name does exist today among his works,[10] the surviving version does not offer an opportunity for judging Conrad's literary gifts at that time, for the story was re-written later. Even if we did not have the author's own revelations to go by, we should be bound to ascribe an early date to this work. Though one does, in fact, find in some places in the final version Conrad's own movement, temperament, and irony, the subject it-self is much more in the vein of the sea stories of W. W. Jacobs. This rather humorous story, probably inspired by an anecdote he had heard, seems a deliberate exercise and never gives that feeling of things seen, re-created and transformed by the temperament of the writer and of the man that makes Conrad's subjects, even when they are not absolutely autobiographical, seem to belong to a special world created by his own vision.

The existing version of "The Black Mate," however un-Conradian it may be, is nevertheless the sole survivor of those first exercises, whether on paper or in his head, that were leading Conrad, quite unconsciously, toward his second vocation, the one that was to bring him undreamed-of glory and to draw continuously upon the ex-periences of his first calling: the sea.

As a subject of the United Kingdom, master mariner in the merchant navy, and finally as an apprentice writer in a language which was the third he had mastered, the year 1886 marked a kind of triple adoption of our Pole by this new homeland to which he had been drawn by the hazards of life and by some secret affinity.

[10] *Tales of Hearsay,* A collection published posthumously.

V

Meeting Almayer

(1887)

. . . that part of the Eastern seas from which I have carried away into my writing life the greatest number of suggestions.

The Shadow-Line. Author's Note

If I had not got to know Almayer pretty well it is almost certain there would never have been a line of mine in print.

A Personal Record

HOWEVER PLEASANT and useful a possession a master mariner's certificate might be, it was not enough to live on. His need was urgent. The interest on the small sum invested in Barr, Moering & Co. could never be anything but a tiny supplement to his income, and the date of his thirtieth birthday was approaching when it had been agreed that Uncle Thaddeus was to stop sending him his usual three-hundred-pound allowance—a decision to which the necessity of supporting Casimir's widow and children gave new weight. Conrad could therefore not afford to wait for a command and on February 18, 1887, he went to Amsterdam to take a position as first mate in the *Highland Forest,* a thousand-ton sailing ship, registered at Glasgow and bound for Samarang.

The ship could not put to sea immediately. The cargo had not ar-

rived and it seemed that it never would. The winter was very severe.
The first mate had nothing to do on board; the prospect of sailing
diminished from day to day. The situation is accurately depicted in
The Mirror of the Sea:

> I call to mind a winter landscape in Amsterdam—a flat fore-
> ground of waste land, with here and there stacks of timber,
> like the huts of a camp of some very miserable tribe; the long
> stretch of the Handelskade; cold, stone-faced quays, with the
> snow-sprinkled ground and the hard, frozen water of the canal,
> in which were set ships one behind another with their frosty
> mooring-ropes hanging slack and their decks idle and deserted,
> because, as the master stevedore (a gentle, pale person, with a
> few golden hairs on his chin and a reddened nose) informed
> me, their cargoes were frozen-in up-country on barges and
> schuyts. In the distance, beyond the waste ground, and running
> parallel with the line of ships, a line of brown, warm-toned
> houses seemed bowed under snow-laden roofs. From afar at
> the end of Tsar Peter Straat, issued in the frosty air the tinkle
> of bells of the horse tramcars, appearing and disappearing in
> the opening between the buildings, like little toy carriages
> harnessed with toy horses and played with by people that ap-
> peared no bigger than children.

The days passed. Conrad was impatient over the delay and, having
nothing to do on board the ship, where he was unable to keep warm,
he used to spend his evenings in a café in the center of the town.

> It was an immense place, lofty and gilt, upholstered in red
> plush, full of electric lights, and so thoroughly warmed that
> even the marble tables felt tepid to the touch. The waiter who
> brought me my cup of coffee bore, by comparison with my
> utter isolation, the dear aspect of an intimate friend. There,
> alone in a noisy crowd, I would write slowly a letter addressed
> to Glasgow, of which the gist would be: There is no cargo,
> and no prospect of any coming till late spring apparently. And
> all the time I sat there the necessity of getting back to the ship
> bore heavily on my already half-congealed spirits.[1]

---

[1] *The Mirror of the Sea.*

He tells us that only his consciousness of the importance of his job gave him a little warmth to fight against the severity of that winter, but for an active man an important job which exists in name only is not much. During the day he would visit his charterer, a certain Mr. Hudig:

> (Mr. Hudig) always began by shoving me into a chair before I had time to open my mouth, gave me cordially a large cigar, and in excellent English would start to talk everlastingly about the phenomenal severity of the weather. It was impossible to threaten a man who, though he possessed the language perfectly, seemed incapable of understanding any phrase pronounced in a tone of remonstrance or discontent. As to quarrelling with him, it would have been stupid. The weather was too bitter for that. His office was so warm, his fire so bright, his sides shook so heartily with laughter, that I experienced always a great difficulty in making up my mind to reach for my hat.[2]

After countless visits to Mr. Hudig, after any number of daily letters (of which none, unfortunately, have survived) to the Scottish owners, the cargo finally did arrive and the day after they finished loading, the very evening before they sailed, the captain made his appearance. This was the man Conrad called "the excellent Captain MacW——," Captain John MacWhirr, whom he later immortalized by conferring his looks and character upon the captain whose terrific obstinacy he depicted in "Typhoon." In *The Mirror of the Sea* he makes two direct allusions to the real-life character, referring to this excellent captain's habit of remaining invisible in his cabin—even at mealtimes—during the early part of the voyage. This put Conrad in sole command of the ship for the first few days of his service as chief mate—to which he certainly had no objection.

He had, however, assumed the entire responsibility for the loading, and the cargo, having exasperated him by its slowness in arriving, was to give him still more trouble when it was there. It had been stowed in the hold with more regard for general textbook principles than for the idiosyncrasies of this ship, which was a stranger to him.

[2] Ibid.

Captain MacWhirr had realized this before setting foot on board and had predicted to his new officer in an ironic tone that they would have "a lively time."

He turned out to be a good prophet. The voyage from Amsterdam to Samarang was "lively but not joyful," for Conrad's method of loading had made the ship roll heavily and violently.

There were days when nothing would keep even on the swing tables, when there was no position where you could fix yourself so as not to feel a constant strain upon all the muscles of your body. She rolled and rolled with an awful dislodging jerk and that dizzily fast sweep of her masts on every swing. It was a wonder that the men sent aloft were not flung off the yards, the yards not flung off the masts, the masts not flung overboard.[3]

This unfortunate stowage had particularly unpleasant consequences for the chief mate. Toward the end of the voyage a spar struck him violently in the back and sent him sliding on his face for quite a considerable distance along the main deck. A strange illness followed: "inexplicable periods of powerlessness, sudden accesses of mysterious pain," so queer that in the end the patient agreed with his captain who, while nursing him with great care, told him he wished it had been a straightforward broken leg. The Dutch doctor he consulted on his arrival in Samarang could give no scientific explanation of the case. All he said was: "Ah, friend, you are young yet; it may be very serious for your whole life. You must leave your ship; you must be quite silent for three months—quite silent." [4] It goes without saying that Conrad followed his advice only halfway. Still, he was ill enough to have to leave the *Highland Forest,* which had arrived in Java in June, having sailed from Amsterdam in March. Early in July Conrad went to Singapore, the nearest British territory, and was admitted to hospital.

In his airy room, which overlooked the town and from which he could see the bay, he had plenty of leisure, as he wrote later, to remember the dreadful cold and snow of Amsterdam while watch-

[3] Ibid.
[4] Ibid. (Tr.)

ing the fronds of palm trees tossing and rustling beside his window. He was also able to enjoy the irony of this passage in a letter from his uncle which he had found waiting for him in Samarang:

> If I were to remind you of the affectionate, loyal interest that both Bismarck and Katkof display towards us, you would get the flavor of our moral and social position. Happy is he who can settle down in Patagonia and enjoy there the fruits of civilization and liberty! What must it be like in Java or Samarang?[5]

From the hospital in Singapore Conrad replied to these sentiments, giving news of himself. Another letter from his uncle shows that the young officer was still not able to explain the exact nature of his trouble:

> I had thought that you were on your feet again, that I had brought you into port, and that after fourteen years of effort and work you were on the right track. But "no luck," as you say, and that is really what it looks like, for if the prospect of continuing your career at sea means rheumatism, you are really too young for that. And as your leg bothers you already, I should be afraid of your never getting over it. It worries me not to know what it is. I should like to think it is just a slight indisposition, and yet the sad experiences I have had with my dear ones makes me fear the worst. With old age come doubts . . . . Alas! What can I send you except words of affection, buried, as I am, in the country, far away from everything, in a land that has no connection with the Indies. . . . I hope that this disappointment will be forgotten as quickly as so many others. . . . I suppose when you get back you will apply to the same shipowners, for even if this illness has broken your connection with them, you fulfilled your responsibilities completely honorably, as you say yourself. The main thing is for you to get well and come back to London soon.[6]

At the very moment when he had reached the peak of his career at sea, was he going to have to leave it on account of his health? As

[5] Letter of April 17, 1887.
[6] Letter of August 20, 1886.

it turned out, this strange indisposition did not keep him out of action as long as the Samarang doctor had expected, for, less than two months after going into the hospital, he managed to embark in Singapore as first mate on the steamship *Vidar.*

Most likely it was practical necessity and his still-precarious health that made him accept a berth in a steamship—something he had done only once before in his life at sea—and then for only a few weeks—ten years earlier. His more regular and less tiring duties would permit his complete recovery, while the relatively short voyages, involving minimum changes of climate, would be good for his rheumatic condition. He did not suspect that the voyage he was about to make during the next few months as chief mate of the *Vidar,* unimportant as they now appeared, were to play a considerable part in his life as a writer—a life of which he still had not the least inkling.

In October, 1924, I had the good fortune to meet Captain David Craig, who commanded the *Vidar* while Conrad was her first mate. Still very young despite his seventy years and his half century of service in Eastern seas, he himself gave me the following information:

The first time I met Conrad was at the Shipping Office of Singapore about the middle of August, 1887. He pleased me at once by his manners, which were distinguished and reserved. One of the first things he told me was that he was a foreigner by birth, which I had already guessed from his accent. I replied that that did not matter in the least as he had his certificate. (It was quite difficult at that time to find officers in the East who were not over fond of the bottle.) The *Vidar* belonged to an Arab called Sven Mosin Bin S. Ali Jaffree. He had been a rich man, but he had been nearly ruined by his two sons-in-law. I had navigated these waters for the past ten or twelve years, and I had got to know that Arab well. I respected him. Some of his creditors were on the point of making him bankrupt; the Chartered Bank had seized the ship, but they could not sell because I was a creditor with a prior claim—for wages, docking-costs, etc. During one voyage among the islands I collected several thousand guilders from his debtors, and on his instructions I placed them with a bank, which, after a credi-

tors' meeting, made an arrangement; there was a sale, and the
steamship *Vidar* became in part my property.

This was the situation of the *Vidar* when Conrad joined her, and
when he speaks, in *The Shadow-Line,* of the ship he has just left, it
is the *Vidar* he is describing.

> She was an Eastern ship, inasmuch as then she belonged to
> that port. She traded among dark islands on a blue-scarred sea,
> with the Red Ensign over the taffrail and at her masthead a
> house-flag, also red, but with a green border and with a white
> crescent in it. For an Arab owned her, and a Syed at that.
> Hence the green border on the flag. He was the head of a great
> house of Straits Arabs, but as loyal a subject of the complex
> British Empire as you could find east of the Suez Canal. World
> politics did not trouble him at all, but he had a great occult
> power amongst his own people.
>   It was all one to us who owned the ship. He had to employ
> white men in the shipping part of his business, and many of
> those he so employed had never set eyes on him from the first
> to the last day. I myself saw him but once, quite accidentally
> on a wharf—an old, dark little man blind in one eye, in a snowy
> robe and yellow slippers. He was having his hand severely
> kissed by a crowd of Malay pilgrims to whom he had done
> some favour, in the way of food and money. . . . Excellent
> (and picturesque) Arab owner, about whom one needed not
> to trouble one's head, a most excellent Scottish ship—for she
> was that from the keel up—excellent sea-boat, easy to keep
> clean, most handy in every way, and if it had not been for her
> internal propulsion, worthy of any man's love.

This eight-hundred-ton ship sailed, in fact, under the Dutch flag
and was registered at Banjermasin, one of the principal ports of
Borneo. The ship left Singapore, went through the Karimata Strait
and along the coast of Borneo to Banjermasin, which was usually
her first port of call. Keeping between the coast of Borneo and the
island of Pulo Laut, where she took on coal, she then proceeded to
Dongola, on the west coast of the Celebes, returned to Coti Broeuw
and finally reached Bulungan, a tiny settlement up a river on the

east coast of Borneo. From there she returned to Singapore by the same route. Most of these ports were situated some ten or twenty miles up the estuaries of winding rivers whose banks were covered with dense vegetation and thickets of all kinds of tropical trees. These little ports tucked away on the river banks generally consisted of one single long street—if it could be called a street—with a row of dwellings and shops facing the river and raised six feet above the ground, with the landing stage always occupying the most important place. They carried on a profitable trade in the natural products of the area: rubber, cane, gutta-percha and resin were the main cargo items. The voyages of the *Vidar* took only about three weeks for the round trip and she would stay at Bulungan only overnight, just long enough to load.

Besides the captain and first mate, there were two European engineers, a Chinese third engineer, a *serang,* and a crew of eleven Malays, not to mention eighty Chinese whom they took along for loading and unloading, for it was impossible to find sufficient experienced deck hands in those ports. Sometimes they carried a few passengers too.

Under these conditions Conrad made five or six voyages between Singapore and Borneo in the *Vidar,* between August 22, 1887, and January 5, 1888.

Bulungan was the place that Conrad later called Sambir, in *Almayer's Folly* and *An Outcast of the Islands,* and it was during these voyages that he got to know the characters whom he was later to turn into the heroes of the novels and stories that make up the "Malayan" part of his work.

There is no doubt that in his conversations with his captain, with whom he soon became friendly, he learned many details about people and events in this part of the world, still quite new to him. During the ten or twelve years he had spent there, Captain Craig had not only had to navigate an often dangerous archipelago and treacherous rivers, but he had also had to deal with the traders—European, half-caste, Malay, Arabian—of all these places. There were few men who could do more than Captain Craig to satisfy the lively curiosity of this first mate whose memory was so reliable and whose thoughts were so unexpected. Captain Craig himself, when he read Conrad's books later, was amazed at the use the writer had made of what little he had had time to see and hear, without seeming to pay any particular attention to it.

At Bulungan lived the Dutch half-caste whose real name was Almayer and whose appearance and character, according to Captain Craig, Conrad portrayed with such staggering accuracy. The author devoted an especially charming chapter of *A Personal Record* to his first meeting with Almayer, of which we shall quote only a few passages:

It was very early morning, and a slight mist . . . promised to turn presently into a woolly fog. Barring a small dug-out canoe on the river, there was nothing moving within sight. I had just come up yawning from my cabin. The serang and the Malay crew were overhauling the cargo chains and trying the winches; their voices sounded subdued on the deck below, and their movements were languid. That tropical daybreak was chilly. The Malay quartermaster, coming up to get something from the lockers on the bridge, shivered visibly. The forests above and below and on the opposite bank looked black and dank; wet dripped from the rigging upon the tightly stretched deck awnings, and it was in the middle of a shuddering yawn that I caught sight of Almayer. He was moving across a patch of burnt grass, a blurred, shadowy shape with the blurred bulk of a house behind him, a low house of mats, bamboos and palm-leaves with a high-pitched roof of grass.

He stepped upon the jetty. He was clad simply in flapping pyjamas of cretonne pattern (enormous flowers with yellow petals on a disagreeable blue ground) and a thin cotton singlet with short sleeves. His arms, bare to the elbow, were crossed on his chest. His black hair looked as if it had not been cut for a very long time, and a curly wisp of it strayed across his forehead. I had heard of him at Singapore; I had heard of him on board; I had heard of him early in the morning and late at night; I had heard of him at tiffin and at dinner; I had heard of him in a place called Pulo Laut from a half-caste gentleman there, who described himself as the manager of a coal-mine; which sounded civilised and progressive till you heard that the mine could not be worked at present because it was haunted by some particularly atrocious ghosts. I had heard of him in a place called Dongola, in the Island of Celebes. . . . I overheard more of Almayer's name amongst our deck passengers (mostly wandering traders of good repute) as they sat all over the ship —each man fenced round with bundles and boxes—on mats, on pillows, on quilts, on billets of wood, conversing of Island affairs. Upon my word, I heard the mutter of Almayer's name faintly at midnight, while making my way aft from the bridge to look at the patent taffrail-log tinkling its quarter-miles in the great silence of the sea. I don't mean to say that our passengers dreamed aloud of Almayer, but it is indubitable that two of them at least, who could not sleep apparently and were trying to charm away the trouble of insomnia by a little whispered talk at that ghostly hour were referring in some way or other to Almayer.

The outward appearance of this man, what he had heard of him and, above all, the pathetic contrast between his dilapidated condition and the enormous ambitions which he still cherished, made a deep impression upon the novelist's sensitivity just then awakening in Captain Conrad's consciousness. Here he suddenly found himself confronted with an unusually eloquent example of the discord between the power of the imagination and the weakness of human resources. This was to form the basis, the dominant theme—heroic, brave, and at the same time desperate—of the whole of his work. Had not he, too, nourished ambitions and dreams? And what was left of them in the monotonous life he was leading aboard this steamer, on a run where nothing unexpected ever happened? After the fiery ardor of his youth the impairment of his health had dampened his self-confidence. Was this, the ridiculous pathos of Almayer, what life held in store for him too? He tried to chase away this haunting idea, this unwelcome troublesome phantom, but all his pondering crystallized in this caricature of his own secret hopes and unavowed ambitions. The importance of this meeting cannot be questioned when we recall Conrad's own statement, later, in *A Personal Record*: "If I had not got to know Almayer pretty well it is almost certain there would never have been a line of mine in print."

During one of these voyages in the *Vidar*, just as they were leaving the Macassar Strait, they met, far out from the shore, a runaway Malayan slave, crouching in a small canoe half full of water, waiting for death. They picked him up and took him to the Celebes, and this episode later became part of *An Outcast of the Islands*. It was at Almayer's, too, that Conrad met the man who was to be the lamentable hero of that same book, Willems, a Dutchman, a former seaman, once a strong man, now ruined by drink.

During these voyages from Singapore to Borneo and back, Conrad also heard of and met Tom Lingard, out of whom he created one of his favorite characters, by combining some of the real features of this man, whose name he calmly borrowed, with memories of Dominic Cervoni, who, from the early days of his sea life to the last pages of his literary life, was to be a sort of familiar demon to him. The real Tom Lingard was the skipper of a sailing ship trading in the Malay Archipelago. His nephew, Jim Lingard, had spent some time aboard his uncle's ship and had then settled at Bulungan. It was actually on board the *Vidar* that he had been nicknamed *Lord Jim* on account of his distant manner. Conrad was to keep only the name and appearance of this character, giving him other adventures, as he did with Babalatchi and Lakamba, who were really just two natives of the Celebes established as traders at Broeuw, one of the *Vidar's* ports of call.

During these five months' navigation, Conrad observed with an intensity which was apparently never noticeable and which may have been unconscious. From the words of Captain Craig, of James Allen, the chief engineer, and of John C. Niven, the third engineer, the *Vidar's* first mate drank in all the information he could about these various people, their antecedents, morals, characters, interests, intrigues, and about those concealed or half-revealed enmities which, in this corner of the world, produced clashes between two or three races and several religions and aroused, at the farthest point of the Far East, moral conflicts, ambitions, passions, follies, ephemeral glories, and lasting failures.

Conrad never liked to take notes and probably took none on what he saw and heard, yet in our conversation Captain Craig repeatedly insisted on the fact that, at the end of his watch, when he went below to his chief mate's cabin, he generally found him writing. Conrad's correspondence at the time was more or less limited to his letters to his uncle, at the rate of one a month, which would not explain the frequent writing that Captain Craig says he so often interrupted. Here we may, without implausibility, risk a guess.

The previous year Conrad had in a way entered upon literary work by writing, as an exercise, that story for the magazine competition in London. We are justified in supposing that at this time, as a result of the compulsory idleness imposed upon him by his six or seven weeks in hospital in Singapore, his intellectual activity had intensified and was looking for an outlet. How could he have resisted the stirring within him of the writer wanting to be born, who was to wait another two years to establish himself and who was not to publish his first book for another seven years?

Captain Joseph Conrad Korzeniowski probably served his literary apprenticeship aboard the *Vidar*. Because of the inspiration he found there and the deep workings of this first gestation, the latter half of 1887 was richer in literary consequences than any other period in the amazing life of Joseph Conrad, except possibly, as we shall see, the second part of 1890, which he was to spend in the Congo. And through a special stroke of irony both these interludes in the life of a sailing-ship man were spent in steamers!

VI

First Command

(1888)

HIS HEALTH WAS improving, as a letter from Uncle Thaddeus implies:

> I send you all my good wishes on your thirtieth birthday.
> You have set my mind at rest with your assurances that you
> are well as regards legs and liver, and that you are sure of be-
> ing able to return to Europe any time life in the Indies has a
> bad effect upon your health. I suppose your idea is to get back
> to Europe without cost to yourself.[1]

His fellow officers on board the *Vidar* were very agreeable companions. Thirty years later he wrote to one of them:

> You could not really have believed that I had forgotten any
> time in the *Vidar*. It is part of my sea life to which my memory
> returns most often, since there is nothing to remember but
> what is good and pleasant in my temporary association with
> three men for whom, I assure you, I have preserved to this day
> a warm regard and sincere esteem.[2]

[1] Letter of December 18, 1887.
[2] Letter to J. C. Niven, December 5, 1923.

And yet, despite the congenial companionship aboard ship, the novelty of the scenery and the unique characters he met, an unbearable weariness was beginning to come over the second officer of the *Vidar*. This time it was not a question of a queer physical discomfort, but of a sort of moral disorder, a discontent with no precise cause, an inner melancholy, a vague nostalgia. As his strength revived, the lack of any element of surprise in these regular voyages proceeding according to timetable and in the routine work connected with the cargo began to seem boring. It was not enough for so active, so ardent a character. At his age he was not going to stagnate in this bourgeois existence and remain the first mate of a steamer for years. One or two more voyages and then he would go back to Europe, he told his uncle, who wrote to him in January, 1888, from the Ukraine:

> I received your letter of December 1st today. Your news and the report of what the doctor told you are as good as New Year candies to me (though that is a French custom not practiced in this country).
>
> Dispose of your time and arrange your return to Europe as you think best. But at the first disturbing liver symptom, come back, for nothing is more valuable than health. Still I did not send you this money with any intention of inducing you to return to Europe.
>
> I ask no sacrifice of you—or only a very little one. Buy some decent writing paper and decent ink. Your paper smudges and your ink runs, and my eyes suffer, though my heart rejoices. You can do them both good by this small outlay.

The uncle adds that he cannot consider meeting his nephew abroad. The political atmosphere, he adds, is one of war, and they cannot think of meeting in the Russian part of Poland as long as the formalities of Conrad's naturalization have not been completed to the satisfaction of the Russian authorities. Conrad hesitates, grows impatient. Every day increases his restlessness. We find this period of his life faithfully reproduced in the opening of "The End of the Tether":

> He could not hope to see anything new upon this lane of the sea. . . . The old ship ought to have known the road better

than her men, who had not been kept so long at it without a change. . . . She made her landfalls to a degree of the bearing, and almost to a minute of her allowed time. At any moment, as he sat on the bridge without looking up, or lay sleepless in his bed, simply by reckoning the days and the hours he could tell where he was—the precise spot of the beat. He knew it well too, this monotonous huckster's round, up and down the Straits; he knew its order and its sights and its people. Malacca to begin with, in at daylight and out at dusk, to cross over with a rigid phosphorescent wake this highway of the Far East. . . . At noon the three palms of the next place of call, up a sluggish river. . . . Sixty miles farther on there was another place of call, a deep bay with only a couple of houses on the beach. And so on, in and out, picking up coastwise cargo here and there, and finishing with a hundred miles' steady steaming through the maze of an archipelago of small islands up to a large native town at the end of the beat. There was a three days' rest for the old ship before he started her again in inverse order, seeing the same shores from another bearing, hearing the same voices in the same places, back again to the *Sofala's* port of registry on the great highway to the East, where he would take up a berth nearly opposite the big stone pile of the harbour office till it was time to start again on the old round of 1,600 miles and thirty days. . . . Not a very enterprising life for a man who had served famous firms, who had sailed famous ships. . . .[3]

This really could not go on. Up until then he had lived almost without thinking at all, with a feeling of eternity before him. Since his stay in the hospital in Singapore he had begun to reflect upon life and his future. Life seemed frightfully monotonous, his future gray and dull. Was this really the end of his youth—so soon, at thirty? Later Conrad was to give a personal interpretation and a suggestive name to this moment of his life: the shadow-line.

> One goes on. And the time, too, goes on, till one perceives ahead a shadow-line warning one that the region of early youth, too, must be left behind.

[3] *Youth and Two Other Stories.*

This is the period of life in which such moments of which I have spoken are likely to come. What moments? Why, the moments of boredom, of weariness, of dissatisfaction. Rash moments. I mean moments when the still young are inclined to commit rash actions, such as getting married suddenly or else throwing up a job for no reason. . . .

My action, rash as it was, had more the character of divorce —almost of desertion. For no reason on which a sensible person could put a finger I threw up my job—chucked my berth— left the ship of which the worst that could be said was that she was a steamship and therefore, perhaps, not entitled to that blind loyalty which . . . . However, it's no use trying to put a gloss on what even at the time I myself half suspected to be a caprice. . . .

I left it in that, to us, inconsequential manner in which a bird flies away from a comfortable branch. It was as though all un-knowing I had heard a whisper or seen something. Well—per-haps! One day I was perfectly right and the next everything was gone—glamour, flavour, interest, contentment—every-thing. It was one of those moments, you know. The green sickness of late youth descended on me and carried me off. Carried me off that ship, I mean.

We were only four white men on board, with a large crew of Kalashes and two Malay petty officers. The captain stared hard as if wondering what ailed me. But he was a sailor, and he, too, had been young at one time. Presently a smile came to lurk under his thick iron-gray moustache, and he observed that, of course, if I felt I must go he couldn't keep me by main force. And it was arranged that I should be paid off the next morning. As I was going out of the chart-room he added sud-denly, in a peculiar, wistful tone, that he hoped I would find what I was so anxious to go and look for. A soft cryptic utter-ance which seemed to reach deeper than any diamond-hard tool could have done. I do believe he understood my case. . . .

The past eighteen months, so full of new and varied experi-ence, appeared a dreary, prosaic waste of days. I felt—how shall I express it?—there was no truth to be got out of them.

What truth? I should have been hard put to it to explain.
Probably, if pressed, I would have burst into tears simply. I
was young enough for that.[4]

On January 5, 1888, the *Vidar's* first mate landed at Singapore and
decided to give up his job, without the least idea of what he was going to do. His intention was to seize the first opportunity of going
back to Europe. He would wait as long as he had to and he settled
down in the Sailors' Home for a few days or a few weeks. He had
not been there a fortnight when, quite unexpectedly, after hoping
in vain for such luck for a whole year, a command fell to him, so
to speak, out of the blue.

The harbor master sent for him and after a brief conversation
entrusted him with the command of a British ship then in the port
of Bangkok, whose captain had just died. The next day, January
19, 1888, he received this official memorandum:

> This is to inform you that you are required to proceed today
> in the S.S.*Melita* to Bangkok and you will report your arrival
> to the British Consul and produce this memorandum which
> will show that I have engaged you to be Master of the *Otago*
> in accordance with the Consul's telegram on a voyage from
> Bangkok to Melbourne, wages at fourteen pounds per month
> and to count from the date of your arrival at Bangkok, your
> passage from Singapore to Bangkok to be borne by the ship.
> Further to receive a passage from Melbourne to Singapore if
> you are not kept in the ship.

His elation over this first command, obtained from one moment to
the next, which Conrad has described so truthfully and minutely in
The Shadow-Line, was soon to yield to a very different feeling: one
of heavy responsibility, made heavier by quite exceptional circumstances.

He left for Singapore that same day, as the memorandum required,
having taken leave of Captain Patterson, a chance acquaintance at
the Sailors' Home who had been the means of his getting the command. As they said good-by, Patterson said laconically: "I expect
you'll have your hands pretty full of tangled-up business." But the
young captain, up in the air over his new command, was not the

---

[4] *The Shadow-Line.*

least bit apprehensive. He knew a good part of the Indian Ocean and the Malay Archipelago well; he had some acquaintance with Australian waters. It is true that the Gulf of Siam, where he was bound, was completely unknown to him, and Captain Patterson's remarks about it: "The Gulf . . . ay! A funny piece of water—that," might well have caused him some uneasiness, but a new surge of youth, a pride in his first real command, filled the heart and mind of the young captain aboard the *Melita* during the four days it took him to reach Bangkok from Singapore.

Bangkok! The city of his dreams in 1883, the magic city endowed with all the seduction, all the perfumes of the East, which he had never reached, due to the burning of the *Palestine*. At last he was to see it, and as master of a ship.

"There! That's your ship, Captain," he said.

I felt a thump in my breast—only one, as if my heart had ceased to beat. There were ten or more ships moored along the bank, and the one he meant was partly hidden from my sight by her next astern. . . . Directly my eyes had rested on my ship all my fear vanished. It went off swiftly, like a bad dream. Only that a dream leaves no shame behind it, and that I felt a momentary shame at my unworthy suspicions.

Yes, there she was. Her hull, her rigging filled my eye with a great content. That feeling of life-emptiness which had made me so restless for the last few months lost its bitter plausibility, its evil influence, dissolved in a flow of joyous emotion.

At first glance I saw that she was a high-class vessel, a harmonious creature in the lines of her fine body, in the proportioned tallness of her spars. Whatever her age and her history, she had preserved the stamp of her origin. She was one of those craft that in virtue of their design and complete finish will never look old. Amongst her companions moored to the bank, and all bigger than herself, she looked like a creature of high breed—an Arab steed in a string of cart-horses. . . . I knew that, like some rare women, she was one of those creatures whose mere existence is enough to awaken an unselfish delight. One feels that it is good to be in the world in which she has her being.[5]

[5] Ibid.

She was the bark *Otago,* belonging to an Australian firm of ship-owners. Conrad was to take her first to Adelaide, her port of registry, and then, during the next fourteen months, was to sail the length and breadth of the Indian Ocean in her.

The circumstances in which Conrad acquired command of this ship and of his stay in Bangkok inspired not only *The Shadow-Line* but also the tale entitled "Falk." From a comparison of these two stories and of documents in our possession it has been possible accurately to reconstruct the course of events.

The port authorities of Singapore had appointed Joseph Conrad ex officio to the command of the *Otago,* left without a master by the sudden death of her captain. Nothing out of the ordinary there. But the captain who had just died had been a most peculiar man. From the first mate Conrad soon learned that this captain, a man of sixty-five, had spent most of his time in the last few weeks of his life in his cabin, playing his violin day and night, not paying the least attention to how his ship was getting on unless it might be to take some sail off her and prevent her putting into any port. It was as though he not only didn't care a thing for his officers and crew, but would actually have been glad to see them all dead of hunger or boredom. One evening, feeling very ill, he had thrown his violin overboard and died, still utterly indifferent to the welfare of his men.

All he left to his successor were some unpaid bills, a few dry-dock estimates hinting at bribery, and a quantity of vouchers of three years' extravagant expenditure—all this in the greatest disorder inside a dusty violin case. There was even an account book filled, not with figures, but with verses of a jovial and improper character, and a photograph of the captain himself, taken at Saigon, showing him in the company of a "female in strange draperies." [6] This senile passion had been the cause of the eccentricities of the late captain, whose intention had really been none other than to lose his ship with all hands.

The new captain must have been profoundly shocked by his predecessor's betrayal of the principles and long traditions of the community of ship captains into which he himself had just been initiated, but he had little time to think of the faults of the dead: he had to see to the needs of the living.

[6] See *The Shadow-Line* and "Falk" (*Typhoon and Other Stories*). (Tr.)

It was impossible to find out where the money for the last two cargoes had gone. No trace of it could be found on board the ship, and there was no receipt. Soon Captain Korzeniowski realized that the situation was even more involved than he had thought, for he discovered that for more than ten months his predecessor had not taken the trouble to keep the owners informed of any of his movements. He learned this from a letter from the owners themselves.

Certainly this first command was not a bed of roses. The new captain could not expect much help from his two officers. The ship's first mate, Mr. Burns, a little older than Conrad, had been in the *Otago* two years and had had hopes of getting the command, although he was not qualified for it. After the captain's death, instead of taking the ship to Singapore, he had brought her into Bangkok, where he thought they would never find a qualified captain, so that his temporary command would be confirmed. Burns was therefore not particularly well disposed toward the intruder.

As for the second mate, he was not likely to become the captain's right-hand man either, if we believe what Conrad said in "Falk":

> All I can say his name was Tottersen or something like that. His practice was to wear on his head, in that tropical climate, a mangy fur cap. He was, without exception, the stupidest man I had ever seen on board ship. And he looked it too. He looked so confoundedly stupid that it was a matter of surprise for me when he answered to his name.

The prospect of a long sea passage—for Bangkok to Sydney in this ship might take sixty days—in the company of these two officers was not very encouraging; neither were some other elements in the situation. The first thing the young captain had to do was get hold of some money for the immediate needs of the ship, for there was not even a yard of canvas or an inch of rope aboard. Furthermore, the health of the crew, almost without exception feverish, was disquieting in this pestilential river. It was essential that she put to sea as soon as possible. But he still had to procure the cargo.

The steward had to be taken to hospital with symptoms of cholera and died within a week. He was replaced by a Chinaman who disappeared after three days with thirty-three gold sovereigns, Conrad's painfully accumulated savings, which he was keeping for emergencies. Mr. Burns, the first mate, took to his bed in his cabin with a violent fever and finally he, too, had to be taken to hospital. He had a wife and child in Sydney and although, when Conrad arrived in Bangkok, he had threatened out of jealousy not to stay with the ship, now he begged him not to leave him behind, although in the state he was in it was out of the question to take him along.

The cargo was held up; the delay went from bad to worse, and each day's delay brought a new outbreak of fever in the crew. Wherever he turned the new captain saw nothing but difficulties, heavy responsibilities, dangers of sickness and even death for his men. As he was to write later:

> Everything in this world, even the command of a nice little barque, may be a delusion and a snare for the unwary spirit of pride in men.[7]

This forced stay in Bangkok lasted about three weeks, until the beginning of February. If we are to believe the account in "Falk," he found the atmosphere of his ship so unbearable at night that he spent most of his evening aboard the German ship anchored next to him in the river: the *Diana* of Bremen, which looked more like a country villa than a regular ship. Conrad had met the captain of the *Diana* while he and his second officer were pursuing the Chinese steward who had stolen his money. Captain Hermann had joined them with such energy in this fruitless chase and had shown Captain Korzeniowski such sincere cordiality that a friendship had sprung up, and in the evening Conrad would go and smoke a pipe aboard the German ship with Captain Hermann, surrounded by his wife and children and that heavily built, silent niece who was to become the heroine of "Falk." It is quite probable that the character of Falk himself, though not the name, came from real life: that he was actually the owner and captain of a river tug who at first refused to take the *Otago* down to the sea because he imagined that Conrad was running him down with Captain Hermann, whose niece he wanted to marry. Obviously it must also have been at Bangkok that Conrad met the hotelkeeper to whom he gave the name Schonberg and who appears successively in "Falk," *Lord Jim,* and *Victory.*

[7] "Falk" (*Typhoon and Other Stories*).

At last the tug did take the *Otago* down-river. The second officer was still very ill: he had had to be brought aboard on a stretcher; the second mate was hardly any better off. Of all the crew the most loyal and efficient was the cook, a very fine sailor who had signed on in this capacity only because a weak heart prevented him from doing any heavier work. He and the captain were the only ones immune to the rigors of the climate.

The ship got under way but her progress was exasperatingly slow. It did not take Captain Korzeniowski long to see why Captain Patterson had called the Gulf "a funny piece of water." There was a dead calm which lasted for days. This painful progress of a ship which seemed to be glued to the sea, without a breath of wind in the sails, with a crew of feverish men whose recovery depended on their getting away quickly from this pestilential estuary, was faithfully related by the author in *The Shadow-Line*.

We can understand why Joseph Conrad said, thirty years later, in a letter to Sir Sidney Colvin:

> The locality does not matter and if it is the Gulf of Siam it's simply because the whole thing is exact autobiography. . . . I am sorry you received an impression of horror. I tried to keep the mere horror out. It would have been easy to pile it on. You may believe me. *J'ai vécu tout cela.*[8]

Now, by an irony of fate, he could not get away from the Bangkok he had dreamed of and taken so long to reach. While the captain was on deck scanning the horizon, checking his sail in the hope of discovering the faintest sign of a breeze, the fever seemed to be having its sport with the crew, laying low one man one day, another the next. Suddenly the captain finds to his dismay that the ship's regulation store of quinine, his only weapon against the fever, has been wasted and adulterated by his predecessor. A silent struggle against malignant invisible powers arrayed against the ship and its men: a struggle against the immobility, the silence, the implacable calm of the water and the sky; an inner struggle—for there was no visible enemy on whom to vent one's fury or despair. It was enough to drive one mad, but Conrad, ever conscious of his responsibility, held on, backed up only by Ransome, the cook, the

---

[8] Letter of February 27, 1917.

man with the weak heart, who thought of everything, kept an eye
on everything, with his carefully controlled movements and a vi-
tality he found it hard to hold back.

The *Otago* took no less than three weeks to reach Singapore
from Bangkok, a distance of about eight hundred miles. At Singapore the crew had to be discharged in a sorry state, all except Mr.
Burns, the second officer, who wanted to go on to Sydney. The
ship put to sea again during March, and we know from a letter
from Thaddeus Bobrowski that Conrad finally arrived at Sydney
early in May. This letter brought him rather bad news: his uncle
had consulted no fewer than five doctors in Kiev: he was to go for
treatment to Odessa since, in view of the state of the ruble and the
drop in his income, it was impossible for him to take a cure abroad.
He had a great desire to see his nephew again, but the latter did
not plan to return to Europe for at least two years, now that he had
his own ship at last.

In all Conrad's work and letters we find only one mention of this
stay in Sydney: the account of how, on the quay, he ran into the
second officer, Mr. B——, under whom he had served as an ordinary
seaman in his first English ocean-going ship—the *Duke of Sutherland*—the man who, whenever he went ashore, came back to the
ship completely drunk.

> He recognized me at once, remembered my name, and in
> what ship I had served under his orders. He looked me over
> from head to foot.
>
> "What are you doing here?" he asked.
>
> "I am commanding a little barque," I said, "loading here
> for Mauritius." Then, thoughtlessly, I added: "And what are
> you doing, Mr. B——?"
>
> "I," he said, looking at me unflinchingly, with his old sar-
> donic grin—"I am looking for something to do."
>
> I felt I would rather have bitten out my tongue. His jet-
> black, curly hair had turned iron-grey; he was scrupulously
> neat as ever, but frightfully threadbare. His shiny boots were
> worn down at heel. But he forgave me, and we drove off
> together in a hansom to dine on board my ship. He went over
> her conscientiously, praised her heartily, congratulated me
> on my command with absolute sincerity. At dinner, as I

offered him wine and beer he shook his head, and as I sat looking at him interrogatively, muttered in an undertone:

"I've given up all that."

After dinner we came again on deck. It seemed as though he could not tear himself away from the ship. We were fitting some new lower rigging, and he hung about, approving, suggesting, giving me advice in his old manner. Twice he addressed me as "My boy," and corrected himself quickly to "Captain." My mate was about to leave me (to get married), but I concealed the fact from Mr. B——. I was afraid he would ask me to give him the berth in some ghastly jocular hint that I could not refuse to take. I was afraid. It would have been impossible. I could not have given orders to Mr. B——, and I am sure he would not have taken them from me very long. He could not have managed *that,* though he had managed to break himself from drink—too late.

He said good-bye at last. As I watched his burly, bull-necked figure walk away up the street, I wondered with a sinking heart whether he had much more than the price of a night's lodging in his pocket. And I understood that if that very minute I were to call out after him, he would not even turn his head.[9]

When he arrived at Melbourne Captain Korzeniowski received instructions to proceed to Mauritius. He called at Sydney and sailed from there in the early days of August. Urged by his love of adventure, he wrote to his owners in Port Adelaide suggesting that he proceed to Mauritius, not by the usual route following the west coast of Australia, but through Torres Strait which separates the north coast of Australia from New Guinea. He never expected the owners to fall in with the suggestion, for this route was more dangerous, but to his great surprise they raised no objection, although an additional insurance premium had to be paid for that route. This proves that they had already come to appreciate their new captain's capability.

The season was already late; there was no time to lose in traversing the Strait. He left Sydney in a terrible southeasterly gale, to the great dismay of the pilot and the tug master, who were scandal-

[9] *The Mirror of the Sea.*

ized by his obstinacy. At the end of his life Conrad recalled with some pride "that particular intensity of life that is the quintessence of youthful aspirations."

It was not without a certain emotion that, commanding very likely the first, and certainly the last, merchant ship that carried a cargo that way—from Sydney to Mauritius—I put her head at daybreak for Bligh's Entrance, and packed on her every bit of canvas she could carry. Windswept, sunlit empty waters were all around me, half-veiled by a brilliant haze. The first thing that caught my eye upon the play of green white-capped waves was a black speck marking conveniently the end of a low sandbank. It looked like the wreck of some small vessel.

I altered the course slightly in order to pass close, with the hope of being able to read the letters on her stern. They were already faded. Her name was *Honolulu*. The name of the port I could not make out. The story of her life is known by now to God alone, and the winds must have drifted long ago around her remains a quiet grave of the very sand on which she had died. Thirty-six hours afterwards, of which about nine were spent at anchor, approaching the other end of the Strait, I sighted a gaunt, grey wreck of a big American ship lying high and dry on the southernmost of the Warrior Reefs. She had been there for years. I had heard of her. She was legendary. She loomed up, a sinister and enormous *memento mori* raised by the refraction of this serene afternoon above the far-away line of the horizon drawn under the sinking sun.

And thus I passed out of Torres Strait before the dusk settled on its waters. Just as a clear sun sank ahead of my ship I took a bearing of a little island for a fresh departure, an insignificant crumb of dark earth, lonely, like an advanced sentinel of that mass of broken land and water, to watch the approaches from the side of the Arafura Sea.[10]

On September 30, 1888, after a voyage of fifty-four days, the *Otago* arrived safe and sound at Port Louis in Mauritius.

[10] *Last Essays.*

VII

The Pearl of the Ocean

(1888)

> . . . a fertile and beautiful island of the
> tropics. The more enthusiastic of its in-
> habitants delight in describing it as the
> "Pearl of the Ocean."
>
> *'Twixt Land and Sea,*
> "A Smile of Fortune"

DUE TO CIRCUMSTANCES connected with the unloading and reload-
ing of his ship, Captain Korzeniowski had to spend almost two
months in Mauritius. His charterers were Langlois & Co., and some
years ago a young director of this company, Mr. Paul Langlois,
who for six weeks was in close touch with the *Otago's* captain,
fortunately put his reminiscences of him into writing. We are
thus indebted to him for an accurate portrait of Conrad at thirty-
one:

> Forceful and very mobile features, passing very rapidly
> from gentleness to an agitation bordering on anger. Big
> black eyes which were as a rule melancholy and dreamy, and
> gentle as well, except for fairly frequent moments of annoy-
> ance. A decisive chin. A beautifully shaped, graceful mouth
> surmounted by a thick, well trimmed dark brown mustache.
> That was his face—good-looking certainly but, above all,

strange in its expression and difficult to forget if you had seen it once or twice.

Apart from his distinguished manners, the most striking thing about the captain of the *Otago* was the contrast he presented with other skippers. As a big sugar exporter, I saw ten or so of them every day in the office of "old Krumpholtz," who for thirty years was the only freight agent in the area. Between ten in the morning and one o'clock in the afternoon, his office, situated on the ground floor of the Mauritius Fire Insurance Co., was the rendezvous of all the captains in search of a cargo. And if you remember that in those days, before the sea had been invaded by steamers, there were always fifteen ships or so in port during the sugar season, you can get an idea of the numerous assembly that packed the outer office of "old Krumpholtz" every day.

Now, these shipmasters, generally dressed in ducks, with caps or straw hats on their heads, their faces and hands tanned by sun and salt water, their nails black with the tell-tale tar of their calling, their language forceful and often coarse, were not models of taste and refinement. Unlike his colleagues, Captain Korzeniowski was always dressed with great elegance. I can still see him (and just because of the contrast with the other sailors my memory is precise) arriving in my office almost every day dressed in a black or dark coat, a vest that was usually light in color, and fancy trousers; everything well cut and very stylish; on his head a black or gray derby tilted slightly to one side. He invariably wore gloves and carried a cane with a gold knob.

From this description you can see what a contrast he made to the other captains, with whom, by the way, he was on strictly formal terms, generally not going beyond a greeting. He was not, of course, very popular with his colleagues, who sarcastically called him "the Russian Count." So much for his physical appearance.

As to his moral character: a perfect education; very varied and interesting conversation—on the days when he felt communicative, which wasn't every day. The man who was to acquire fame under the name of Joseph Conrad was quite often taciturn and very excitable. On those days he had a nervous tic in the shoulder and the eyes, and anything the least bit unexpected—an object dropping to the floor, a door banging—would make him jump. . . .

Before his ship was chartered, he would appear at Krumpholtz's only for a few minutes each day, and afterwards not at all. He was always on board his ship; he was never to be seen at the Hotel Oriental, where most of the captains took their lunch and spent the afternoon and where they could always be reached if they were wanted. During his whole stay in Port Louis I don't believe the taciturn Conrad ever took a walk in the country, or—still less—ever made any contact with fashionable society, to which his culture, his perfect education, his impeccably correct manners and the elegance of his appearance would certainly have given him the entrée.

Joseph Conrad's English and French were both equally pure and fluent, but he *preferred* the latter language, which he handled with elegance. Our conversations were always in French.

On one single point the facts do not bear out this account of Mr. Paul Langlois, with whom Captain Korzeniowski had only business dealings during his stay in Port Louis. Conrad's social contacts were not confined to his consignees or charterers. The very day after his arrival, at the office of Blyth Bros., his consignees, he met the brother of one of their employees, a young merchant-navy officer whom he had done a favor in Bombay four years earlier. This young man, Gabriel Renouf, who belonged to one of the best French families of Mauritius, not only showed real pleasure at seeing him again, but found the captain of the *Otago* so superior to the average master mariner that he could safely be introduced to a family which did not usually receive "people of that sort." This family consisted of three sisters and two brothers, orphans who lived with their eldest sister, married to Mr. L. E. Smith who held the position of treasurer in the firm.

The captain's perfect manners made an excellent impression on this whole family. He spoke elegant French and was unusually courteous. Not only was he warmly welcomed but he was urged to come again. He came again: his conversation was interesting, he knew how to listen, and he seemed to enjoy the often frivolous talk of the young girls. He appeared vivacious, expansive, even cordial. This traveler told of picturesque memories which enchanted them in their cramped provincial existence. One of the girls, Mademoiselle Eugénie, who was particularly pretty and lively, took a leading part in the conversation: with great animation she got the young captain involved in the question of "feminism"—and the captain showed no sign of rebelling.

Sometimes he would remain cold and preoccupied and seemed uninterested in the girls' talk of a forthcoming ball or the last race meeting and he would take his leave formally. They did not expect to see him again, but hardly had a few days gone by than the captain was back knocking at the door of the house on the corner of the Rue de la Bourdonnais and the Rue Saint-Georges. They had a wide balcony overhanging this street and it was there that they usually sat, in this early Mauritian summer.

The captain had his worries. The chartering was delayed. Port Louis harbor was full of sailing ships trying to undercut one another's freight rates. Captain Korzeniowski, dogged and suspicious, did not want to let anyone get the better of him but in the end he had to accept the season's lowest rates. All the same—and this is typical of the attention he gave to essential details—he was the first person to think of inserting in the charter party a clause making the charterer responsible for any pilot and tug charges incurred in entering Melbourne, where his cargo was bound. This subsequently became standard practice.

Moreover, on its voyage out the ship had carried a cargo of fertilizer, so it was now necessary to cover the dunnage and bottom boards with jute matting before proceeding to load the twelve thousand sacks of sugar which were to be her cargo on the homeward voyage. It turned out that this matting, which was made locally, was not available as a result of a fire in the factory of Valaydon & Co. which had a monopoly on its manufacture in the island.

The captain was bored to death. Compelled to wait, he went back to the Rue Bourdonnais to the old French family that he was later to describe as "one of the old French families, descendants of the old colonists; all noble, all impoverished, and living a narrow, domestic life in dull, dignified decay. The men, as a rule, occupy inferior posts in Government offices or in business houses. The girls are almost always pretty, ignorant of the world, kind and agreeable and generally bilingual; they prattle innocently both in French and English." [1]

The mixture of reserve and simplicity in Conrad's manner gave the girls courage to subject their guest to the ordeal of the confession album—which was then having a vogue. He submitted with good grace. The questionnaire was in French, the language the captain used to speak with all members of the family, yet he wrote his answers in English. Wasn't he a British subject? Perhaps there was still another reason. The tangible evidence of the "ordeal" has been preserved in this family. We shall see that Captain Korzeniowski replied to the extremely indiscreet questions in a bantering tone in which we can nevertheless find traces of the sincere and reticent character of the future author of *Lord Jim*. This is how he answered:

1. What is the principal trait of your character? — Laziness.

2. By what means do you try to please? — By making myself scarce.

3. Whose name makes your heart beat faster? — Ready to beat for any name.

4. What is your dream of happiness? — Never dream of it; want reality.

5. Where does the lady of your dreams live? — A castle in Spain.

6. What is your favorite quality in a woman? — Beauty.

7. What would you like to be? — Should like not to be.

8. Which is your favorite flower? — Violet.

9. Which country would you like to live in? — Don't know. Perhaps Lapland.

[1] *'Twixt Land and Sea,* "A Smile of Fortune."

10. What color eyes do you prefer?	Grey.
11. What gift of nature would you like to be endowed with?	Self-confidence.
12. What do you enjoy most at a ball?	Not dancing can not tell.
13. Which is your favorite *promenade?*	Hate all "promenades."
14. Do you prefer blondes or brunettes?	Both.
15. What is your favorite occupation?	Chasing wild geese.
16. State your present state of mind.	Calm.
17. What do you hate most?	False pretences.
18. Do you think anyone is in love with you?	Decline to state.
19. Your motto?	————
20. Your name?	J.C.K.

One afternoon Captain Korzeniowski invited all the family to tea in the Jardin des Pamplemousses. They went in horse-drawn carriages; it was a journey of about six miles. The sumptuous tea was served by the *Flore Mauricienne* and the captain, as usual, was a model of urbanity and refinement. Another time he invited his friends to tea aboard the *Otago* and proudly did the honors of his ship.

The chartering had been concluded. The loading of sugar sacks was proceeding smoothly. The captain was relieved of his commercial worries. To be sure, there was still this man who absolutely insisted that he accept a small load of potatoes along with his jute matting—just a little matter of blackmail!

The captain's troubles were almost over. His visits to the Rue Bourdonnais became more frequent. As friendly and courteous as ever, the visitor would plunge into sudden silences, into thoughts unrelated to the subject of the conversation; then he would get up quite brusquely and, after formally taking his leave, go away as if he were never coming back. The girls found him alternately charming and queer. They had never met a Pole in their lives before and foreigners, as everyone knows, are peculiar.

One day passed, then another; the captain did not reappear. One evening when he came home from the office, one of the brothers told his sisters that the captain had come to see him and had gravely requested the hand of Mademoiselle Eugénie in marriage. The captain had fallen in love. Apparently the girls were not particularly surprised. The brother, however, had had to express to the captain his sincere regret, for Mademoiselle Eugénie was already engaged and her marriage had even been arranged for the middle of the following January.

All the castles in Spain that Captain Korzeniowski had been building for the last month in the solitude of his cabin aboard the *Otago* crumbled to nothing. He had been dreaming of an attachment, a family, a home. Once more, circumstances threw him back into isolation. He was obviously born not to have roots anywhere.

Until the moment his ship sailed, two days later, the captain stayed aboard. He sent a letter to Gabriel Renouf bidding him farewell and asking him to present his compliments to his sisters and informing him of his decision never to return to Mauritius. He added magnanimously: "On January 14, at the time when Mademoiselle Eugénie is standing before the altar, I shall be near you in my thoughts."

On November 22, 1888, the *Otago* sailed for Melbourne. The mountains of Mauritius receded under the approaching darkness. The captain resolutely turned his back on the bewitching attractions which the "Pearl of the Ocean" had held out to him.

Toward the middle of January the ship arrived in Melbourne harbor after a normal voyage. There had been an unprecedented drought that year in Australia, the original cause of the famous "land crack," the effects of which Australia was to feel for many years. The small shipment of potatoes which the captain had been forced to take along was literally worth its weight in gold. For his disappointed heart that, at least, was a "smile of fortune."

On his arrival he found a letter from his uncle giving him rather bad news about his health and adding:

You don't tell me how long you expect to stay in Australian waters. Since you are happy, I don't want to prolong or cut short your stay in Australia, but for an old man the time he has left is a matter of some interest, and so is the knowledge that he may see once more those who are dear to him.

Couldn't you ask Mr. Krieger to inquire at the Russian Embassy whether the formality exempting you from allegiance has gone through? I read in the Polish papers that it had gone through in 27 cases. Perhaps yours was among them: they didn't give any names. Perhaps this important matter has already been decided. In that case we could consider meeting in the Ukraine.[2]

But Conrad was satisfied with the performance and profits of his ship and had no intention of returning to Europe just yet. His relations with his Australian owners were excellent. As soon as she had unloaded at Melbourne, the *Otago* went to Port Minlacowie, in southern Australia, to pick up a cargo of grain for Port Adelaide, her home port.

There he found another letter from his uncle, just as disquieting about his health. It said that, well or sick, he was hoping to see his "dear captain" once more. He thanked him for having asked his friend Krieger to inquire at the Russian Embassy:

I did not find your name in the *Official Gazette* for the whole year 1888, but there is no need to be surprised, because they had to check your papers in Berdichev, where you were born, and in Chernikov, which you left with your father.

Uncle Thaddeus is obviously beginning to find the time long, and his anxieties about his approaching end are revealed in the arrangements he has made, of which he informs his nephew. He has placed with Madame Cécile Zaleska—or, in case of her death, with her son Stanislas—fifteen thousand rubles exempt from inheritance tax, which will come to Conrad one year after his uncle's death. He gives him the names of his executors: Mr. Stanislas Syroczynski and Mr. Thaddeus Florkowski.

On his arrival at Port Adelaide Captain Korzeniowski has a

2 Letter of September 24, 1888.

long talk with his owners and tells them of his desire to take the *Otago* for a year to the China Seas. The owners appreciate the seamanlike and businesslike qualities of their new captain, but his passage of the Torres Strait has also given them the impression that he is not without his eccentricities. The ship's voyage to Mauritius turned out profitably after all; prospects are favorable there. Simpson & Co., friendly but unshakable, express to Captain Korzeniowski their determination to send the *Otago* back to Port Louis. The captain brings up all the arguments he can think of in favor of a voyage to China, but the owners are adamant.

No, he will not go back to Port Louis. He does not want to risk a meeting with the object of his unhappy love; he does not wish to see any member of that family; he has taken a dislike to the island and all its inhabitants. He will not return to Mauritius. He seeks in vain for a solution to this problem. Giving up at last, he finally comes to a heroic decision: on March 26, with a heavy heart, he writes to the owners that certain obligations compel him to return to Europe and that he is relinquishing his command. The following letter shows that the decision rested entirely with himself:

Port Adelaide,
April 2nd, 1889.

Captain J. Conrad Korzeniowski,
Port Adelaide.

Dear Sir,

Referring to your resignation of the command (which we have in another letter formally accepted) of our bark *Otago,* we now have much pleasure in stating that this early severance from our employ is entirely at your own desire, with a view to visiting Europe, and that we entertain a high opinion of your ability in the capacity you now vacate, of your attainments generally, and should be glad to learn of your future success.

Wishing you a pleasant passage home, we are, dear Sir,

Yours faithfully,
HENRY SIMPSON & SONS
Owners of the Black Diamond Line.

Three years later Conrad was to make two more visits to the Australian ports, but when he laid down the command of the *Otago* he broke forever his connection with the East, whose various shores he had haunted almost without a break since 1883.

Death had given him command of this ship, far from this Australian port; love deprived him of it. Once more the unknown stretched before him. So he would go back to Europe: he would go and see his uncle again: borrow for a few weeks the illusion of the home he had dreamed of aboard his ship in Port Louis in Mauritius.

If his proposal of marriage had been accepted, Joseph Conrad's life would have been entirely different. He would not have experienced another quite novel adventure in Africa the following year—one that was to have major consequences. Perhaps, married to a Mauritian, living in French-speaking surroundings, his latent literary genius would have sought its expression in that language, in which he was quite at home. Who knows . . . ? We may make all kinds of conjectures about the possible consequences of this event. At least we know what a heavy sacrifice the "Pearl of the Ocean" had exacted of this sailor and why he would not set foot there again at any price.

VIII

Heart of Darkness
(1889-1890)

The bitter knowledge that one gains
from travel.

Baudelaire

Land in a swamp, march through the
woods, and in some inland post feel the
savagery, the utter savagery, had closed
round him—all that mysterious life of the
wilderness that stirs in the forest, in the
jungles, in the hearts of wild men.

"Heart of Darkness"

HE WOULD HAVE to start life all over again. No job in sight; a little
money in his pocket: that was how things stood with Captain
Korzeniowski when he took passage on a steamer bound for
Europe in April, 1889. When he arrived in England early in
June, it seems that he made a short visit to his friends, the
Kliszczewskis, in Cardiff. The only reason he did not go straight
to the Ukraine to see his uncle, as he had intended, was that after
three years the Russian authorities had still not completed their
formalities. The notice of his exemption from allegiance had just
appeared in the *Official Gazette,* but Conrad still had to make an
application to the governor of the province of his birth in order to
set foot on imperial territory without difficulties.

While he was waiting for the document that would permit him to go to Poland, since Thaddeus Bobrowski was prevented by his uncertain health and his limited means from going abroad to meet him, Conrad, giving up the rooms where he had always stayed before in North London, went to live in two furnished rooms in Bessborough Gardens, in the south of the city, not far from the Thames. There he lived for several months a life of leisure to which he had grown completely unaccustomed.

He had by no means given up the idea of going back to sea: but a command is not always to be had for the asking. Months went by and all his efforts came to nothing. He was in exactly the same situation as Marlow, the narrator of "Heart of Darkness":

> "I had then, as you remember, just returned to London after a lot of Indian Ocean, Pacific, China Seas—a regular dose of the East—six years or so, and I was loafing about, hindering you fellows in your work and invading your homes, just as though I had got a heavenly mission to civilize you. It was very fine for a time, but after a bit I did get tired of resting. Then I began to look for a ship—I should think the hardest work on earth. But the ships wouldn't even look at me. And I got tired of that game too."

Days and months passed without bringing him the least hope of a command: the memory of the *Otago* was always in his heart. Captain Korzeniowski wandered about the town, went frequently to the City, either to the offices of Barr, Moering & Co. in Camomile Street where he would meet his friend Adolf Krieger, or to Fenchurch Street where he would go to see if Captain Froud, the helpful secretary of the Shipmasters' Society, had managed to hunt him up a ship.

Days and months passed; the summer was almost over and Captain Korzeniowski was still navigating "without maps or compass" in the streets of London. After roaming so many seas this novel kind of wandering was not altogether out of tune with his mood. Up to then he had lived entirely in the present: now, whether as a result of weariness, maturity, or an obsession with half-glimpsed scenes, this thirty-two-year-old captain fell to daydreaming. The eager adventurous carelessness of his early youth was giving way to a mood of reminiscence, not about theories and systems, but about human beings, seen, sensed, or spoken to for a brief moment, whose faces, gestures, desires, and illusions he was able to re-create in these days of indolence in London.

One morning in September, "an autumn day with an opaline atmosphere, a veiled, semi-opaque, lustrous day . . . one of those London days that have charm of mysterious amenity, of fascinating softness," in his furnished room in Bessborough Gardens, the captain got up from table after breakfast, pushed his chair back, and rang the bell resolutely, contrary to his usual habit which was to dawdle over his breakfast. The landlady's daughter appeared, surprised.

"Will you please clear away all this at once?" asked the captain in a final but perfectly calm tone. He was not at all sure that he wanted to write, that he meant to write, or that he had anything to write about. He heard her put the tray down in the passage and shut the door, and he went on smoking and looking out of the window. Then, at the urging of a sudden incomprehensible impulse, he put down his pipe, took a pen and "thinking of nothing whatever," began to write the story of Almayer's illusions.[1]

Never did a writer's life begin so late or so casually. If it was true that on that morning in September, 1889, Captain Korzeniowski began to make way for the novelist Joseph Conrad, he himself was far from suspecting it and far from desiring it. He said himself in *A Personal Record*:

> I never made a note of a fact, of an impression, or of an anecdote in my life. The conception of a planned book was entirely outside my mental range when I sat down to write; the ambition of being an author had never turned up amongst these gracious imaginary existences one creates fondly for oneself at times in the stillness and immobility of a daydream; yet it stands clear as the sun at noonday that from the moment I had done blackening over the first manuscript page of *Almayer's Folly* (it contained about two hundred words and this proportion of words to a page has remained

---

[1] See *A Personal Record*. (Tr.)

with me through the fifteen years of my writing life), from the moment I had, in the simplicity of my heart and the amazing ignorance of my mind, written that page the die was cast. Never had Rubicon been more blindly forded, without invocation to the gods, without fear of men.

Every morning of that misty London autumn Captain Korzeniowski pursued the memory of those tropical scenes, but, haunted as he was—despite himself—by Almayer's misfortunes, his main concern was still his maritime career. He had not the least idea of giving up the sea. For fifteen years he had owed the sea his livelihood—meager as it was and—as we have seen—strongly seasoned with dangers and risks; he felt he had been born to it. Besides, the profits he had accumulated during his year's command of the *Otago* were not substantial enough to allow him to contemplate a very long stay ashore. In any case, what would he have done ashore for any length of time? He had only a tiny group of friends in London: the Kriegers, a former master mariner named Hope and his wife, a few passing acquaintances. He had no home, nothing but temporary lodgings. He thought only of getting away.

His friend Adolf Krieger had had him taken on as supercargo by the Antwerp shipowners, Walford & Co., who offered him some prospects of a voyage as captain to the West Indies and New Orleans, but that command, too, was a long time coming. Conrad's situation and his mood are both attributed to Marlow at the beginning of "Heart of Darkness":

". . . I have a lot of relations living on the Continent, because it's cheap and not so nasty as it looks, they say. I am sorry to own I began to worry them. This was already a fresh departure for me. I was not used to get things that way, you know. I always went my own road and on my own legs where I had a mind to go. I wouldn't have believed it of myself; but, then—you see—I felt somehow I must get there by hook or by crook. So I worried them. The men said 'My dear fellow,' and did nothing. Then—would you believe it?—I tried the women. I, Charlie Marlow, set the women to work— to get a job. Heavens! Well, you see, the emotion drove me.

I had an aunt, a dear enthusiastic soul. She wrote: 'It will be delightful. I am ready to do anything, anything for you. It is a glorious idea. I know the wife of a very high personage in the Administration, and also a man who has lots of influence . . .' "

Of all the notions that might have come into the head of a captain of sailing ships, Conrad had suddenly been seized by the most unexpected, the most incomprehensible: to go to the Congo and command a wretched little steamboat of a few tons, a sardine can with a stern wheel. Many years ago, when he was a very little boy in Poland, he had announced that he would go to the heart of Africa:

> It was in 1868, when nine years old or thereabouts, that while looking at a map of Africa of the time and putting my finger on the blank space then representing the unsolved mystery of that continent, I said to myself, with absolute assurance and an amazing audacity which are no longer in my character now:
> "When I grow up I shall go *there*."
> And of course I thought no more about it till after a quarter of a century or so an opportunity offered to go there—as if the sin of childish audacity was to be visited on my mature head.[2]

Perhaps, as Conrad makes Marlow say, a map of the Congo seen in a bookseller's window in Fleet Street stirred up these childhood desires. Perhaps a change in his relations with the Antwerp shipowners played a role in this unexpected move. In any case, at the end of September a letter from G. de Baerdemacker, shipbroker in Ghent, recommended Captain Korzeniowski to Mr. Albert Thys, staff captain, aide-de-camp to King Leopold, and managing director of the Société Anonyme Belge pour le Commerce du Haut-Congo at Brussels. "This gentleman," stated the letter, "is very warmly recommended to me by friends in London. Besides being a past master of his profession and holding the highest certificates, his general education is superior to that of most sea-

2 Ibid.

men and he is a perfect gentleman." Early in November Joseph Conrad presented himself at the office of this Brussels company.

In 1889 the Congo was very much in the foreground. Since September, 1875, when King Leopold had founded the International Association for the Civilization of Central Africa, and since Stanley's expedition from Zanzibar to the Lower Congo in 1876 and 1877, Africa had aroused at once the most ardent interest and the most violent greed. A few months earlier, on February 17, 1889, Stanley, repeating the exploits of his search for Livingstone, had discovered and joined Emin Pasha in Kavali's camp. Scientific, journalistic, and political circles in Europe had followed these excursions with attentive and breathless interest. Brussels had become a focus of adventure. The daredevils of the whole world met there, as well as the missionaries. Men of good will and rogues came there to enter into contracts which would enable them to make use of their faith, talents, energy, greed, violence, or even their innocence, in the heart of what Stanley had called the "Dark Continent." England and Belgium were at that very moment getting ready to give Stanley a hero's welcome.

This atmosphere of adventure and discovery had reawakened in Conrad the geographical passions of his childhood. The young captain's imagination was still lively enough to flare up. He suddenly took it into his head to command one of the little steamboats of the Upper Congo. Conrad's impulses, as we have seen, were often no less obstinate than urgent.

They needed a captain who could speak French. Captain Korzeniowski met this requirement perfectly. The impression he made on Albert Thys must have been satisfactory, because there and then Thys promised him a job in the Congo as soon as there was a vacancy in the company's fleet.

The Société Anonyme Belge pour le Commerce du Haut-Congo was still comparatively new; in its permanent form it had existed only since December 10 of the year before; but under the direction of enterprising men this commercial venture was about to expand considerably. New stations were soon to be set up; new steamers built; plans were being studied for the possible layout of a railroad from Matadi to Stanley Pool, which would establish rapid communication between the two navigable stretches of the Congo. New perspectives were opening up for adventurous undertakings.

The captain hurriedly broke his connections, such as they were, with Walford & Co. of Antwerp, but a final reply from Brussels still did not come. He grew impatient and, for want of anything else to do while he was waiting, he went on with *Almayer's Folly.* Meanwhile, Uncle Thaddeus, hearing that he was going to Brussels, reminded him that he had a relative there, a distant cousin, Alexander Poradowski, whom he had known long ago in Cracow.

In the middle of January, 1890, Conrad, thinking that this relative in Brussels might perhaps have some connections that would help to speed up his appointment, wrote to him in Polish that he expected to return to Brussels and would be happy to see him again, for he had not forgotten the kindness he had shown him long ago in Poland. He added that he would also be happy to make the acquaintance of his aunt, whom he knew only from a photograph which Alexander Poradowski had once shown him in Cracow.

Alexander Poradowski, cousin of Conrad's maternal grandmother, had fled to Brussels after the failure of the insurrection of 1863. He had later married a Frenchwoman from Lille, the daughter of a man with a high reputation in the scientific world, Émile Gachet, a philologist and paleographer. Madame Marguerite Poradowska, who was then about thirty, was very pretty and quick-witted and had created around her in Brussels a circle of friends and admirers. She had lived with her husband in Galicia for several years, and two years previously had published in the *Revue des Deux Mondes* a sketch of Ruthenian life in the form of a novel entitled *Yaga,* and a year later in the same periodical a novel of Polish life *Demoiselle Micia.* Uncle Thaddeus had kept his nephew informed of this latest literary distinction in the family.

Alexander Poradowski hastened to reply to his young cousin, restored to him from the bosom of the sea, but only to say that he was ill and was soon to have an operation and would therefore not be able to see him in March, as Conrad suggested. Conrad therefore decided to go to Brussels on his way to the Ukraine instead of on his way back, and left London on February 5. He arrived in Brussels that same evening. Two days later the uncle, whom he had not seen for sixteen or seventeen years, died.

In spite of the sad circumstances in which he had met his aunt, of whose existence he had known nothing, Conrad was by no means blind to her charm and lively intelligence. During the two days he spent there, the captain had time to confide some of his ambitions to Madame Poradowska and she, impressed with the personality of this nephew, promised to do all she could for him. Their conversations and promises were interrupted by the sudden death of Alexander Poradowski. Conrad left Brussels before the funeral, taking with him a copy of Madame Poradowska's first novel. On February 11 he was in Warsaw. After an absence of sixteen years the prodigal son was on his way back to his native land for the first time.

Whether due to the sad ending of his stay in Brussels or the impression made on him by Madame Poradowska or by her novel *Yaga,* the traveler forgot one of his bags at the restaurant in the Friedrichstrasse station in Berlin. If it had not been for the watchfulness of a worthy and intelligent *Kofferträger,* he might have lost it for ever. The bag contained the first seven chapters of *Almayer's Folly.*

Conrad spent two days in Warsaw, where he had not been since his earliest childhood. Uncle Thaddeus must have alerted his relatives and friends to the mariner's return. An evening at a sporting club, where he was taken by a childhood friend, suddenly plunged the visitor into an atmosphere of patriotic talk and speculation such as he had not experienced for many a year.

From Warsaw and then from Lipovetz, where his uncle had sent a carriage and a servant to meet him, Joseph Conrad wrote in French to his new aunt. He apologizes for his style: "These badly written thoughts spring from the heart which knows neither the grammar nor the spelling of studied commiseration." [3] He stopped at Lublin, where his Zagórski cousins lived. He told them about the death of their uncle Alexander and from this family, with whom Madame Poradowska was very popular, he learned some new details about his French aunt, to whom he wrote that he had read her book twice during his journey.

It was at least eight hours by carriage from the railway station to Kazimierowka. While the traveler who had got off the train was dining, served by a Hebrew waiter, in an enormous barnlike bedroom, the door opened and, in a traveling costume of long boots, big sheepskin cap and a short coat girt with a leather belt, appeared

---

[3] Letter of February 14, 1890.

the confidential servant of Mr. Thaddeus Bobrowski, his mustache gleaming with little icicles, for it was bitterly cold outside. He had come to take delivery of that queer traveler who, as they said down there in the Ukraine, had been to the ends of the earth and farther and who spoke goodness knows what foreign language. When he heard his master's odd nephew speaking the purest Polish, his initial anxiety gave way to astonishment.

The next morning, following his master's instructions, the major-domo wrapped the captain in an enormous bearskin traveling coat and took his seat protectively by his side, as though he were in charge of a little boy going off to school. On this wintry day, in a sledge drawn by four bay horses, harnessed two by two, to the jingling of bells, the captain set out for the distant home, isolated and still unknown to him, lying beyond this infinite stretch of snow-covered plain, good wheat land, gently undulating, with little clumps of dark trees scattered here and there in the hollows.[4]

Once more he sees the sun setting on the plain as he used to see it on his childhood journeys. It is twenty-three years since he saw the sun setting on that land. Night is falling. Lulled by the rapid even movement of the sledge, the captain gives himself over to childhood memories, while in the dusk vast unfenced fields glide by, with a cottage here and there. At last the lights of Kazimierowka shine out, and waiting on the threshold is Uncle Thaddeus, with a warm embrace for the nephew he has not seen since that too brief glimpse at Marienbad, ready to clasp to his generous temperate heart *"Monsieur le capitaine au long-cours de la marine marchande britannique."*

As we can imagine, the days went by quickly in the two months the visitor spent with his uncle. The captain had to tell all about his voyages. The uncle, who had recently been working on his memoirs, described the family's past life—a melancholy past—and his loneliness, filled now with responsibility for his numerous wards, for his good judgment was so widely respected that he had been made guardian of many orphans in the vicinity.

To the record that the exact and scrupulous Thaddeus Bobrowski had kept since December 13, 1869, of his nephew's income and expenses, below the line on which three years earlier he had noted:

---

[4] See *A Personal Record*. (Tr.)

"Thus Mr. Conrad's progress to the estate of man has cost 17,454 rubles," he added these final lines:

> On February 16 you came to visit me at Kazimierowka and I take this opportunity of presenting you with this financial statement together with my cordial good wishes for your future success.

The next day he handed the captain this little "record book."

Early in March the captain was able to revisit the setting of his childhood memories. Accompanied by his uncle, he spent ten days on the estate at Nowofastov, some fifty miles away, where he lived as a little child and which Thaddeus Bobrowski had deeded to his sister-in-law, Madame Montrésor, after the death of his daughter. At Nowofastov relatives and friends listened, spellbound, to this born storyteller who was not reluctant to tell his tales.

Back at the Kazimierowka house there was a constant coming and going from one room to another. Late at night as he was going to bed, Conrad would hear his uncle's quick footsteps on the waxed floor of the next room, crossing the anteroom lined with bookshelves and entering the drawing room, where they became inaudible on the thick carpet. Through the closed blinds of his room, illuminated by two candelabra with four candles each, the visitor would hear the gentle sound of sleigh bells dying away beyond the village.

On a writing desk was lying, unostentatiously, a brown paper packet: the manuscript of *Almayer's Folly*. But how was he to work on it amid all these memories? Deep in this snow-covered Ukrainian plain the captain hardly gives a thought to the heavy scents of the tropical forest, to Almayer's vast hopes or his daily disappointments. Yet he thinks of Africa. For all his childhood memories, his uncle, his relatives, his friends, the captain does not lose sight of his African project. Moreover, his aunt in Brussels, in spite of her bereavement, has not forgotten her promises and has written that she is doing all she can. Her help is very useful, for letters arrive from London implying that Captain Korzeniowski's references have not satisfied the Société du Haut-Congo. "The prospect of seeing you in Brussels," he writes to Madame Poradowska after a month's absence, "will be a comfort to me when the time comes to leave my uncle." Their liking is mutual. The young widow does not forget her literary pretensions; Conrad, the writer-to-be, lets himself go in letters in a serious vein. In the silence of the country house in the Ukraine, the English sea captain applies himself to exercises in French literature:

> Life rolls on in bitter waves like the dark, cruel ocean under a sky covered with sad clouds. There are days when it seems to the poor souls embarked on the hopeless voyage that no ray of sun has ever managed to pierce this dreary veil, that the sun will never shine again, that it has never even existed.
>
> Eyes which the biting wind of grief has filled with tears must be forgiven if they refuse to see the blue sky: lips which have tasted the bitterness of life must be forgiven if they refuse to utter words of hope. . . .[5]

Another letter from his Aunt Marguerite at the beginning of April gives him better news of his projects. The prodigal's taste for adventure revives; his taste for the fatted calf has not replaced his appetite for *la vache enragée*. He informs the Société du Haut-Congo that he will present himself at their offices toward the end of the month. On April 18 he takes leave of his uncle; on the twenty-second he is in Lublin, where he spends forty-eight hours with his Zagórski cousins, on the twenty-ninth he is in Brussels. He cannot afford to devote much time to the charms of his Poradowska aunt, for he is suddenly appointed captain and promised the command of one of the Upper Congo steamboats. He barely has time to go back to London to pack his belongings, buy a few articles, return to Brussels to sign his contract, go back to London, then to Brussels again to say good-by to his aunt. He leaves Brussels by train on May 11, 1889, for Bordeaux, where he takes passage for Boma on the *Ville de Maceio* belonging to the Compagnie des Chargeurs Réunis.

At the beginning of "Heart of Darkness" Marlow, who is Conrad himself, has this to say about the reasons for the company's sudden hurry to engage him as a captain:

> "I got my appointment—of course; and I got it very quick. It appears the Company had received news that one of their captains had been killed in a scuffle with the natives. . . . It

---

[5] Letter of March 23, 1890.

was only months and months afterwards, when I made the attempt to recover what was left of the body, that I heard the original quarrel arose from a misunderstanding about some hens. . . . Through this glorious affair I got my appointment, before I had fairly begun to hope for it.

"I flew around like mad to get ready, and before forty-eight hours I was crossing the Channel to show myself to my employers, and sign the contract. In a very few hours I arrived in a city that always makes me think of a whited sepulchre . . . I had no difficulty in finding the Company's offices. . . . A narrow and deserted street in deep shadow, high houses, innumerable windows with venetian blinds, a dead silence, grass sprouting between the stones. . . ."

And then Marlow gives his unforgettable account of his visit to the company's office. The women dressed in black, knitting in the outer office like impassive Fates; the huge, many-colored map of Central Africa; the interview with the managing director which lasted only a few seconds; the compassionate secretary; the visit to the doctor; the farewells to his aunt—this succession of details and scenes, all extraordinarily vivid and all bearing the imprint of a biting irony, are nothing but the memory of actuality.

Just before leaving London, in a letter to one of his first cousins, Madame Tyska, née Bobrowska, a letter intended for all his relations in Lublin, Joseph Conrad announced that he was leaving "for a stay of three years in the middle of Africa." In fact, he left more like someone who has taken himself at his own word than like an enthusiastic traveler. During the ship's call at Teneriffe, he wrote to Madame Poradowska:

We left Bordeaux on a rainy day. A sad day; not a very cheerful departure. Haunting memories; vague regrets; hopes that are still more vague.[6]

And a few weeks later, on June 10, he writes to her again from Libreville. He speaks tenderly of his uncle and declares: "You have enriched my life with a new interest, a new affection." He asks her to write to him and adds:

[6] Letter of May 15, 1890.

If one could get rid of one's heart and memory (and brain, too) and then get a whole new set of these things, life would become ideally amusing. . . . Pending the inevitable fever I am very well. . . . After this I shall not be able to write until we get to Léopoldville. It takes twenty days to get there: on foot, too. Horrors!

The ship had called at Teneriffe, Dakar, Konakri, Sierra Leone, Grand-Bassam, Kotonu, Libreville, Loango, Banana at the mouth of the Congo, and Boma, the seat of the government of the Free State since 1886. All these ports of call explain why, after leaving Bordeaux on May 10, Captain Korzeniowski did not reach Boma until June 13. From there he went to Matadi in a little steamboat. His work was not to begin until he reached Stanley Pool, some two hundred and fifty miles away, above the rapids.

Conrad's traveling companion all the way from Bordeaux had been an agent of the Free State named Prosper Harou, who was going back to his station. This Belgian official, who had done several tours of duty in Africa, knew its dangers and did not hide from the newcomer the fact that actual circumstances were a little different from the official statistics. These revelations cast a slight pall over the journey, but the traveler tried to make the best of things, as we can see from a letter in Polish which he wrote on board the *Ville de Maceio* to his cousin Charles Zagórski:

22 May, 1890, Freetown, Sierra Leone.

My very dear Charles,

It is just a month today since you were horrified by my hasty departure from Lublin. You can see from the date and address of this letter that I had to hurry. Only now am I beginning to breathe a bit more calmly. If you only knew what a confounded lot of things I had to see to. From London to Brussels, back to London; then back to Brussels again. You should have seen all the tin chests and revolvers, the high boots and the touching farewells. One more handshake and one more pair of trousers! And if you only knew how many bottles of medicine and affectionate wishes I am taking with me, you would understand the typhoon, cyclone, hurricane, earthquake —no! the universal cataclysm—the fantastic atmosphere of shopping, business matters and sentimental leave-taking in which I spent two whole weeks! . . . I shall be at Boma no doubt on the 7th of next month and then leave Boma with my caravan to go to Léopoldville. As far as I can make out from my contract letter, I am destined to command a steamboat belonging to Mr. Delcommune's exploring party, which is now getting under way. I am delighted at this prospect, but I don't know anything definite, because it seems that everything is supposed to be kept secret. What does worry me is that I have been told that 60% of the company's employees go back to Europe without even staying six months. . . . Others are hastily sent back after a year so that they won't die in the Congo. Heaven forbid! That would spoil the statistics, which are excellent, you see! In brief, it seems that only 7% can stand three years' service. . . . Ah yes, but a Polish gentleman, soaked in British tar! How that will confuse them! We shall see. In any case I can console myself by remembering that—faithful to our national traditions—I got myself into this of my own free will.

Obviously Conrad was no longer unaware of the risks of this adventure, though they had certainly not been put to him frankly in Brussels before his departure.

A little later, on June 24, Uncle Thaddeus wrote to his nephew from the Ukraine:

I am following you through space in my thoughts, wondering what is happening to you. I suppose that if you haven't yet been put on a spit and eaten broiled (or perhaps in a stew) I shall get a letter from you sooner or later. . . . Your last letter is dated from Teneriffe, and according to my calculations you ought to be at Léopoldville by now. Don't wait to sum up your opinions on people and things and on the civilizing mission in which after all—confound it! you are a cog, but, while all that is crystallizing into sentences, tell me quickly how you are and what your first impressions are like.

And he ends another letter along the same lines as his nephew, though less philosophically and confidently.

Your letter of May 28 was dated from Libreville, so it took seven weeks. You wrote it on the frontier of civilization and barbarism. What am I to expect if you go to the very heart of Africa, where the mail only arrives once a month? . . . Your only consolation and your only hope of adding to your pertinacity and optimism in the present struggle for life will lie in Molière's famous phrase: *"Tu l'as voulu, George Dandin!"* I for my part will count the days and weeks of the three years that separate us no less impatiently, wondering if my carcass can hold out so long.

On June 18 the traveler writes to Madame Poradowska from Matadi:

I leave tomorrow, on foot. No donkeys here, except your very humble servant. A twenty day caravan.

He did not leave the next day, not until ten days later. In 1890 Matadi was already a fairly important station; there were almost two hundred Europeans there and five or six trading stations of various nationalities. What gave Matadi new life and would rapidly increase its importance was that work had just begun on the Matadi-Kinchassa railway, which was to facilitate the rapid transport of goods from the Upper Congo to the ports of embarkation for Europe. At that time these goods all had to be carried on the backs of porters along caravan tracks.

Conrad's call at Matadi did nothing to raise his spirits. This part of the Congo looks like a lake surrounded on all sides by high mountains, but nature is not at her most attractive there, according to Captain Thys, the man whom Conrad had talked to in Brussels before leaving.

When you arrive in Matadi (he wrote), you seem to have reached an accursed land, a real barrier erected by nature to impede progress.

Joseph Conrad cared little about fostering so-called progress, which he regarded with considerable scepticism, expressed later in "An Outpost of Progress" and "Heart of Darkness." His stay in

Matadi seemed endless, for he was impatient to start on the two-hundred-mile march that would take him to his ship.

One note he wrote about his stay in Matadi tells us a great deal about his impressions of the people he met in his first few days there:

> Think just now that my life amongst the people (white) around here cannot be very comfortable. Intend avoid acquaint-ances as much as possible.[7]

This sentence occurs at the beginning of a document which is quite exceptional in Conrad's life: a diary which he kept in English from June 13 to August 1, 1890, that is, for the period of his stay at Matadi and the long trek from Matadi to Kinchassa.

At all events, he made the acquaintance of the head of the station, a Belgian named Gosse, a former officer, who was to die six months later, and of another man, who subsequently attained an extraordinary notoriety, Mr.—afterward Sir—Roger Casement, who was then twenty-six and was in the Congo for the third time, currently with the Société Anonyme Belge. He was, in fact, one of the few people in Africa who made a good impression on Conrad: "Thinks, speaks well, most intelligent and very sympathetic," he wrote in his diary shortly after his arrival, and on leaving Matadi he notes again: "Parted with Casement in a very friendly manner."

While waiting to start, he passed the time as best he could in activities which had very little to do with his proper functions. "Have been busy packing ivory in casks. Idiotic employment." And the same day he notes again: "Prominent characteristic of the social life here: people speaking ill of each other." The atmosphere of this colonial outpost certainly did not appeal to him.

At last, on June 28, together with Prosper Harou, he left Matadi with a caravan of thirty-one porters. At their first halt, before crossing the river at M'poso, two Danish officials joined them and they all made the ascent of the mountainous Pataballa region together. The fatigue and unpleasantness can be imagined from what Captain Thys had written about this region a short time previously:

> If, on leaving Matadi you take the land route and head for M'poso and the Pataballa Range, the same impression con-

[7] *Last Essays*, "Congo Diary."

tinues: and when you arrive at Pataballa, sweating and panting, your legs aching, there falls from your lips an exclamation
which doubtless never varies: "What awful country!"

At the end of this long climb, toward Congo da Lemba, his traveling companion began to suffer from fainting spells which were to
occur repeatedly during the journey so that he had to be carried most
of the way. For eleven days, from Matadi to Manyanga, it was a
monotonous march, at the rate of fifteen to twenty miles a day, along
an uneven track, sometimes through forest, sometimes over a plain
covered with tall grass—a weary and dismal expedition of which he
has given this striking picture:

> "Paths, paths, everywhere; a stamped-in network of paths
> spreading over the empty land, through long grass, through
> burnt grass, through thickets, down and up chilly ravines, up
> and down stony hills ablaze with heat; and a solitude, a soli-
> tude, nobody, not a hut."

They would start very early in the morning on a tiring march
which lasted until eleven o'clock, along a track broken now and
again by a native market or a river to be forded or crossed by means
of a bridge of lianas. Once they met an officer of the Free State on a
tour of inspection and a few minutes later saw the body of a Negro
who had been shot. Pitch camp, cook, sleep, strike camp, and off
again. They marched through gray-yellowish country "with reddish
patches (soil) and clumps of dark green vegetation scattered sparsely
about." They marched through steep gorges or along the crest of a
mountain chain. The nights were damp and cold, the mornings
misty, the middle of the day scorching. The camp sites were dirty,
the water often brackish, and the mosquitoes kept up their activity
night and day. Often there was an argument with the porters just
before setting out. After a week of this, Conrad notes in his diary:
"Getting jolly well sick of this fun."

At last, on the morning of July 8, they arrived at Manyanga. They
were very kindly received there by the director of the Transport
Company of the Upper Congo, an Englishman, Reginald Heyn,
and his assistant, Jaeger.

Up to now Conrad's health had been satisfactory. During his stay

8 "Heart of Darkness."

at Manyanga he fell ill, probably with an attack of fever. Harou's health was no better.

After a sixteen-day rest, they set off again in a rather poor state and resumed their march day after day, during which the noonday heat was rivaled by the dangerous coolness of the nights.

On Sunday, July 27, they spent the day at the Sutili mission station, where they were received by the missionary's young wife, Mrs. Annie Comber. Little did Conrad suspect that on that very day, far away at Luri in Corsica, Dominic Cervoni, his master in seamanship and the comrade of his Mediterranean years, was dying, at the age of fifty-six, after thirty-seven years in the service of the sea.

The march continued, monotonous as ever, except for an occasional skeleton tied to a stake or a heap of stones in the form of a cross marking the grave of a white man. Harou was seriously ill with one attack of fever after another and had to be carried again. He was heavy; the porters complained and deserted at night with their loads. Conrad had to use his authority to put down the beginnings of a mutiny. After nine days they arrived somehow or other, limping and stumbling, at Kinchassa, the home port of the Upper Congo flotilla.

There the company had set up a shipyard, or rather an assembly yard. It was there that they assembled the shells of ships sent out in sections from Europe and carried on men's backs from Matadi to the Pool. Damaged ships were also repaired there.

When Conrad arrived they were at work on repairs to the ship intended for him, the *Florida,* for she had been wrecked a few days previously. Captain Korzeniowski did not, however, have to wait two months for them to repair his ship, as Marlow did in "Heart of Darkness." He embarked as second officer that same day on a little steamboat of fifteen tons, the *Roi des Belges.* Captain Koch, a Dane who had been upriver several times, undertook to initiate him into the difficulties and dangers of this fresh-water navigation. Arriving in Kinchassa on August 2, he left the next day, as the manuscript heading of a second diary proves: "Up River Book, commenced 3rd August, 1890, S.S. *Roi des Belges."*

In Kinchassa he got in touch with Camille Delcommune, temporary acting manager, whom he calls "the manager" in "Heart of Darkness":

"My first interview with the manager was curious. He did not ask me to sit down after my twenty-mile walk that morning. He was commonplace in complexion, in feature, in manners, and in voice. He was of middle size and of ordinary build. His eyes, of the usual blue, were perhaps remarkably cold, and he certainly could make his glance fall on one as trenchant and heavy as an axe. . . . He was a common trader, from his youth up employed in these parts—nothing more. He was obeyed, yet he inspired neither love nor fear, nor even respect, . . . He had no genius for organizing, for initiative, or for order even. That was evident in such things as the deplorable state of the station. He had no learning, and no intelligence. His position had come to him—why? Perhaps because he was never ill . . ."

We shall refer later to an impression of this same Camille Delcommune which occurs in Conrad's own correspondence and confirms this one.

On August 4 the S.S. *Roi des Belges,* carrying Camille Delcommune, Captain Koch and Captain Korzeniowski, the agents Keyaerts, Rollin, and Van der Heyden, and the engineer Gossens, left Kinchassa with two lighters and two native canoes in tow. On August 26 the ship reached the confluence of the Ubangi; on September 1 she arrived at her destination, Stanley Falls, only twenty-eight days after her departure from Stanley Pool. This voyage, which in those days was considered remarkably quick, must have seemed interminable to Conrad, for he says in "Heart of Darkness": "It was just two months from the date we left the creek when we came to the bank below Kurtz's station."

Nothing could give a more vivid feeling of this thousand-mile trip up the Congo aboard that wretched little fifteen-ton steamboat than the series of admirable descriptions that make up the greater part of "Heart of Darkness," from which we quote the following passage:

"Going up that river was like traveling back to the earliest beginnings of the world, when vegetation rioted on the earth and the big trees were kings. An empty stream, a great silence, an impenetrable forest. The air was warm, thick, heavy, sluggish. There was no joy in the brilliance of sunshine. The long stretches of the waterway ran on, deserted, into the gloom of over-shadowed distances. On silvery sandbanks hippos and alligators sunned themselves side by side. The broadening waters flowed through a mob of wooded islands, you lost your way on that river as you would in a desert, and butted all day long against shoals, trying to find the channel, till you thought yourself bewitched and cut off for ever from everything you had known once—somewhere—far away—in another existence perhaps. There were moments when one's past came back to one, as it will sometimes when you have not a moment to spare to yourself; but it came in the shape of an unrestful and noisy dream, remembered with wonder amongst the overwhelming realities of this strange world of plants, and water, and silence. And this stillness of life did not in the least resemble a peace. It was the stillness of an implacable force brooding over an inscrutable intention. It looked at you with a vengeful aspect. I got used to it afterwards; I did not see it any more; I had no time. I had to keep guessing at the channel; I had to discern, mostly by inspiration, the signs of hidden banks; I watched for sunken stones; I was learning to clap my teeth smartly before my heart flew out, when I shaved by a fluke some infernal sly old snag that would have ripped the life out of the tin-pot steamboat and drowned all the pilgrims; I had to keep a look-out for the signs of dead wood we could cut up in the night for next day's steaming. When you have to attend to things of that sort, to the mere incidents of the surface, the reality—the reality, I tell you—fades. The inner truth is hidden—luckily, luckily. But I felt it all the same; I felt often its mysterious stillness watching me at my monkey tricks."

The ship did not stay long at Stanley Falls and there is in "Heart of Darkness" no description of this farthest point of navigation on the river, but another page from the writer's work gives us an impression of Captain Korzeniowski in the heart of Africa. In it we find an echo of the feeling of solitude that came over him at this time, which was due not only to his being plunged into a mysterious silence, "into the heart of an immense darkness," but also to the fact that he no longer felt between his white companions and himself that innate solidarity, that common conception of human dignity, that fidelity to a few very simple and, so to speak, tacitly assumed principles which throughout his childhood and his fifteen years at sea had been the constant atmosphere of his life and, at the bottom of his heart, his safeguard and his pride.

Everything was dark under the stars. Every other white man on board was asleep. I was glad to be alone on deck, smoking the pipe of peace after an anxious day. The subdued thundering mutter of the Stanley Falls hung in the heavy night air of the last navigable reach of the Upper Congo, while no more than ten miles away, in Reshid's camp just above the Falls, the yet unbroken power of the Congo Arabs slumbered uneasily. Their day was over. Away in the middle of the stream, on a little island nestling all black in the foam of the broken water, a solitary little light glimmered feebly, and I said to myself with awe, "This is the very spot of my boyish boast."

A great melancholy descended on me. Yes, this was the very spot. But there was no shadowy friend to stand by my side in the night of the enormous wilderness, no great haunting memory, but only the unholy recollection of a prosaic newspaper "stunt" and the distasteful knowledge of the vilest scramble for loot that ever disfigured the history of human conscience and geographical exploration. What an end to the idealized realities of a boy's daydreams! I wondered what I was doing there, for indeed it was only an unforeseen episode, hard to believe in now, in my seaman's life. Still, the fact remains that I have smoked a pipe of peace at midnight in the very heart of the African continent, and felt very lonely there.[9]

The purpose of the voyage of the *Roi des Belges* from Kinchassa to Stanley Falls was to relieve one of the company's agents at the Falls whose health was causing the greatest anxiety. This explains the haste of the steamboat's departure from Kinchassa and its passage upriver.

This dying agent, whom Conrad turned into the abominable hero

[9] *Last Essays,* "Geography and Some Explorers."

of "Heart of Darkness," Kurtz, actually had quite a similar name, Georges-Antoine Klein. He had arrived in the Congo late in 1888 and was put in charge of the company's station at Stanley Falls in 1890. He died on September 21 aboard the S.S. *Roi des Belges* and was buried at Bolobo by the ship's company.

It is impossible without formal proof to be sure of the exact resemblance between Kurtz and Klein, but it is beyond doubt, when one is familiar with Conrad's habit of using in his work elements drawn from reality, that these two characters, one real, the other fictitious, were alike in more than name.[10]

Going upriver Captain Korzeniowski was only the first mate of the *Roi des Belges* but he brought the steamer back to Kinchassa as captain, as the following letter shows:

SOCIÉTÉ ANONYME BELGE
POUR LE COMMERCE DU HAUT-CONGO
9, rue Bréderode.
Stanley Falls, Sept. 6, 1890

Mr. Conrad Korzeniowski,
Captain.

I have the honor to ask you to take over the command of the S.S. *Roi des Belges* as of today, until the recovery of Captain Koch.

Yours etc.
Camille Delcommune.

Thus Conrad owed his official command solely to Captain Koch's illness—a fact which will explain some later events.

This date, September 6, probably coincided with their departure from the Falls, since, due to the current, the passage back took only half as long as the trip upriver. In any case, the date of Klein's burial

---

[10] This is confirmed by an examination of the manuscript of "Heart of Darkness" now in the library of Yale University. On p. 55 of this manuscript Conrad had written: "In the interior you will no doubt meet Monsieur Klein. . . ." He later crossed out the last two words and changed them to Mr. Kurtz, a correction he repeated in three other places in the same paragraph. (Note from Mr. John Gordan, Harvard University, November 11, 1938.)

(September 21) must correspond to that of the ship's call at Bolobo. On September 24 the *Roi des Belges* returned to her base at Kinchassa and Conrad's one experience as a fresh-water mariner came to an end.

From "Heart of Darkness," which parallels so closely Conrad's own life at this period, we can assume that Captain Korzeniowski's relations with the manager had soon become cool and even somewhat strained. The captain's disappointment, his conviction that they wanted to keep him in a subordinate position and that the promises made in Brussels would never be fulfilled in the Congo, his growing discontent, his outright indignation at the hypocritical greed of these traders and their methods—all these feelings had been in evidence even before his meeting with Kurtz-Klein, which, as Marlow said, "seemed to shed a kind of light on all the things around him and on his own thoughts." Even before he left Kinchassa to go upriver, he had confided his first disappointments to his uncle, as the following reply clearly shows:

> Three days ago I received your letter from Stanley Pool. . . . I see that you are very angry with the Belgians, who are exploiting you unscrupulously. You must admit that this time nothing forced you to put yourself in the Belgians' hands. *"Tu l'as voulu, tu l'as voulu, George Dandin."* . . . If you had paid attention to my opinion in the whole business, you would have gathered, after our conversation, that I was not very keen on your project. As a Polish gentleman, I have always preferred what is safer and less brilliant to what is more brilliant and less safe. . . . If you break your contract, you risk expense and being accused of irresponsibility, which might harm your future career.[11]

Conrad did not need this advice from Thaddeus Bobrowski (which, in any case, did not reach him until long afterward) to persuade him to go ahead with the adventure he had so unfortunately engaged in. He was not going to give in. The day of his return to Kinchassa, in the course of a long letter to his cousin, Madame Tyska, he said:

[11] Letter of September 14, 1890.

I am very busy getting ready for a new expedition on the Kasai River. I think in a few days I shall leave Kinchassa again for several months, possibly more than ten months.

And two days later in a letter in French to Madame Poradowska he tells her that he is back from Stanley Falls, where he went "to learn the river." He adds:

My days here are dreary. There is no doubt about it. I decidedly regret having come here: indeed, I regret it bitterly. Everything here repels me. Men and things, but especially the men. And I repel them, too. From the manager in Africa—who has taken the trouble of telling a lot of people that he can't stand me, down to the lowest mechanic—they all have the gift of getting on my nerves. . . .

The manager is a common ivory-dealer with sordid instincts who considers himself a trader when he is nothing but a kind of African shopkeeper. His name is Delcommune. He hates the English, and of course I am regarded here as an Englishman.[12]

He says he has had fever four times in two months, and at the Falls ("its native country") he had an attack of dysentery which lasted five days. He feels demoralized. "And besides," he adds, "I'm homesick for the sea."

He wanted to hold out and he still hoped to get command of the *Florida,* which was to transport the Katanga expedition directed by Alexandre Delcommune, brother of the acting manager, who no doubt persuaded Alexandre not to give Conrad command of the steamboat.

We have no firsthand evidence as to the cause of his final break with Camille Delcommune, but we have an extremely valuable secondhand item: a letter dated November 29, 1890, from Lublin in Poland, from Madame Marguerite Poradowska to the director of the Société du Haut-Congo in Brussels, paraphrasing several passages from a letter of September 26 which she had just received from Conrad in Kinchassa:

[12] Letter of September 26, 1890.

Moreover, the ship he was to command will not be ready until June, *if then,* and the manager, Mr. Delcommune, has told him frankly that he cannot hope for a promotion or a raise in salary as long as he stays in the Congo. Mr. Delcommune also stated that he is not bound by promises made in Europe unless they are in the contract, and the promises you were good enough to make to him are not in his contract.

After expressing the anxiety felt by Captain Korzeniowski's whole family about the reports of his health, Madame Poradowska informed the managing director of the company of Conrad's wish to be appointed to the command of one of the ocean-going vessels belonging to one of the trading companies in the Congo that carried on a shuttle service between Banana and Antwerp. If he could be recalled for this purpose, Captain Korzeniowski was quite willing to pay the expenses of his passage home. Madame Poradowska added this significant sentence:

It is sad to think that a man of Mr. Conrad Korzeniowski's abilities, experienced in the command of ships, should be reduced to this subordinate position and exposed to such noxious diseases.

It is obvious from this letter that the principal cause of Conrad's discontent was Delcommune's refusal to give him command of a ship and his fixed determination to keep him subordinate. Their decision, when Alexandre Delcommune arrived, not to give Conrad command of the *Florida,* was the last straw for him.

By October 19 he had decided to give up everything and go back to Europe with nothing left but the rather vague hope of commanding a sea-going vessel. A few weeks later, just before he reached Europe, Thaddeus Bobrowski wrote to him:

On the 24th I received your letter of October 19 from Kinchassa informing me of the unhappy ending of your expedition to the Congo and your return to Europe. Madame Marguerite told me of it too, from Lublin, where she heard about it from the director of the Company to whom she had written for news of you.

Although you assure me that the first sea breeze will restore your health, I find your handwriting so changed—no doubt due to the fever and dysentery—that my thoughts since then have not been at all cheerful. I never kept it a secret that I was not in favor of your African venture, but I have been faithful to my principle of letting everyone be happy in his own way.

See a specialist in tropical diseases immediately, for our doctors here know nothing about them and I am not even in a position to tell you to come here for a rest.

Tell me also about the state of your finances, so that I may perhaps help—so far as my circumstances permit.[13]

Captain Korzeniowski had held out as long as he could; he was beaten as much by the effects of the climate as by human malice. His health was seriously impaired. Delcommune's ill will toward Conrad must be regarded as a stroke of luck, for if he had obtained command of the vessel going up the Kasai it is unlikely that Captain Korzeniowski would have come back alive.

We know nothing of the circumstances of his return. He must have left Kinchassa early in November at the latest, since he was at Matadi on December 4. In any case he made the journey from Kinchassa to Léopoldville in a native canoe, as we are told in *A Personal Record*:

. . . A good many of my other properties . . . remained behind through unfortunate accidents of transportation. I call to mind, for instance, a specially awkward turn of the Congo between Kinchassa and Leopoldsville—more particularly when one had to take it at night in a big canoe with only half the proper number of paddlers. I failed in being the second white man on record drowned at that interesting spot through the upsetting of a canoe. The first was a young Belgian officer, but the accident happened some months before my time, and he, too, I believe, was going home; not perhaps quite so ill as myself—but still he was going home. I got round the turn more or less alive, though I was too sick to care whether I did or not, and, always with *Almayer's Folly* amongst my dimin-

[13] Letter of December 27, 1890.

ishing baggage, I arrived at that delectable capital Boma, where, before the departure of the steamer which was to take me home I had the time to wish myself dead over and over again with perfect sincerity.

The immediate result of this voyage to the Congo was, as Conrad said himself, "a long, long illness and a very dismal convalescence." For the rest of his life his health was to show the permanent effects of this African expedition. He suffered from attacks of fever and gout which made his existence an intermittent martyrdom and his correspondence a long, courageous lament.

On the other hand, we are justified in thinking that this voyage to the Congo and its deplorable consequences played a big part in turning Captain Korzeniowski into the novelist Joseph Conrad.

Edward Garnett, whose role in Conrad's literary life will emerge later, told me that Conrad once said to him: "Before the Congo, I was just a mere animal," meaning that for his first fifteen years at sea he had lived almost without being aware of it, carried along by the ardor of his temperament in response to an almost unconscious desire for adventure, without ever thinking about the reasons for his or other people's actions. The illness he contracted in the Congo, by immobilizing him, cutting down his physical activity, and keeping him shut up for long months, forced him to look into himself, to think over the experiences of which his life was so extraordinarily full—though he was still only thirty-three.

It was just before his departure for the Congo that Captain Korzeniowski's literary vocation had begun to take shape. In the baggage he took to Stanley Falls and almost lost on the way back from Kinchassa, was a notebook of a few hundred pages containing the first seven chapters of *Almayer's Folly*. So it is not true that the Congo awoke the latent novelist whom John Conrad Korzeniowski had borne within himself ever since the studious years of his lonely childhood. However, it was the Congo and its consequences that finally shaped his destiny and threw the painful weight of illness into the balance on the side of the novelist, while the seaman was still struggling with him for supremacy.

He was to sail again, but never with the same confidence. From now on he always felt threatened. Despite his unconquerable energy, in the incessant struggle against his old pitiless enemy, the sea, he no longer had that absolute confidence in his own strength that had kept him going so long. A voyage, a victory, as the English saying goes—but he was no longer quite sure of victory.

It is not altogether correct to say, as John Galsworthy does, that "that lingering Congo fever which dogged his health fastened a deep, fitful gloom over his spirit." This gloom was the very basis of his character; he had breathed it since he was born: a gloom not only personal but national: that brave and at the same time desperate attitude of Poland at one of the darkest hours in her history; a gloom intensified by his contact with distant countries, in the solitude of the sea, and revived—horribly—by the sight of colonial greed. If the Congo did not create this deep gloom, it did cause it to spring forth from the very depths of his being, and without any doubt it contributed to those magnificent floods of bitterness which, issuing from the very heart of human darkness, broaden out like a vast river or well up like a cataract to carry to the farthest reaches of its dreams the strength of an unquiet soul and a generous spirit.

IX

'Twixt Land and Sea
(1891-1894)

The sea is the sailor's true element, and
Marlow, lingering on shore, was to me
an object of incredulous commiseration,
like a bird, which, secretly, should have
lost its faith in the high virtue of flying.

Chance

ON HER RETURN to Brussels from Poland early in January, 1891,
Madame Poradowska anxiously inquired at the Société du Haut-
Congo about the ship on which Captain Korzeniowski was to return to Europe, so that she might inform Thaddeus Bobrowski,
who, she said in her letter, "thinks that his nephew is so ill that
he will go straight to London." That was, in fact, exactly what he
did a short time later. The crossing had had a beneficial effect. He
left the ship almost well and in fair spirits. Before the month was
out he had gone to Brussels to ascertain his chances of a sea command. There he found his aunt Poradowska in the same frame
of mind, or even more optimistic. A few days after his visit she
wrote to him: "The two days you were here were splendid." He is
assured of her complete support: she will move heaven and earth to
get him a command, since that is what he wants. With this in view,
Conrad, now back in London, gives her a few picturesque details:

You may also add that judging by the appearance of my
nose I only get drunk once a year, that I don't look as though

I have any leanings towards piracy and that, from what you
know of me, you do not think me capable of embezzlement.
I have never been in a police court and I am capable of a
discreet glance at a pretty face without making eyes at it.
It is true that I limp. But I am in distinguished company.
Timoléon was lame and there is even a devil who is lame
too, from what I hear.[1]

Yet in spite of his bantering tone, in the same letter he admits
having seen a doctor who put him to bed because of the swelling
in his legs. As soon as he is well he proposes to go to Antwerp
with his friend, Captain Hope. A few days later he is decidedly
better and goes to Glasgow "on business." He writes to his aunt
that he has given up the trip to Antwerp, but is thinking of coming to Brussels "for a little visit." However, at the end of February his legs are so swollen that he can no longer stand, and his
friend Krieger loses no time in taking him to the German Hospital
in London.

"Rheumatism in the left leg and neuralgia in the right arm," he
tells Madame Poradowska in twisted handwriting the day after
his admission to the hospital. A fortnight later he can still only
scrawl a few words in pencil to Madame Poradowska and to his
uncle, who has invited him to spend some time in the Ukraine and
sent him some money, saying:

Your note has given me the impression that you are very
weak and depressed, in spite of the message from the excellent Krieger, who told me what Dr. Ludwig said.

By the end of March he can get up for a bit. "I have been in bed
a month and I think that is the longest time in my whole life,"
he writes to his aunt, adding that through the influence of Mr.
Pécher of Antwerp he has received from Mr. Knott of Newcastle
some inquiries about the command of a steamer, but how can
he accept in his present state?

To reassure his uncle he tries to put the situation in a humorous
light, but his uncle is not fooled. His convalescence is extremely
slow. When his aunt tells him of the death of his uncle, Jean

[1] Letter of February 1, 1891.

Zagórski, in Lublin, he apologizes for not being able to send a letter of condolence:

> I take such a discouraged view of everything; everything looks gloomy. . . . The work of assembling my ideas and turning them into Polish is—for the moment—beyond me.[2]

At the beginning of May he is suffering from palpitations and shortness of breath and ten days later he writes: "Once again I am plunged in deepest darkness and my dreams are nothing but nightmares; I am having less trouble breathing than for several days."

It is out of the question for him to go to the Ukraine as his uncle urges him to, and Dr. Ludwig, who is looking after him, advises him to go for treatment to the hydropathic sanatorium at Champel, near Geneva.

After almost three months of suffering and insomnia he finally leaves the hospital, spends a day resting in Paris, and arrives in Champel on May 21 in a state of extreme melancholy and depression.

This man of thirty-four, who had for so long shown such determination in his struggle against material and mental difficulties and who had so recently reached the goal of his career: that is, the responsibilities, initiative, and active duty involved in a command, now had to face the bitter fact that his health was ruined, his future compromised, his strength insufficient to carry on any longer the inspiring but exhausting battle of the sailor against the sea.

During his visit to Champel, which lasted until June 14, Joseph Conrad stayed at the Hôtel-Pension de la Roseraie, situated at a turning in the road from Geneva, where it runs for some distance along the Arve before coming to the suburb of Carouge. It is a big, square, white house, with four stories and a flat roof, in a shady garden with a lawn bounded by the road which overlooks the Arve, forming a sort of tree-lined embankment. At this spot the rapid current of the river is checked by a wier, whose monotonous echo may have reminded the traveler unpleasantly of the Congo falls. On one side can be seen the Pinchat hillside and, on the

[2] Letter of April 14, 1891.

horizon, the massive bulk of the Salève; on the other, a little plain half covered with the low buildings, workshops, sheds, and factories of Carouge.

It was only a short walk from La Roseraie, across the road and through the gate leading up a little hill, to the hydropathic baths. If he turned to the left along the Roseraie-Plainpalais road he could be in the center of Geneva in less than half an hour.

The treatment at the sanatorium, the rest, the air of this sheltered spot, did the patient good immediately. On June 3 he wrote to Madame Poradowska: "I feel much better, if not completely well."

Whether because his physical improvement was really very quick or because he discovered new mental reserves, Conrad soon pulled out of his depression and with new energy went back to work on the manuscript of *Almayer's Folly,* which he had not touched for a year. As he was to say ironically in *A Personal Record:*

> Geneva, or more precisely the hydropathic establishment of Champel, is rendered for ever famous by the termination of the eighth chapter in the history of Almayer's decline and fall.

While he was at Champel he received an offer—probably thanks to Adolf Krieger—to serve in a ship sailing for—or on—the Niger, but he was completely disgusted with Africa and, although he was convinced that the climate of Nigeria was less dangerous than that of the Congo, he lost no time in declining the offer and went back to London in the middle of June after spending a day in Paris with Madame Poradowska who was staying there.

Back in London, he took up a new kind of navigation which he was to go in for intermittently during the next few years: he made a short cruise on the Thames and in the estuary in his friend Hope's yacht.

He obviously does not know where he is going. His health is better, but he has no confidence in it:

> What is the good of planning, since it is always the unexpected that happens? As soon as the unexpected does hap-

pen, I shall write and tell you. I am very curious myself to know what it will look like,[3]

he writes to his aunt, shortly after his return to London. The following month he says again: "All my plans have failed, so I am not making any more." And a fortnight later: "All my plans have failed and I think I shall have to stay in London for good."

We have no idea what these plans and projects were, but there is reason to think that they were not solely concerned with a position as captain or first mate. This is indicated by a letter of July 30, 1891, from Thaddeus Bobrowski, in which he reproaches his nephew for a lack of perseverence in his projects:

. . . a weakness [he adds] which you get from the Nalecz Korzeniowskis. Your grandfather and your uncle were always wrapped up in schemes of a practical nature which existed only in their imagination. Your father was an idealistic dreamer. He loved mankind and desired its happiness, but he had two standards: he was full of indulgence for the poor and very hard on the rich. All three of them had a great deal of pride and suffered keenly from their lack of success. Unfortunately, you get carried away by your imagination in all your undertakings, and when they fail you give yourself up to a discouragement which goes entirely too far.

On the very same day his uncle wrote him this letter, Conrad was writing to Madame Poradowska:

Here I am, ill again. Just when I was going to begin work. An attack of malaria! I am just about stunned by this new disaster.

He abandons all his plans and rather reluctantly accepts the friendly offer made him by Barr, Moering & Co. through Krieger's influence. On August 5 he tells his aunt about it:

I am in charge of Barr, Moering's warehouse. If I find I can get used to this life, I shall stay in London. . . . I have a slight fever every day.

[3] Letter of June 22, 1891.

He had to supervise in detail the management of a warehouse on the Thames. This job, which he accepted in order to get used to a normal existence again, was not to last more than a few months in all, but after a week or two Conrad was already finding it tedious. He seemed to have no interest in anything.

> In the evening when I get home, I feel so lazy that I look at the pens with horror, and as for the ink-well, I banished that from my room long ago.[4]

Nevertheless, to take his mind off the melancholy that haunted him, and notwithstanding his aversion to the inkwell, he sought relief from his own troubles in narrating those of Almayer. The major part of the ninth chapter, which he had postponed so long, dates from this period.

"The earth," he said, "had nothing to hold me with for very long." He felt sure that only the sea could set him free from his doubts and depression, and he made new efforts to find a command.

A year of compulsory inactivity, of physical suffering, of introspection and long meditations about the conditions of life itself and of his own existence had dredged up from the depths of his soul that inborn bitterness that twenty years of eager, adventurous life had succeeded in allaying or at least repressing. A letter from Thaddeus Bobrowski at this time—November 9, 1891—reveals Conrad's state of mind:

> My dear boy,[5]
> I begin as I always do, but I ought to begin: "My dear pessimist" [5] because that has been the tone of your letters for some time and that is the description that fits you best. I can't say I am pleased with your frame of mind and, knowing it, I can't look forward to your future without misgivings. I am grateful for your frankness. Don't keep your real state of mind from me; that would be no use. I know people too well and I am too fond of you not to be able to read between the lines of your letters. . . .
> After thinking over carefully the reasons for your pessi-

---

[4] Letter to Madame Poradowska, August 26, 1891.

[5] In English in the original.

mism, I cannot attribute it either to youth or to old age, considering your thirty years and the busy life you have led. I have to put it down to ill health, to the awful adventures of your African expedition and the serious illness which resulted from it, which gave you plenty of time to think and to devote yourself to something I have noticed in you, which derives from the make-up of your character and the heritage you received from your parents—your tendency to mull things over, in spite of your very practical occupation.

I may be mistaken, but I think that this pessimistic tendency already existed years ago, when you were in Marseilles, but then it sprang from your youth. I am sure, therefore, that with your melancholy nature you ought to avoid all this meditation, which leads you to pessimistic conclusions. I advise you to take up a more active, gayer way of life.

Our country, as Slowacki rightly says (although he himself was not above reproach on this score), is the "pan" among nations, which in plain words means a collection of people who think their greatness is not appreciated, who are—and always will be—unrecognized. If individuals, like nations, would take duty as their aim instead of grandiose ideals, the world would be a happier place.

You may tell me that I talk like someone who has "always had a place in the sun," but that is not true. I have been through plenty of trouble. I have suffered from my own destiny, my family's, and my country's, and it is through those very sufferings and mortifications that I have attained a calm view of the duties of life, in which my motto has been and will be *usque ad finem*: the love of duty as demanded by circumstances.

Uncle and nephew had every reason to understand and love one another, but their characters were so fundamentally opposed that the Polish country gentleman was incapable of conceiving the very depth and extension of his nephew's chronic melancholy, which was born of a constant painful awareness of man's greatness and misery. Yet they had both arrived at the same conclusion: that salvation, transitory as it might be, could be found in action.

In fact, Captain Korzeniowski had not waited for his uncle's letter to come to a decision. On November 14 he wrote to Madame Poradowska:

> Yesterday afternoon I had a letter from an acquaintance of mine in command of the *Torrens* offering me the position of first mate. I accepted and today, at 7:30 A.M., I took over from my predecessor. We leave in six days. Destination: Port Adelaide. The voyage will take seventy to eighty days.

True, he had hesitated, not feeling sure of being able to carry out his duties properly because of his health, but he had been told that "moping ashore never did anyone any good." Moreover, Captain Cope's offer was not only satisfactory but flattering. The *Torrens* was a magnificent clipper of thirteen hundred tons, one of the best and fastest sailing ships ever built, and for years the favorite ship of passengers bound for Australia. She had been nicknamed "the wonderful *Torrens.*" Captain H. R. Angel, who had commanded her up to then, had made fifteen voyages in her at a record average speed for sail at that time: seventy-four days from Plymouth to the Adelaide Semaphore. To serve in a ship like this, even as mate, was flattering, besides putting an end to his homesickness for an occupation he had been away from for two and a half years.

After his service in the *Torrens,* Conrad paid her this tribute:

> . . . Apart from her more brilliant qualities, such as her speed and her celebrated good looks (which by themselves go a long way with a sailor), she was regarded as a "comfortable ship" in a strictly professional sense, which means that she was known to handle easily and to be a good sea boat in heavy weather. I cannot say that during my time in her we ever experienced really heavy weather; but we had the usual assortment of winds, up to "very strong gales" (logbook style), from various directions; and I can testify that, on every point of sailing, the way that ship had of letting big seas slip under her did one's heart good to watch. It resembled so much an exhibition of intelligent grace and unerring skill that it could fascinate even the least seamanlike of our passengers.[6]

[6] *Last Essays,* "The Torrens: A Personal Tribute."

Captain Cope, in fact, never managed to match the prowess of his predecessor in this ship. The *Torrens,* with Captain Korzeniowski as chief officer, left Plymouth on November 25, 1891, and did not arrive in Adelaide until February 28, 1892, a passage of ninety-five days. It was in Adelaide that the captain of the *Otago* had been compelled to give up his command three years ago.

Before leaving London, he had urgently begged Madame Poradowska to write to him in Australia and she did not fail to do so. He found several letters from her awaiting him, all full of literary matters. Neither were the captain's letters entirely nautical, as we see from one he wrote her on April 6, the eve of his departure from Adelaide:

> We leave tomorrow for the Cape of Good Hope. From there we go to Saint Helena and then to London. . . . I have just been re-reading *Madame Bovary* with an admiration tinged with respect. Here we have an author with enough imagination for two realists. There are few writers so creative as he. One never for a moment questions his characters or his events; one would as soon doubt one's own existence.

Conrad had forgotten the exact date of this reading when, much later, in 1918, he wrote to the novelist Hugh Walpole:

> You say that I have been under the formative influence of *Madame Bovary.* In fact, I read it only after finishing *A.[lmayer's] F.[olly]*, as I did all the other works of Flaubert, and anyhow, my Flaubert is the Flaubert of *St. Antoine* and *Ed[ucation]: Sent[imentale]:* and that only from the point of view of the rendering of concrete things and visual impressions. I thought him marvelous in that respect. I don't think I learned anything from him. What he did for me was to open my eyes and arouse my emulation. One can learn something from Balzac, but what could one learn from Flaubert? He compels admiration,—about the greatest service one artist can render to another.[7]

The homeward voyage was uneventful and lasted almost five months, including two calls, at the Cape and at Saint Helena. Conrad was hardly back in London before he began to think of

[7] Letter of June 7, 1918.

leaving again and his name appears in the ship's register for the next voyage. The day after his arrival he replies to Madame Pora-dowska, who wants him to come to Brussels or Paris, that it is out of the question for him to take a leave, for material reasons, or to give up this ship. Nonetheless, he is worried about his uncle's health, for he has, he says, been ailing the whole winter:

> He feels better in summer, but I am afraid it will not last. I may be wrong, for I take a gloomy view of everything since my own health broke down. It is ridiculous, but that is how it is.[8]

In a letter from Uncle Thaddeus just after Conrad's return, we have definite proof that the voyage had helped to set him up physically, and that his responsibilities and active duties as an officer had revived his spirits:

> I received your letter of September 24 the day before yester-day and I was very pleased by its cheerfulness. I am delighted at this change in your spirits. As you say you are leaving again on October 25, I am writing to London. . . .

Another letter from his uncle, dated a fortnight previously, indi-cates Conrad's ambitions for his career at sea:

> I share your feelings and understand that you want a com-mand. You might have had one if you had stayed in Aus-tralia, but that would have kept you away from Europe and your friends, and from me, for a long time—perhaps forever. You say my letters give you courage. That is the essence of my philosophy: we must wait patiently for fortune to look favora-bly upon us and graciously accept her gifts, meanwhile doing what has to be done. . . .
>
> . . . Madame Marguerite writes me voluminous letters, so illegibly written that I have to use a magnifying glass. Now her enthusiasm has waned a bit, and she hasn't written since April. The good soul is a terrible bluestocking and has the romantic ideas of a sixteen-year-old schoolgirl.[9]

[8] Letter of September 4, 1892.
[9] Letter of October 17, 1892.

To tell the truth, Uncle Thaddeus is not very fond of Madame Poradowska. It is obvious that he was afraid at one time that she might be playing a leading role in his nephew's life. The previous year he reproached Conrad in one of his letters for flirting with his aunt and showed some anxiety about their relations, but Conrad's departure for Australia convinced him that there was not much ground for his fears, and his second departure reassured him completely. He sent good wishes for his safe return, the more so as they had agreed that when he got back to Europe next year Conrad would come and visit him. As these Australian voyages lasted eight to nine months, he would be back in summer, and Thaddeus Bobrowski would be happy to be his host in the Ukraine during the season.

In the same letter Uncle Thaddeus gives him a long account of an event which has deeply disturbed the family. Conrad's cousin, Uncle Casimir's son, Stanislas Bobrowski, has just been arrested by the Russian authorities and is soon to stand trial for having given clandestine lessons in Polish. This reawoke in Conrad painful memories of his early childhood.

On October 25, 1892, he left London again as first mate of the *Torrens,* and after an even longer passage—ninety-seven days— arrived in Adelaide on January 30, 1893. This voyage was marked by an important incident, though it had nothing to do with Conrad's shipboard duties.

Among other passengers in the *Torrens* was a young man, W. H. Jacques, a Cambridge man, who was traveling for the sake of his health. In a sailing ship of this type the passengers were not ordinary tourists. The voyages were long; those aboard led a kind of family life, and daily contact quickly brought about a certain intimacy between officers and passengers. Conrad, with his natural courtesy and his growing curiosity about people, was especially interested in the passengers, since his relations with his captain were confined to duty and he felt nothing but a respectful indifference for him.

The first mate of the *Torrens,* being a great reader, had no trouble in finding topics of conversation with this young man just down from the university. They became friendly, lent each other books. There were long talks on the poop deck or in the mate's cabin.

One evening, on a sudden impulse, Captain Korzeniowski opened a drawer, took out a stack of paper covered with handwriting, and handed it to his companion. It was the first nine chapters of *Almayer's Folly*.

"Would it bore you very much reading a MS. in a handwriting like mine?" I asked him one evening on a sudden impulse at the end of a longish conversation whose subject was Gibbon's History. Jacques (that was his name) was sitting in my cabin one stormy dog-watch below, after bringing me a book to read from his own travelling store.

"Not at all," he answered with his courteous intonation and a faint smile. As I pulled a drawer open his suddenly aroused curiosity gave him a watchful expression. I wonder what he expected to see. A poem, maybe. All that's beyond guessing now. He was not a cold, but a calm man, still more subdued by disease—a man of few words and of an unassuming modesty in general intercourse, but with something uncommon in the whole of his person which set him apart from the undistinguished lot of our sixty passengers. His eyes had a thoughtful introspective look. In his attractive, reserved manner, and in a veiled, sympathetic voice, he asked:

"What is this?"

"It is a sort of tale," I answered with an effort. "It is not even finished yet. Nevertheless, I would like to know what you think of it." He put the MS. in the breast-pocket of his jacket; I remember perfectly his thin brown fingers folding it lengthwise. "I will read it tomorrow," he remarked, seizing the door-handle, and then, watching the roll of the ship for a propitious moment, he opened the door and was gone. In the moment of his exit I heard the sustained booming of the wind, the swish of the water on the decks of the *Torrens,* and the subdued, as if distant, roar of the rising sea. I noted the growing disquiet in the great restlessness of the ocean, and responded professionally to it with the thought that at eight o'clock, in another half-hour or so at the furthest, the top-gallant sails would have to come off the ship.

Next day, but this time in the first dog-watch, Jacques

entered my cabin. He had a thick, woollen muffler round his throat and the MS. was in his hand. He tendered it to me with a steady look but without a word. I took it in silence. He sat down on the couch and still said nothing. I opened and shut a drawer under my desk, on which a filled-up log-slate lay wide open in its wooden frame waiting to be copied neatly into the sort of book I was accustomed to write with care, the ship's log-book. I turned my back squarely on the desk. And even then Jacques never offered a word. "Well, what do you say?" I asked at last. "Is it worth finishing?" This question expressed exactly the whole of my thoughts.

"Distinctly," he answered in his sedate veiled voice, and then coughed a little.

"Were you interested?" I inquired further, almost in a whisper.

"Very much!"

. . . "Now let me ask you one more thing: Is the story quite clear to you as it stands?"

He raised his dark, gentle eyes to my face and seemed surprised.

"Yes! Perfectly."

This was all I was to hear from his lips concerning the merits of *Almayer's Folly*.[10]

This was the first time Conrad had shown anyone his literary efforts. Ever since 1889 this manuscript had gone everywhere with him: from London to the Ukraine, from the Congo to Champel, from Australia to London, but he had never alluded to it or let anyone read it. Very likely Madame Poradowska had urged him, as his uncle used to, to write down some of his impressions and memories, but up until then he had not even told her that he was trying to write.

This short conversation with his first reader took place off the Cape of Good Hope, just before they rounded it. It was followed by a long spell of bad weather, during which the chief mate of the *Torrens* had plenty to do. Mr. Jacques had to keep to his cabin. His health grew worse and he was to die shortly after landing in

[10] *A Personal Record.*

Australia. Conrad himself was very ill for a fortnight before they arrived in Adelaide, on January 30, 1893, with "a souvenir of Africa," as he called it. Immediately on landing he took a week's leave, which he spent in the hills near Adelaide where the climate was better than on the coast. On his arrival he had found a very literary letter from his Aunt Marguerite accompanied by the two latest numbers of the *Revue des Deux Mondes,* containing a story she had recently finished, "Popes et Popadias."

Despite the encouragement given him in this laconic fashion by the passenger in the *Torrens,* the manuscript of *Almayer's Folly* was kept firmly in the drawer during the six weeks the ship spent in Adelaide and the four months of the homeward voyage. The chief mate of the *Torrens* was out of sorts. His ship had lost her reputation for record speeds; he found his captain the most boring of men. He wrote to Madame Poradowska:

> I am getting a bit tired of this whole existence. It is not my present trouble (for I feel much better just now) but the uncertitude of the monotonous grey in store for me that discourages me.[11]

The homeward voyage, however, was to bring him an unexpected and lasting satisfaction.

A few months earlier two young men, one just down from Cambridge, the other from Oxford, had sailed from London for the Pacific islands, attracted by the bright prospect of a long cruise in a sailing ship, the desire to see new lands and, most of all, perhaps, by the possibility of visiting Robert Louis Stevenson in Samoa. For about six years Stevenson had been roaming the Pacific archipelagoes and cruising in the South Seas and had settled in Samoa, with no hope of ever returning to England. The only way for these young men to meet the famous and charming author was to go to the other side of the world to see him. They had resolved to do so, but a series of events—among other things the depletion of their funds, which had run out sooner than they expected—had held them up in New Zealand. Forced—very regretfully—to return to Europe, they came to Adelaide to sail on the first ship leaving, which was the *Torrens.*

[11] Letter of February 3, 1893.

Struck by the first mate's unusual appearance, courtesy, and personality, they lost no time getting into conversation with him. These young men, who had left Europe to make the acquaintance of one great writer at the height of his career, thus made contact, without knowing it, with another great writer on the threshold of his literary life. One of these young men was none other than John Galsworthy, the future author of *The Forsyte Saga*.

Captain Korzeniowski did not, as has frequently been claimed, show his literary efforts either to John Galsworthy or to his companion, Edward Lancelot Sanderson. The two young men had many long conversations with the mate while he was off duty. They were impressed and attracted by this sailor's extraordinary personality, by the unusual scope of his reading, by the artistic qualities of his stories, but they never suspected that he had begun to write.

The day after Conrad's death, John Galsworthy set down these recollections of his youth—a page which logically belongs here:

It was in March, 1893, that I first met Conrad on board the English sailing ship *Torrens* in Adelaide harbour. He was superintending the stowage of cargo. Very dark he looked in the burning sunlight, tanned, with a peaked brown beard, almost black hair, and dark brown eyes, over which the lids were deeply folded. He was thin, not tall, his arms very long, his shoulders broad, his head set rather forward. He spoke to me with a strong foreign accent. He seemed to me strange on an English ship. For fifty-six days I sailed in his company.

The chief mate bears the main burden of a sailing ship. All the first night he was fighting a fire in the hold. None of us seventeen passengers knew of it till long after. It was he who had most truck with the tail of that hurricane off the Leeuwin, and later with another storm: a good seaman, watchful of the weather; quick in handling the ship, considerate with the apprentices—we had a long, unhappy Belgian youth among them, who took unhandily to the sea and dreaded going aloft. Conrad compassionately spared him all he could. With the crew he was popular; they were individuals to him, not a mere gang; and long after he would talk of this or that among them, especially of old Andy the sail-maker: "I liked that old fellow, you know."

With the young second mate, a cheerful capable young seaman, very English, he was friendly; and respectful, if faintly ironic, with this whiskered, stout old captain. Evening watches in fine weather were spent on the poop. Ever the great teller of a tale, he had already nearly twenty years of tales to tell. Tales of ships and storms, of Polish revolution, of his youthful Carlist gun-running adventure, of the Malay seas, and the Congo; and of men and men; all to a listener who had the insatiability of a twenty-five-year-old.

On that ship he told of life, not literature. On my last evening he asked me at the Cape to his cabin, and I remember feeling that he outweighed for me all the other experiences of that voyage. Fascination was Conrad's great characteristic —the fascination of vivid expressiveness and zest, of his deeply affectionate heart, and his far-ranging, subtle mind. He was extraordinarily perceptive and receptive.[12]

John Galsworthy landed at the Cape, where the *Torrens* called on May 17. There Captain Korzeniowski found another letter from his eager aunt and in his reply assured her that "Popes et Popadias" was a little masterpiece and that he was delighted at the success it was having, for he had predicted it. As for himself, life seemed to hold no charm for him:

My life is bounded by the dark circle where the blue of the sea and the blue of the sky meet without merging. Moving forward in that perfect circle traced by the hand of the Creator, of which I am always the centre, I follow with my eyes the rising and falling line of the swell—the only movement I am sure of.[13]

The conversations between the chief mate and the young Cambridge student continued—conversations and games of chess—from the Cape to Saint Helena and from Saint Helena to London, where the ship arrived, overdue, on July 26, 1893.

12 John Galsworthy. "Reminiscences of Conrad."
13 Letter of May 17, 1893.

Two urgent letters from his uncle were awaiting him in London. One, written two months previously, said:

I want to talk to you as soon as possible about the plan we made three years ago to meet again, that is, for you to come here, since it is impossible for me to go to London.

It would really be a terrible disappointment to me not to see you. I don't want to give up the prospect of this pleasure, which might be my last. I don't want to resign myself to it, whatever pretexts reason may claim for opposing your desire and mine. So I hope for and expect your visit, my dear boy, because at my age to procrastinate is really to tempt fate. No doubt you will share my sad point of view.

If the demands of your service do not prevent you, come to me, *monsieur mon frère,* and if after my death there are a few rubles less, I shall at least be the richer for some happiness.

This time, like last, you will probably come via that horrible Berlin—the Byalystock express leaves from there—avoiding Warsaw, which is already empty and will be emptier still in summer. You will arrive via Brzesc and Koszyatyn and after a few hours' wait there, you will change to a modest mixed train (freight and passengers) which will bring you to the Oratov station at 11:30, seven versts from Kazimierowka.

Send a telegram from Brzesc for the horses, but in Russian, because Oratov does not accept or receive telegrams in any foreign language. As you see, here we live in a country that is "in its artistic infancy." We have no express: just one train a day.

If for any reason you have to spend an hour or two in Koszyatyn, hire a carriage to drive you to the château of M. Wasintyncki, a friend of your parents, because he was grieved that you didn't go to see him last time. You can go back via Lublin and Lowicz if you prefer. Travel any way you like. You know the country now. It will be a pleasanter time of year than three years ago.

His uncle's other letter implies that the captain of the *Torrens,* probably disheartened at not being able to achieve the speed that had made his predecessor famous, had considered transferring to a steamship, which would have given Conrad the chance of succeeding him. But back in London Captain Cope changed his mind, and some time later Conrad, who had now had enough, decided not to make a third voyage with him.

Apparently, judging by his uncle's letter, he left for the Ukraine from Flushing early in August and spent almost two months there. Although the latter part of the summer was beautiful, he was seriously ill at the beginning of September and had to spend five days in bed, but he wrote to Madame Poradowska: "It is good to be ill here. My uncle looks after me as if I were a little boy." At the end of September he returned to London via Amsterdam, without breaking the journey anywhere. He was in a great hurry to find a berth, if not a command.

Two months later he declares to Madame Poradowska that since his return from Poland he has done nothing, but has spent his days in a disheartening idleness. It really was "the idleness of a haunted man who looks for nothing but words wherein to capture his visions," [14] for he spent most of his time finishing the ninth chapter of *Almayer's Folly*.

About five o'clock almost every afternoon he would go to the Shipmasters' Society in Fenchurch Street and stay there chatting with the secretary, Captain Froud, who was trying to find him a ship. At the end of November Captain Froud told him that a steamship captain had called on him looking for a second mate who could speak French. A steamship and a berth as second mate for a man who had his master's certificate and whose heart was in sail! After all, why not—if only to avoid embarrassing the nice, obliging Captain Froud? In any case, in an interview with the steamer's captain Conrad obtained several privileges to compensate him for taking a subordinate position below his rank. On November 26, 1893, he informed his aunt that he was sailing the next day on the *Adowa*. He had received his assignment that morning and his service was to begin that same evening at eleven o'clock. "It was time. I was beginning to fall into a black melancholy. Result of idleness."

This steamer had been chartered by a new French concern, the Franco-Canadian Company, which intended to establish a monthly service transporting emigrants from France to Canada. The *Adowa* arrived in Rouen on December 4 and anchored in the center of the city, near the opera. Before they left London they had installed four hundred and sixty bunks for emigrants in the 'tween decks. There had been a lot of talk in Rouen about the founding of this company, and some of the directors came from Paris to inspect the ship, managing to knock their silk hats cruelly against the deck beams in the process. Conrad has related that some Rouen families came to inspect the ship and that he was always in evidence, in his best uniform, to give information, as though he had been a Cook's interpreter. Then one fine day everything was changed. The ship had to leave its luxurious berth and anchor farther down the Seine at a muddy, shabby quay.[15] The winter that year was particularly severe. The Seine was full of drifting ice, and river traffic, including the ferry service, had to be suspended for a time. Captain Korzeniowski sought relief from his boredom in writing to his aunt. After telling her that they were to leave for La Rochelle bound for Halifax toward the middle of December, he says that the Franco-Canadian Company seems not to have kept its agreement with the owners and the ship's departure has been postponed. There is to be a trial in Paris that week to determine the damages to be awarded.

> We shall not go to Canada. As soon as the case has been decided, we shall return to England to load for India, the Persian Gulf—I don't know where.[16]

And a few days later:

> It is true that life is not exactly amusing, but still I do get paid for being bored. All the same, this is leading to nothing and I am beginning to get old.[17]

Steps are being taken, he says, to find him a job in an Australian pearl fishery, and at the same time he asks his aunt if she doesn't know someone on the Suez Canal Board. He would like to know how to go about getting a position as pilot on the Canal and what

[15] See *A Personal Record*. (Tr.)
[16] Letter of December 18, 1893.
[17] Letter of December 20, 1893.

salary he could expect. He would prefer Suez. The work is light,
one is not too far away, and he supposes that one can earn a living
at it. That is all he asks. He has lost his appetite for adventure.

He fills in his time as best he can, and in his cabin aboard the
Adowa, alongside the quay in Rouen, in that bitter winter weather,
he tries to paint in words a sunset in the Malayan Isles. He is beginning the tenth chapter of *Almayer's Folly* and he likes to think
that just here the shade of old Flaubert floats with amused interest
above the deck of his ship. Raising his eyes, he mechanically looks
through the porthole.

> The round opening framed in its brass rim a fragment of
> the quays, with a row of casks ranged on the frozen ground
> and the tail-end of a great cart. A red-nosed carter in a blouse
> and a woollen nightcap leaned against the wheel. An idle,
> strolling custom-house guard, belted over his blue *capote,* had
> the air of being depressed by exposure to the weather, and
> the monotony of official existence. The background of grimy
> houses found a place in the picture framed by my port-hole,
> across a wide stretch of paved quay, brown with frozen mud.
> The colouring was sombre, and the most conspicuous feature
> was a little *café* with curtained windows and a shabby front
> of white woodwork, corresponding with the squalor of these
> poorer quarters bordering the river. We had been shifted
> down there from another berth in the neighbourhood of the
> Opera House, where that same port-hole gave me a view of
> quite another sort of *café*—the best in the town, I believe, and
> the very one where the worthy Bovary and his wife, the ro-
> mantic daughter of old Père Renault, had some refreshment
> after the memorable performance of an opera which was the
> tragic story of Lucia di Lammermoor in a setting of light
> music.[18]

In this dingy little café Captain Korzeniowski spent his dreary
mornings and went on writing to his aunt. He has received a new
book from her: *Le Mariage du Fils Grandsire, a Novel of Life in
Little.* Not wanting to be outdone, he finally tells her that he is
writing a book himself. In a letter of January 7, 1894, he promises

[18] *A Personal Record.*

her that if she is good, he will let her read his story of Almayer when he has finished it.

At the rate it is going he wonders if he will ever finish it. Two days later he reports to his aunt that the *Adowa* is definitely leaving Rouen. Not a single emigrant has shown up: the company has broken its chartering contract; the ship is going back to London, and no one knows when or where it will go next. On January 18 [19] he writes to his aunt from London: "I am very disappointed at having had to leave the *Adowa*. It was very convenient to have a job near Europe. I am afraid I shall soon have to leave on a long voyage."

He never left on a long voyage again. January 14, 1894, the date when Captain Korzeniowski went ashore from the *Adowa,* marked the end of his sea life—though he was far from suspecting it. This life ended, as it had begun, almost unconsciously, as a result of events in which his decision and his will had no say. Begun in Marseilles and ending, more or less, in Rouen, his twenty years as a British sailor were bounded by these two French ports.

He had not the least intention of giving up the sea. His transfer from maritime to literary life came about imperceptibly, without his desiring it or realizing it, under the pressure of circumstances, secret impulses, and what the novelist was later to call "the unknown powers that shape our destinies."

[19] In *Letters of Joseph Conrad to Marguerite Poradowska,* Gee and Sturm date this letter January 20. (Tr.)

X

Within the Tides
(1894-1896)

A free man, a proud swimmer striking
out for a new destiny.
                "The Secret Sharer"

ON FEBRUARY 18, 1894, a little over a month after Captain Korzeniowski had returned to London and installed himself once more
in his rooms at 17 Gillingham Street, near Victoria Station, he received a telegram with a message which completely overwhelmed
him. He immediately informed Madame Poradowska:

My uncle died on the 11th of this month and I feel that
everything in me is dead. He seems to have taken my soul
with him. I had been ill for several days and was just getting
better when I received this news.

Death had taken from him a being whom he loved deeply, the
only relative he had known intimately, the man who had cared
for him in childhood, watched over his adolescence, contributed to
his success and, through the years of his sea life, whether near to
him or far, had never ceased to show him constant benevolent affection.

Ten years later, he wrote to Casimir Waliszewski, the Polish
historian:

I cannot speak of Thaddeus Bobrowski, my uncle, tutor and benefactor, without emotion. To this very day, after ten years, I still have the feeling of a terrible bereavement. He was a man of great character and remarkable intelligence. He did not understand my desire for the sea, but he did not oppose it on principle. In the course of my twenty years of wandering (from 1874 to 1893), I saw him only four times, but I owe the good sides of my character to his affection, protection and influence.[1]

Later still, in 1915, he was to say:

He . . . had been for a quarter of a century the wisest, the firmest, the most indulgent of guardians, extending over me a paternal care and affection, a moral support which I seemed to feel always near me in the most distant parts of the earth.[2]

Throughout the twenty years of his adventurous nomadic life, the house at Kazimierowka had been the one fixed point on which his thoughts could center. Uncle and nephew had, indeed, met only four times in twenty years, but these meetings, looked forward to for so long, often postponed, always desired, had been the more valuable for that. Not only did they rekindle an affection kept alive by their letters; they also revealed to Conrad—through the reminiscences of Thaddeus Bobrowski—many of the circumstances of his past of which he was ignorant or which he had never suspected himself in his ardent, melancholy childhood. Their meetings had crystallized the early impressions of his life, provided food for his meditations, helped to form his character and mind, his attitude to people and things.

His uncle's death suddenly deprived him of the illusion of a home. While he was at sea, he had rarely felt the need for this, but it left a gap which was becoming more noticeable now that his health had broken down and the urgings of his literary vocation, though still vague, were making him aware that he was no longer a sailor whose only domain was the sea, his only home a ship.

A few days later a letter from one of the executors of the will

[1] *Lettres françaises.*
[2] *A Personal Record.*

informed him of his late uncle's bequests, which proved the particular affection and esteem Thaddeus Bobrowski had held for his nephew. He left him fifteen thousand rubles and expressed the wish that he sit on the small committee appointed to examine the manuscript of his memoirs deposited in the Ossolinski Library in Lwow.

Six months earlier Conrad had found his uncle so animated, so full of life and energy and memories that no one could have guessed that his end was so near, at the age of sixty-six. For weeks he did not get over this blow. "I am like a wild animal. I try to hide when I am suffering in body or mind, and just now I am suffering in both," he writes to Madame Poradowska at the beginning of March, and at the end of that month he says again: "I haven't been very well for the last fortnight. No sleep and no appetite."

He would like to go to Brussels to see his aunt but he does not know whether that will be possible. He is looking for a job and does not dare to leave London for fear of missing an opportunity. He asks her if she thinks the Suez Company is going to answer, or if he is to take their silence for a refusal.

His thoughts cannot free themselves from the memory of his uncle. In his solitude and his enforced idleness he has only one way of paying his debt of love to that memory: to finish the book he wanted to dedicate to him. In a burst of energy, between January and May, 1894, he writes the last three chapters of *Almayer's Folly*, the last quarter of a story the beginning of which dates back more than four years.

It is not accomplished without violent fits of discouragement. His only literary confidante is his aunt Marguerite and he tells her at the end of March: "I have just written 'XI' at the top of a blank page, and it may stay blank for ten days. . . ." [3] And a few days later: "I am struggling with Chapter XI, a struggle to the death, you know! If I give it up I am lost." And he sends her the manuscript of the first page of this chapter.

In mid-April, from Elstree, near London, where he is staying with the family of young Sanderson, whom he had met the year before on board the *Torrens,* he writes to Madame Poradowska:

[3] Gee and Sturm assign this letter to 1895, in which case it would refer to *An Outcast of the Islands,* not *Almayer's Folly.* (Tr.)

"Chapter XI is finished (9,000 words). I am beginning XII in a quarter of an hour."

On April 24, 1894, he informs her of the end of Almayer's misfortunes in these words:

> It is my painful duty to inform you of the death of Mr. Kaspar Almayer, which occurred this morning at 3 A.M. It's finished! A scratch of the pen writing the last word and suddenly all those people who have been whispering in my ear, gesticulating before my eyes, living with me, for so many years, become a troop of phantoms who withdraw, fade away, merge into one another, indistinct and pale in the sunshine of this brilliant and dark day.
>
> Since I woke up this morning I have the feeling that part of myself is buried in these pages lying here before me. And yet I am happy—a little.

He has been inquiring, probably at the suggestion of the Sanderson family, for someone whose advice he can ask as to his work's merit, for a few days later he writes to his aunt:

> Forgive me for not sending you Chapter XII. The manuscript is in the hands of a pretty distinguished critic, Edmund Gosse. How long will he keep it? I have no idea.

Whether this was the source from which he received some criticism is uncertain, but on May 2 he wrote again to his aunt:

> I find the work of revising my last three chapters not only disagreeable but downright painful. And difficult too. But it absolutely must be done.
>
> I will send you the last chapter soon. It begins with a trio: Nina, Dain, Almayer, and finishes with a long solo for Almayer which is almost as long as Tristan's in Wagner. Well, you will see, but I'm afraid you will find the thing colorless.

He was still giving plenty of thought to the really serious question of his life: a sea command. In April he told his aunt that "the command of a ship has fallen through," and in May that he was "almost sure of obtaining a command." It was actually in the office of the Shipmasters' Society, where he went regularly to see if they had found him a berth, that he decided, early in June, to send *Almayer's Folly* to a publisher just on the chance. He hesitated for a moment between two of them and tossed a coin to decide. Then he called a messenger to take this interminable book to T. Fisher Unwin in Paternoster Square. Quite a decision! He later gave this as one of the reasons:

> At that period of his existence T. F. Unwin had published some paper-bound books by various authors and I bought one or two of them, *Mademoiselle Ixe* and *The Pope's Daughters,* I believe. My ignorance was so great and my judgment so poor that I imagined *Almayer's Folly* would be just suitable for that series. As a matter of fact it was much too long, but this was my motive in the choice of a publisher. I sent the MS. by messenger boy, instructing him to get a receipt which the boy brought me all right, but I did not preserve that document of the literary history of our time. The acceptance came some three months later, in the first typewritten letter I ever received in my life.[4]

As though they had just been waiting for this decision, his "souvenirs of Africa" redoubled in violence, and at the beginning of July Madame Poradowska received a note in which Conrad said: "I have just got up. I have been in bed ten days—ten centuries! I am ill all the time. It is really monotonous!"

At the same time he complains that he hears nothing from Fisher Unwin and is afraid his manuscript will not be accepted.

Madame Poradowska must have read a copy of it, or possibly Conrad gave her the outline of his book during a short visit he paid to Brussels, for she is already toying with the idea of publishing a French translation of it in the *Revue des Deux Mondes*. Faced with the possibility of having *Almayer* refused in England, Conrad thinks about publishing his book in French:

> If you have not spoken to the *Revue,* perhaps we might offer *Almayer* not as a translation but as a collaboration.[5]

[4] Letter to Mr. Chesson, May 6, 1918.
[5] Letter of July 30(?), 1894.

Worried by the recurrence of his illness, early in August he suddenly decides to go back to Champel for the hydropathic treatment. He stays there until the beginning of September and it is from there that he writes Madame Poradowska a really astonishing letter.

Tired of hearing nothing about his manuscript, he has written to London asking that it be returned. As soon as he receives it he will send it to his aunt to be translated. He will use the pseudonym *Kamudi,* a Malayan word pronounced *Karmondi* and meaning "rudder." The book would then appear in French over the name of Madame Poradowska with a note that *Kamudi* collaborated in writing it. In the same letter he thanks his aunt for having approached Mr. Pécher again about a command. He tells her that his funds are almost exhausted, but that on March 1, 1895, he will have at his disposal some fifteen thousand francs coming to him from Poland, and that he is prepared, if necessary, to take an examination in seamanship in Belgium.

He adds that he is reading Maupassant with delight, that he has just finished *Le Lys Rouge* by Anatole France, which means nothing at all to him, and finally that the night before, he began to write the opening of a short story, "twenty to twenty-five pages in the *Revue,*" which he has called "Two Vagabonds." It was a first sketch of what was to become his second book: *An Outcast of the Islands.*

A literary career is obviously the last thing he has in mind, and his own came quite close to beginning—or ending—in this secret, devious fashion, in a French periodical. Nor would that have been the strangest of his adventures!

September passes. To show her skill, his aunt writes to him in English. The "Two Vagabonds" sleep on. Conrad admits that he has run out of ideas. He has written again to Fisher Unwin to ask for either a reply or the return of the manuscript. If he finds a ship —as he hopes—the manuscript will be at Madame Poradowska's disposal with Barr, Moering & Co.

October comes. Conrad is negotiating for various ships. He has asked twice for the return of his manuscript; both times he has been told that it is being considered. He has had enough: a few days more and he intends to demand its return, when suddenly on the morning of October 4 he hears that the editor is accepting it. He offers only twenty pounds, but Conrad cares little about the terms.

I have taken what I was offered, because really getting it published is in itself of the greatest importance. . . . Now I only need a ship to be almost happy.

The manuscript had fallen into the hands of a very young man who had recently been working as a reader for the publisher Fisher Unwin. His name was Edward Garnett and he was the son of the erudite Dr. Garnett, Keeper of Printed Books at the British Museum. This reader had found his attention immediately seized and captivated. The strangeness of the tropical atmosphere, the poetic realism of this romantic story, aroused his curiosity and awoke in him a desire to meet the author, who, he thought, must be of oriental origin.

Edward Garnett lived most of the time outside London and it was not customary for him to meet the authors of the books that he recommended Fisher Unwin to publish. On this occasion, however, he had written such a positive report and seemed so mystified and curious about the author's identity that Mr. Fisher Unwin invited the author and the reader to meet at the National Liberal Club. The reader was quite surprised, we may be sure, to find himself face to face with a master mariner of Polish birth, and the latter was no less astonished to meet so young a critic.

The publisher did his best to start a general conversation and tried to interest his guest in political personalities and third-class novelists such as John Oliver Hobbes and S. R. Crockett. The captain, in spite of the extreme politeness of his manners, began to show a certain tension in his answers, and the strain became acute when, in reply to an allusion by Mr. Fisher Unwin to "your next book," Conrad threw himself back in his seat and said in a clear, slightly cutting tone: "I don't expect to write again. It is likely that I shall soon be going to sea."

A silence fell. A statement like this gave the publisher little hope for his new author's future and induced Mr. Fisher Unwin to go and talk to another club member at the far end of the room. He excused himself and went off.

As soon as he was alone with this strange author who spoke

English with such a strong foreign accent but whose extraordinary personality had immediately attracted him, the very young reader felt himself carried away by a kind of indignation. He maintained that Conrad had no right to let everything he had witnessed on land and sea during thirty-odd years vanish into the mist of oblivion. *Almayer's Folly* showed the qualities of a true writer. Why not try another book?

Touched by this young man's warmth and conviction, Joseph Conrad listened attentively. He had accepted this invitation partly out of curiosity, but also as a man standing at a crossroads and hoping, for quite plausible reasons, to be encouraged to write. He certainly had the "temperament"; of that he felt sure; but this sailor approaching his fortieth birthday was at a point in his life when he badly needed a warm, sincere voice to persuade him to become a writer.

The day after this meeting and another visit to his publisher, he wrote to Madame Poradowska to tell her that he had succeeded in reserving the French translation rights to *Almayer's Folly* and that the publisher's two readers had seen him and complimented him effusively. "Were they by any chance making fun of me?" he added.

Despite this encouragement he is not exactly forging ahead with his second book. He is busy with plans for departing and when they fail to materialize he is in a state of irritation which prevents his becoming absorbed in his novel; he does nothing, he says, but bad work. He is very discouraged. "Ideas don't come. I don't see either the characters or the events."

The remainder of the year goes by like this in indecision and the hope and desire to go back to sea. *Almayer's Folly* is not to be printed until February. All corrections are made. The proofreaders, he says, will take care of typographical errors. He, for his part, hopes with all his heart to have left London by then.

> My work is not getting on and my health is gone. If I stay ashore much longer, everything will be ruined.[6]

He is negotiating for a ship in Antwerp. It is a fortnight, he says in November, since he has written a word. He is tempted to

[6] Letter of November 14 or 21 (?), 1894.

throw everything he has done into the fire. He plunges into reading, and it is in French books that he studies the technique of the novel.

> I have been studying *Pierre et Jean,* thought, method and everything, with the deepest discouragement. It looks like nothing at all but it is really such a complex mechanism that it makes me tear my hair. I want to howl with rage when I read it.[7]

And he says he has been sitting for three days before a blank page and the page is still blank except for a "IV" at the top. He is compelled—and this annoys him extremely—to change his title, "Two Vagabonds." A successful novelist, Mrs. Wood, has just published a book under that title. His title will be *An Outcast of the Islands.* Still nothing from Antwerp. He has an iron in the fire in Liverpool. "They have such a pretty little ship with such a pretty name— *Primera.*"

Along with his New Year greetings to his aunt, he tells her that he has not only changed the title of his book:

> The thing itself is changed. Everything is changed except the doubt: everything except the fear of those phantoms which one calls up deliberately and which often refuse to obey the brain that has created them. Chapter VIII is finished at last! Four more to go. Four centuries of agony—four minutes of happiness and then the end—an empty head, discouragement and infinite doubt.

On Christmas Eve he receives the first proofs of *Almayer.* Seeing himself in print does not give him the least satisfaction. No reply from London about his ship.

He has seen his "reader" again. A mutual liking has sprung up, soon to develop into a firm friendship, which was to last until the novelist's death. They met frequently that winter, in little French-Italian restaurants in Soho, in Newgate Street, in a little Mecca Café in Cheapside. They were enfolded, as Edward Garnett later said, in "an atmosphere of humble conspiracy *à deux"*—humble since Conrad was then more obscure than any publisher's reader. He was

[7] Letter of October 29 or November 5 (?), 1894.

depressed and sceptical and sometimes boyishly eager; he was finding his first acquaintance with what Baudelaire called "the sterility of nervous writers" discouraging. That whole winter Conrad and Edward Garnett exchanged questions and advice, proposals and suggestions. Garnett took the development of this emerging genius for granted, and was enthusiastic over the romantic magic of the scenes in his book. "My part indeed," he said, "was simple—to appreciate and criticize all that he wrote, and to ask for more, more."

From time to time his "souvenirs of Africa" recur. At the beginning of 1895 he is obliged to stop all his work and stay in bed for a time at the house of his friends, the Hopes. On his return to London, he writes to his aunt: "The *Outcast* drags on amid the usual wailing and gnashing of teeth." He was supposed to be leaving for Newfoundland, but the voyage has been postponed and he doesn't feel fit to undertake it. He asks this question, quite touching in its reverence and modesty, which shows again that he leaned naturally toward the French writers, with whom he had long been familiar.

> You know my worship of Daudet. Do you think it would be silly of me to send him my book—I, who have read all of his, under all skies? Not asking him to read it—just as an act of homage. For, after all, he is one of my youthful enthusiasms that has survived—even grown. What do you think? [8]

A short time later he leaves for Brussels to see both his aunt and a firm of ship commissioners with whom he has been corresponding. He is living among a fleet of phantom vessels.

On March 12, 1895, he writes to his publisher from Brussels:

> As you have been good enough to mention to me several times your willingness to arrange for a French translation of *Almayer's Folly,* I venture now to ask you for your good offices in that matter. My aunt is too unwell to undertake the work now, and she will be too busy with her own forthcoming novel to make any arrangements for the future. . . .
>
> I have sent the proof sheets to Paris to "Th. Bentzon" [9] (Mme. Blanc) who writes on England and America in the

[8] Letter of February 23, 1895.

[9] George T. Keating in *A Conrad Memorial Library* reads this name as "The Bentron." (Tr.)

Revue des Deux Mondes and knows the literature and institutions of both countries. My aunt (who is her colleague on the staff of the *Revue*) is writing to her today asking her to read the work and if possible to write a short appreciation of it. . . . They do have, now and then, an analysis of the work of more known men; but in my case I am afraid it would be too much of an uphill drag to obtain Brunetière's consent. Still, we shall try; for the thing is well worth trying.

Returning from Brussels in mid-March, he goes to stay with the Sandersons again at Elstree, near London, and is there for ten days, crippled with gout, almost incapable of working, yet making heroic efforts to finish this *Outcast of the Islands* which has grown into something far more ambitious than he had originally expected. Back in London in April, he says he is on the seventeenth chapter of this book, which will run to twenty or twenty-one. Toward the end of this same month he is ill again and he is bedridden when he receives the first copy of *Almayer's Folly*. Almost six years have gone by since the day when he wrote the first line of it in this same city.

The author came into the world—the public world—under the name of "Joseph Conrad." He had not needed a pseudonym. It was out of the question to add to the ambiguity of his position by signing his books with his real Polish name. In any case, there were two arguments against that. There had been in Poland, in the first half of the nineteenth century, a very good novelist and dramatist who, though in no way related, shared his last name and one of his Christian names: Joseph Korzeniowski. Even if it had not been for this risk of confusion, Joseph Conrad would still have been "Joseph Conrad," for long ago the impossibility he was always up against in the British Navy of hearing his last name correctly pronounced or spelled had led him to give up calling himself by anything but his two Christian names that came most easily to English tongues.[10]

On the first page of the book appeared this dedication, enclosed in black lines, noticeable but at the same time discreet: "To the memory of T. B."—a posthumous homage to the memory of the

[10] See Appendix.

uncle who had died eighteen months too soon to see the new incarnation, so unexpected, of this nephew whose field of adventure was henceforward to be the vast domain of his memories and dreams.

The new author did not even wait to see what the critics thought of his book. Impatient at several recurrences of his illness within a few weeks, he decided to go to Champel again, not only for his health this time, but in the hope of finding more favorable conditions for finishing *An Outcast of the Islands.* On the night before his departure he wrote to Edward Garnett:

> I am going to try what mountain air combined with active fire-hose (twice a day) will do for divine inspiration. I shall try it for about three weeks and maybe the lenient gods will allow me to finish that infernal Manuscript.[11]

He spent the whole of May at Champel, at La Roseraie as usual, working systematically on his book, but with a lack of self-confidence which he said he had never experienced throughout the long years when he was trying to finish *Almayer's Folly.*

The reports from London about the reception of his book could not fail to encourage him. The reaction of the press was, in fact, extraordinarily favorable.

> We were struck by this book [said the critic of the *Daily Mail*]. Nothing like it has appeared during the last few years. Mr. Conrad may go on, and with confidence; he will find his public and he deserves his place.

In *The Speaker* the reviewer expressed a wish to see another book by this new author:

> It is impossible to forget this book. If Mr. Conrad can give us a work as gripping and alive as this, he can be sure of a place in our literature.

The Spectator went even further:

> Beyond a doubt we have here a strong story of an unusual kind which opens up a new domain to the novel. . . . The

[11] Letter of May 1, 1895.

name of Mr. Conrad is new to us, but it appears to us as if he might become the Kipling of the Malay Archipelago.

He certainly cannot complain about his debut. The first printing of the book is sold out almost immediately. And it was not only the London press that gave him such a favorable welcome. He writes to Madame Poradowska from Champel:

> All the provincial press has spoken kindly—and some enthusiastically—of my *Folly* . . . I am working very little and badly, very badly.[12]

And to Edward Garnett:

> I am working every day: tolerably bad work. Like poor Risler the Elder's cashier "I haf' no gonfidence." Some people I have sent the book to wrote very kindly. They seem rather surprised—and I am amused.
>
> I dread the moment when you shall see my *Outcast* as a whole. It seems frightful bosh. I never felt like that even in the first days of my *Folly*.[13]

Nonetheless he comes back from Champel in a better physical and mental state, which is reflected in the joking, ironical tone of his letters to Edward Garnett:

> I received in the morning an invitation *by wire!!!!!* to dine with the Enlightened Patron of Letters. . . .[14] So I have added the festive and hospitable board of "my publisher" to my other experiences—and life seems tolerably complete. What else may I expect? What else that is new? Don't you think, dear Garnett, I had better die? True—there is love. That is always new—or rather startling being generally unexpected and violent—and fleeting. Still one must have some object to hang his affections upon—and I haven't. Oh! the world—since this morning—is one big grey shadow and I am one immense yawn. Do come to the rescue early next week and put some heart into me with your dear, precious brazen flattery. Will

---

[12] Letter of May 20, 1895.

[13] Letter of May 12, 1895.

[14] Conrad's nickname for Mr. T. Fisher Unwin.

you? If so—please say so. Say when, and I shall try to go to sleep till then.

The reviews of his first book have encouraged him, although he takes things as they come and although literary vanity is not much in his line. He writes to Madame Poradowska:

> I have gone back to writing, very much encouraged by the seven and a half columns in the *Weekly Sun* in which T. P. O'Connor buried me under an avalanche of compliments, admiration, analysis and quotations: all this with an enthusiasm which has made him talk a lot of completely ridiculous bosh. Well, that places one, since the *Sun* specializes in this kind of literary note—and I am pleased.[15]

He had returned from Champel with almost a third of his second book written. He spent the end of July and the beginning of August yachting with his old friend, G. F. W. Hope, between Chatham and Harwich and the Dutch coast, and made three unexpected trips to Paris to use his knowledge of French on behalf of a friend involved with some bankers in some business of a gold mine.[16] Meanwhile the *Outcast of the Islands* was growing, page by page— the manuscript was over five hundred pages long. At last, on September 17, 1895, he wrote Edward Garnett this picturesque, humorous letter:

> It is my painful duty to inform you of the sad death of Mr. Peter Willems late of Rotterdam and Macassar who has been murdered on the 16th inst at 4 P.M. while the sun shone joyously and the barrel organ sang on the pavement the abominable Intermezzo of the ghastly Cavalleria. As soon as I recovered from the shock I busied myself in arranging the affairs of the two inconsolable widows of our late lamented friend and I am glad to say that—with the help of Captain Lingard who took upon himself all the funeral arrangements—everything was decently settled before midnight. You know what strong affection I had for the poor departed so you won't be surprised to hear that to me—since yesterday life

[15] Letter of June 11, 1895.
[16] See Appendix.

seems a blank—a dumb solitude from which everything—even the shadows—have completely vanished.

Almayer was the last to go, but, before I succeeded in getting rid of him, he made me perfectly wretched with his grumblings about the trouble and expense connected with the sad event and by his unfeeling remarks about the deceased's little failings. He reviled also Mrs. Willems, who was paralyzed with grief and behaved more like a cumbersome dummy than a living woman. I am sorry to say he wasn't as sober as he ought to have been in these sad conjunctures and as usual he seemed not aware of anybody's grief and sufferings but his own—which struck me as being mostly imaginary, I was glad to see him go, but—such is the inconsequence of the human heart—no sooner he went than I began to regret bitterly his absence. I had for a moment the idea to rush out and call him back but before I could shake off the languor of my sorrow he was gone beyond recall.

There's nothing more to tell you except that the detailed relation of the heartrending occurrences of the last two days will be deposited tomorrow in Paternoster Bdgs for your perusal.

For over a year Conrad had been sending this book to Edward Garnett chapter by chapter, asking and following his advice, and more than a month earlier the reader had already persuaded Fisher Unwin—quite easily considering the success of *Almayer's Folly*—to guarantee its publication even before it was finished. In November part of the print shop where it was being set up was destroyed by fire and it could not appear until six months later.

Preoccupied now with the resources and means of artistic expression, he even played with the idea of writing a novel on this theme. It was called *The Sisters* and its hero was a young painter, son of a rich Ukrainian peasant, but on Edward Garnett's advice he abandoned this book at about the fortieth page.

Captain Korzeniowski had other things in mind, too, at this time. Two years previously, in October or November, 1893, at the house of some friends in London, he had made the acquaintance of a young girl, Miss Jessie George, who had been somewhat aston-

ished—not to say awed, at the appearance of this sailor, so unlike
an Englishman in accent, animation, nervousness, gestures, and punctilious politeness. She was twenty-one and this was the first foreigner
she had met, but her surprise had by no means prevented her from
being interested. She did not see this strange foreigner again for
several months: then she suddenly received a basket of flowers and
a letter in which the traveler announced his intention of visiting
the girl and her mother. Then again weeks and months went by
without the visitor reappearing, until the day when she saw a
hansom cab stop before their door—something that rarely happened
at this time of day in their quiet London suburb. The captain got
out and invited them to dinner that evening. The invitation was
accepted: the captain talked about matters of no account. She saw
him again several times. One day when they had taken refuge
from the terrible weather in the National Gallery, the captain
suddenly said to the young woman:

> Look here, my dear, we had better get married and out
> of this. Look at the weather. We will get married at once
> and get over to France. How soon can you be ready? In a
> week—a fortnight? [17]

Having made his proposal to the slightly startled girl, the captain lapsed again into shadows and silence. A few days later he
invited the girl and her mother to dinner again and informed the
mother of his intentions. He added that he had not very long to
live and intended to take his wife abroad indefinitely. Presented
like that, his proposal was not very encouraging. The young woman,
who was getting to know the captain, sensed some exaggeration,
caused by nervousness, in what he said. She was not afraid of marriage under such auspices and early in 1896 the wedding was
arranged. During his six months' engagement, the captain, having
heard of a bark for sale at Grangemouth, could not rest until
he had had a look at her, but she made such a poor impression
on him that he relinquished this idea in favor of his original plan
of taking his bride to the Continent as soon as they were married.
A fortnight before his marriage, Joseph Conrad announced the

[17] Jessie Conrad, *Joseph Conrad and His Circle.*

event to his cousin Charles Zagórski in a letter in Polish proving that, although the sailor had only recently become aware of the urgings of his literary vocation, he was in future to heed them with the same feeling of confidence and the same personal surrender that had accompanied the start of his maritime life twenty years earlier.

March 10, 1896

My dear Charles,

I am sending you another masterpiece—my second this time. Last year I sent three copies of my novel to your country. Two of them arrived all right; the third, addressed to your wife and yourself, no doubt never reached you. I am trying again and I hope this time my book and my letter will reach you.

At the same time I solemnly announce to dear Aunt Gabrielle and to both of you—I solemnly announce (as the occasion demands) that I am getting married. Perhaps no one is more surprised than I am myself. But I can't say that I am terrified—being, as you know, accustomed to a life full of adventures and to struggling against terrible dangers. I must also confess that my fiancée does not appear at all dangerous. Her Christian name is Jessie: her last name is George. She is a little person who is very dear to me. When I met her, a year and a half ago, she was earning her living as a secretary in the office of the American firm "Calligraph." Her father died three years ago. She has eight brothers and sisters. Her mother is a very respectable person. Anyhow, I am not marrying the whole family. Our marriage will take place on the 24th of this month and we shall immediately leave London to hide our happiness (or our foolishness) from human eyes on the wild and picturesque shores of Brittany, where I intend to rent a little cottage in a fishing village—probably somewhere around Plouaret or Pervengan. There I shall begin work on my third book—for I have to write to live.

A few days ago I was offered the command of a sailing ship —and Jessie liked the idea very much, for she loves the sea, but the pay was so poor that I refused.

The only means of existence remaining to me is writing. You understand, my dear friend, that if I have gone into this, it is with the firm resolution to make myself a reputation—and in this respect I have no qualms about my success. I know what I am capable of. It is just a matter of earning money—which is something quite distinct from literary merit. Well, I am not sure, but my needs are very modest and I can wait, so I look forward to the future calmly.

He was plunging resolutely into this new career, yet at the bottom of his heart he had still not renounced the one he had pursued for twenty years. As he had done all his life, he was obeying a mental compulsion—obeying it resolutely, and the very evening before his marriage he wrote to his friend and confidant Edward Garnett:

> . . . You have driven home the conviction and I *shall* write the sea-story—at once (12 months). It will be on the lines indicated to you. I surrender to the infamous spirit which you have awakened within me and as I want my abasement to be very complete I am looking for a sensational title. You had better help, O Gentle and Murderous Spirit! You have killed my cherished aspiration and now must come along and help to bury the corpse decently. I suggest:

THE RESCUER
A Tale of Narrow Waters

> Meditate for a fortnight and by that time you will get my address and will be able to let me know what your natural aptitude for faithlessness and crime has suggested to you.

The marriage took place in London on March 24, 1896, a sunny day. The bride's numerous family was represented only by her mother. Joseph Conrad had with him only his two friends, Captain Hope and Adolf Krieger, as witnesses.

As we have seen, he had decided to spend the first few months of his new life in Brittany, and the very next day the couple embarked at Southampton for Saint-Malo. In the meantime the weather had changed, and they arrived, after a very rough crossing, almost eight hours overdue. As soon as they had recovered they took the train for Lannion, where they decided to try to rent a farm house which had to be "very small and very retired and very cheap" and near the sea.

They installed themselves in the Hôtel de France and spent a fortnight there, having themselves driven about the country in a carriage in the afternoons. The coachman who drove them told them about the district and the people, about their characters and morals, in which Conrad took a great interest. At the hotel they ate every day at the big *table d'hôte,* together with some twenty other people: bachelors who took their meals there, transient commercial travelers, an engineer who had come to install electricity in the village, with whom Conrad made friends, and a young man with a dreamy, absorbed manner, who observed them without entering into contact and who was none other than Charles le Goffic.

Conrad was hardly in France before he was reminded of Poland. He got a letter from Madame Zagórska congratulating him on his marriage and thanking him for the copy of *An Outcast of the Islands.* Charles Zagórski added some more significant lines to his wife's letter:

> We heard of your literary début from Marguerite [Poradowska]. As I held your book in my hand, I felt, so to speak, a double sadness: first, I was sorry not to be able to get to know the work of your mind, and then I regretted that as a result of the exceptional conditions of your life your talent should be lost to our literature and become the fortune and heritage of foreigners, although they are not foreigners to you, since you have found among them the wife who loves you.

A first appeal from his fatherland to the writer who was later to hear more passionate ones, more unjust ones, until the day when they became wistful but full of admiration!

The young couple had thought briefly of going to live on the island of Bréhat,[18] but their coachman showed them a newly built house, still vacant, barely furnished, quite close to a rather primitive hotel and not far from Lannion on the Ile-Grande. It was a little house with four rooms, one of which was a huge kitchen

---

18 Cf. unpublished letter to E. L. Sanderson, Lannion, March 28, 1896.

with an enormous fireplace with beds like ship's bunks along the walls, but fitted with doors like cupboards. There were two rooms upstairs and above them a big attic overlooking the sea on all sides. They settled down in this house and spent almost five months there.

"I am quite oppressed by my sense of importance," Conrad wrote to his friend Sanderson, "in having a house—actually a whole house!!—to live in. It is the first time—since I came to years of discretion—that such an event happened in my life." [19]

The island, connected with the mainland by a permanent road, is big, as its name implies, but mainly by contrast with the many tiny islands that strew the bay. It is rocky, with a few patches of grass here and there, and almost completely bare of trees.

As rocky and barren an island as the heart of (right-thinking) men would wish to have [Conrad wrote to Edward Garnett just after he went to live there]. And the people! They are dirty and delightful and very Catholic. And most of them are women. The men fish in Iceland, on the Great Banks of Newfoundland and devil knows where else. Only a few old old fellows forgotten by the capricious death that dwells upon the sea shuffle about amongst the stones of this sterile land and seem to wonder peevishly at having been left so long alive. [20]

Conrad was enchanted by the view of this wild coast, these great stretches of sand, the infinity of the green and blue sea. The inhabitants of the region were mostly quarry workers or stonecutters. The owner of their house, Madame Coadou, was a "granite merchant." A master mariner named Le Bras, who had retired to Lannion, where Conrad got to know him, rented him a little four-ton cutter, *La Pervenche,* the crew of which was a navy pensioner, a native of the Ile-Grande. The young couple often cruised round the island in this little boat, along the coast and up the Lannion or Morlaix river to Roscoff, going off on little two or three-day voyages whenever Conrad decided to take a break. Immediately on arriving in Lannion, without waiting to get settled, he had gone

[19] Letter of April 14, 1896.
[20] Letter of April 9, 1896.

back to work and had begun to write that *Rescuer* of whom he had talked to Garnett before leaving. The setting and plot of this book were again Malayan; it was a natural sequel to *Almayer's Folly* and *An Outcast of the Islands:* several of their characters were to reappear; some of their allusions were to be elaborated.

To tell the truth, it was not only the haunting power of his memories of the Far East, nor even the success accorded *Almayer's Folly* that drove him to work: it was need. A couple of weeks before his marriage the failure of a gold-mining company had swallowed up the small inheritance he had received from his uncle. For a moment he had even thought of canceling his marriage plans, but with a tenacity entirely in keeping with his character, he had once more decided to risk the unknown. During the preceding winter he had written hardly anything except the first four chapters of a novel entitled *The Sisters* which, on Edward Garnett's advice, he decided to abandon. He had left London without worrying about the fate of his second book, *An Outcast of the Islands,* which appeared on March 4, 1896. He was thinking of nothing but the next one.

By April 13 he was able to send Garnett the first twenty-four pages of *Rescuer* together with these lines:

> I am so afraid of myself, of my likes and dislikes, of my thought and of my expression that I must fly to you for relief—or condemnation—for anything to kill doubt with. For with doubt I cannot live—at least—not for long. Is the thing tolerable? Is the thing readable?

Garnett strongly encouraged him to go on. Seventy pages were already written when he was interrupted by a recurrence of his "African trouble." This developed into a very violent attack of gout, accompanied by fever and delirium. Mrs. Conrad was in a pitiful situation: speaking almost no French, with an old navy doctor who knew almost no English, while Conrad was raving in Polish. This young, inexperienced woman had the terrifying feeling of having been abandoned at the end of the world. An echo of this situation will be found in a story Conrad wrote later: "Amy Foster."

This crisis and the subsequent convalescence kept him in bed for a fortnight. Once he had recovered, he went back to the *Rescuer,* but could not get into the swing of it again, and, putting the novel aside, tried to write a short story. He took the plot from an event that had just recently happened and the setting from the place where he was living:

On May 24 he wrote to Edward Garnett:

> In the intervals of squirming I wrote also a short story of Brittany. Peasant life. I do not know whether it's worth anything. . . . I want to know what you think of it. The title is: "The Idiots."

In the course of their drives through the country, he had been struck by an encounter with four unfortunate idiots, dressed in long garments, their heads nodding and shaking, who were usually sprawling in the bushes along the roadside. "Four, eh?" the coachman said, turning round in his seat and pointing at them with his whip. "Four! And all in the same family. And the priests say it's God's will."

From this remark was born the story, a bitter, dramatic story, into which Conrad incorporated, with slight changes in scene and character, the coachman himself, their landlady, Madame Coadou, people he had heard of in the region, and the region itself, countryside and coast. Neither the writer's genius nor his real personality came through in this story, but it did show, in a way never to be repeated, the effect of his admiration for a French writer, the obvious influence of Maupassant.

He went furiously back to work on the *Rescuer* but with no luck. Every day his task became not only harder but more uncertain, and he had trouble in finishing the first part of this novel. At the beginning of June he sent it to Garnett with this commentary:

> I do not know what to think of the pages I am sending you. Mostly they fill me with dismay. . . . Here I have used up 103 pages of manuscript to relate the events of 12 hours. I have done it in pursuance of a plan. But is the plan utterly wrong? . . . I doubt the sincerity of my own impressions. . . . Meantime I live with some passing notions of scenes

of passion and battle—and don't know how to get there. I dream for hours, hours! over a sentence and even then can't put it together so as to satisfy the cravings of my soul.[21]

A week later he writes to the same friend:

> Since I sent you that part 1st . . . I have written one page. Just one page. I went about thinking and forgetting—sitting down before the blank page to find that I could not put one sentence together. To be able to think and unable to express is a fine torture. I am undergoing it—without patience. I don't see the end of it. It's very ridiculous and very awful. Now I've got all my people together I don't know what to do with them.[22]

And a month later he is still unburdening himself of his qualms:

> I trust I will live long enough to finish that story but at the pace I am going now I am preparing for myself an interminable old age.[23]

In her published memoirs of their stay in Brittany the novelist's wife has recalled that shortly after the violent attack which had laid Conrad low, there arrived at the Ile-Grande a metal trunk which had accompanied him on his unfortunate Congo expedition. It contained clothes, various objects, the manuscripts of his first two books, and various papers. It probably also contained the little notebook in which he had recorded the impressions of the pedestrian interlude in his African adventure, which was to be published posthumously.

The sight of this trunk and its contents superimposed a vision of the banks of the Congo upon the Breton coast where he actually was and the Malayan landscape where he was trying to be, and in five days, from July 17 to July 21, he wrote the short story called "An Outpost of Progress" in which he made use of a ghastly adventure which he had been told about in the heart of Africa.

Once again he went back to his novel and once again became a prey to the same torture. On August 5 he wrote to Garnett:

[21] Letter of June 10, 1896.
[22] Letter of June 19, 1896.
[23] Letter of July 10, 1896.

I am in desperation and I have practically given up the book. . . . There is 12 pages written [of the second part] and I sit before them every morning, day after day, for the last 2 months and cannot add a sentence, add a word! . . . When I face that fatal manuscript it seems to me that I have forgotten how to think—worse! how to write. It is as if something in my head had given way to let in a cold grey mist.

And a few days later, abandoning the "fatal manuscript," he wrote at one go one of his most beautiful stories, "The Lagoon," again drawing on his Malay memories. This story was also to appear in the collection *Tales of Unrest*.

Toward the end of May he had received a bundle of clippings from the London and provincial papers about *An Outcast of the Islands*. Its reception by the press did not seem so generally favorable as that of *Almayer's Folly*. In fact, some of the reviews put forth some rather queer opinions, such as the one in the *Illustrated London News*, which saw in the author "a disciple of Victor Hugo."

Despite some reservations, the tone and style of an article in the *Saturday Review* of May 16 so impressed Conrad that he wrote to the magazine in an attempt to get behind the anonymity of its author. The latter lost no time in replying and proved to be none other than H. G. Wells. He was still quite young but had already written *The Time Machine* and was beginning to become known. He wrote to Conrad: "You have everything it takes to become a splendid novelist except skill, but that comes with practice." This was the beginning of a relationship which was to develop into friendship in the next few years.

The summer went by in this way, varying between an exasperated, almost sterile perplexity about the *Rescuer* and the great ease with which Conrad had written three short stories straight off. In between there were cruises, some of them rather foolhardy, aboard *La Pervenche* and walks through the Breton countryside.

A change was occurring in the writer's personality. During the five years he had spent putting the finishing touches, page by page—line by line almost—to *Almayer's Folly*, Joseph Conrad had been concerned with nothing beyond his personal edification, so to speak, without any regard for a literary career. For his own satisfaction he had deliberately set himself the task of making tangible and visible something that obsessed him. He had come upon his style and method, not by chance and unthinkingly, but without ever considering any hypothetical reader. The prolongation of his stay ashore, Edward Garnett's "demand" for another book, the feeling, still vague and disquieting, that the sea was retreating from his life, the success of his first book—all these things had combined to bring the "literary being" in him to consciousness. The state of artistic innocence in which he had lived from the moment when he penned the first sentence of *Almayer's Folly* had been succeeded by a concern for and preoccupation with systems and theories which he had discussed all winter long with Edward Garnett and which had only resulted, in *An Outcast of the Islands,* in an excess of the literary, in a superfluity of descriptions and epithets, which in places hid the human interest of the story.

He sensed and understood that only contact with reality could free him from the seductiveness of literary artifice and that he would only find this reality in recalling his own experiences. His voluntary exile on the Breton coast was breaking the Malay spell that had held him, literally, for almost ten years. In "The Idiots" he had tried to depict something that was before his eyes; in "An Outpost of Progress" a recollection of his own misadventures. Gradually he was getting in touch with himself.

The subject of the *Rescuer* was growing too foreign to him. During the month of August he abandoned it again and for the first time he began an attempt to recapture with both accuracy and lyricism a period in his own life and one of his sea experiences. It was in the little house on the Ile-Grande, with a view embracing the green expanse of the Channel, that Conrad wrote the first twenty pages of a story provisionally entitled "The Forecastle: A Story of Ships and Men" in which he proposed to narrate the passage of a sailing ship from Bombay to Europe in 1884. This story, which in the author's head seemed quite short, was not finished until the following year; it was *The Nigger of the Narcissus.*

The summer was drawing to its close. Feeling at home again in France, Conrad had planned to spend the autumn in the Basque country.

A stranger making a tour of Brittany had heard about the "English people on the Ile-Grande" in Lannion and was curious to see what they looked like. He received a friendly welcome. He was a middle-aged man, intelligent and well read. He displayed considerable knowledge of medicine, on which the conversation had touched, and Conrad told him about his own state of health. The visitor was interested and remarked that "the winter in that house, exposed to the four winds of heaven, was scarcely an ideal spot for anyone subject to sudden illness." He said that a man who depended on his pen for his livelihood needed to live under more stable conditions. "You see, sir," he added, "this is how it strikes me. You are a younger author than you are a man, and although you must have ample material to draw upon, it has got to be written. I should not consider your health good enough to risk the chance of making yourself sufficiently comfortable in out-of-the-way places. That is if I may offer you my opinion." [24]

The young couple accompanied the stranger back to the mainland. A genuine mutual liking had sprung up during these few hours of conversation. They parted cordially and never saw each other again, but such friendly interest and sincerity on the part of this passer-by persuaded Conrad to give up his nomadic plans. Before the month of September was over the young couple embarked at Saint-Malo for Southampton and after a calm crossing the captain saw dawn break over the familiar shores of the Isle of Wight. Once again he set foot on this English soil which, through another turn of fate, he was not to leave again for long.

[24] Jessie Conrad, *Joseph Conrad and His Circle.*

XI

The Weight of the Burden
(1897-1904)

To snatch in a moment of courage, from
the remorseless rush of time, a passing
phase of life, is only the beginning of
the task. The task approached in tender-
ness and faith is to hold up unques-
tioningly, without choice and without
fear, the rescued fragment before all eyes
in the light of a sincere mood.

Preface to *The Nigger of the Narcissus*

ON THEIR RETURN from France, the young couple spent a few days
in London in the Gillingham Street rooms where for many years
Joseph Conrad had lived when he was ashore. There was never any
question of their staying there, for the captain had a sort of loathing
for towns in general. All his life he spent only brief periods in
London. To live by the sea was as unthinkable for him as for most
of his fellow sailors. That left a village or the country. Although
he appreciated a certain amount of solitude, he wanted his young
wife, who was still inexperienced, to be able to enjoy the advice and
company of his old friends, Mr. and Mrs. Hope. In order to be
near them, they began looking for a farmhouse in Essex, near
Stanford-le-Hope. They could find nothing but a small new villa,
devoid of charm, in a street leading to the station. There they

installed themselves for want of anything better, resolved to move after the Christmas holidays, which they were to spend in Cardiff with the Kliszczewskis, Conrad's only Polish friends in England. When they returned from Cardiff they found an old farm near Stanford-le-Hope called Ivy Walls, dating from the time of Queen Elizabeth, where, according to local tradition, the Queen had actually slept. It was a small one-story dwelling, screened in front by great elms and flanked by two-story wings whose upstairs windows offered a wonderful view of sunsets over the Thames.

Conrad did not even wait to get properly settled down before beginning work, and, although he was repeatedly interrupted by violent attacks of gout, he grimly set himself to finishing *The Nigger of the Narcissus*.

By October he was writing to his friend Edward Garnett:

> I must enshrine my old chums in a decent edifice. Seriously do you think it would be too long? There are so many touches necessary for such a picture.[1]

He worked at it continuously, even during the holiday week in Cardiff. That winter he took no time off except to go cruising on the Thames, without regard for fog or rain, in his friend Hope's yacht.

> I am letting myself go with the *Nigger* [he wrote to Garnett]. He grows and grows. I do not think that it's wholly bad, though.[2]

And again a few weeks later:

> Of course nothing can alter the course of the *Nigger*. Let it be unpopular—it *must* be, But it seems to me that the thing—precious as it is to me—is trivial enough on the surface to have some charm for the man in the street. As to lack of incident, well—it's life. The incomplete joy, the incomplete sorrow, the incomplete rascality or heroism—the incomplete suffering. Events crowd and push and nothing happens.[3]

[1] Letter of October 25, 1896.
[2] Letter of November 1, 1896.
[3] Letter of November 29, 1896.

This story meant more to him than the first three works he had ventured on. The description of the return of a sailing ship from Bombay to Europe allowed him to relive the years of his youth. The faces, characters, virtues, faults and vices of the crew members whose life he had shared for twenty years—the fatigue and the dangers—all came to life again in his mind. He wanted to make something so universal out of his personal adventure that all sailors might recognize it as their own and thus give his portrait of reality the quality of a work of art. There could be no doubt about the interest of his subject—for twenty years his whole life had centered round it—but in the last three years his artistic standards had grown considerably more exacting.

> If I do not talk to you much about my work [he wrote to his young friend Edward Lancelot Sanderson], it only means that I am working,—with difficulty, as ever. The more I go, the less confidence in myself I feel. There are days when I suspect myself of inability to put a sentence together: and other days when I am positively incapable to invent anything that could be put into a sentence. Gone are, alas! those fine days of *Alm: Folly* when I wrote with the serene audacity of an unsophisticated fool. I am getting more sophisticated from day to day. And more uncertain! I am more conscious of my unworthiness and also of my desire of perfection which—from the conditions of the case,—is so unattainable.[4]

Despite difficulties and misgivings he is never in doubt as to the final goal. He has confidence in his strength; he knows where he is going. This book is his own: no one else could write it. It is not only a product of the mind; it is the author's own flesh. He is depending on the power of his imagination to make visible and tangible this period in his past.

On January 10, 1897, he writes to his dear Edward Garnett:

> Nigger died on the 7th at 6 P.M.; but the ship is not home yet. Expected to arrive tonight and be paid off tomorrow. And the end! I can't eat—I dream—nightmares—and scare my wife. I wish it was over! But I think it will do! It will do!

4 Letter of November 21, 1896.

—Mind I only think—not sure. But if I didn't think so I would jump overboard.

All this time he has very little money to live on. His publisher, who does not seem to have much confidence in this queer writer's future, haggles with him or refuses an advance on his next book. Committed though he is to this publisher, Edward Garnett tries to get Conrad another who will be more generous. Conrad still knows almost no one in London; he goes there infrequently and then only for a few hours. Edward Garnett and the two former passengers in the *Torrens*, Sanderson and John Galsworthy, are almost his only visitors. In the literary world he has met only two critics, Edmund Gosse and E. V. Lucas—brief encounters which were never followed up.

Not that he is taking refuge in proud isolation, but the conditions of his life are difficult, his work exhausting. For one writer he does show a special deference and admiration. As soon as he returned from the Ile-Grande he sent Henry James a copy of *An Outcast of the Islands*—"with a pretty dedication; it fills the fly leaf."

The American novelist's fame was still very limited. At first one is surprised that this subtle analyst of worldly matters of conscience should have attracted the particular attention of a budding writer whose character and way of life were so remote from these subjects, but, looking deeper, one understands how Henry James' perfectly pure art, his research into the technique of the short story and the novel, his analytical richness, the content of his books, the nature of the characters created by this man whom Conrad, a few years later, was to call "the historian of delicate consciences"—how all these factors would attract and grip the author of *The Nigger of the Narcissus*. Some time later Henry James reciprocated with a copy of *The Spoils of Poynton* with this dedication: "To Joseph Conrad in dreadfully delayed but very grateful acknowledgement of an offering singularly generous and beautiful," and, a few days later, with an invitation to luncheon. Personal acquaintance heightened the sympathy which their appreciation of each other's books had aroused. During subsequent years Henry James and Joseph Conrad were to see quite a lot of one another. The circumstances of their birth and life had turned them into two cosmopolitans and, to a certain extent, two foreigners in England, and their points of view were often similar. Henry James' extremely distinguished and slightly ceremonious manners went well with Conrad's Polish courtesy. He always called James very respectfully "mon cher Maître"—for they spoke French by preference, as is confirmed by the long dedications in French that we find in Joseph Conrad's writing in the copies of *The Nigger of the Narcissus* and *The Mirror of the Sea* that he gave to Henry James.

It was at this same time that Conrad made a much more difficult conquest: that of William Ernest Henley.[5] This poet, the highly personal, vigorous author of *A Book of Verse* and *Improvisations on London* was at the same time a redoubtable and ruthless critic in a country where the law of libel and the sporting spirit applied to the appraisal of the arts have often annihilated genuine literary criticism. W. E. Henley, a sound, impassioned judge, had played a considerable part in R. L. Stevenson's rise to fame and, more recently, in Rudyard Kipling's. Through the medium of William Heinemann, a very cultured and open-minded man, Edward Garnett sent Henley the first few chapters of *The Nigger of the Narcissus*. "If the rest is up to the sample it shall certainly come out in the *New Review,*" he declared. Thus *The Nigger of the Narcissus* appeared between July and December, 1897, in the *New Review,* and Conrad wrote to Edward Garnett: "Now I have conquered Henley I ain't 'fraid of the divvle himself."

The *New Review* even published as an appendix the remarkable "Preface" in which Conrad set forth his *ars poetica,* a preface which was not to appear in the editions of *The Nigger of the Narcissus* until much later.[6]

During this same year several other magazines had accepted his stories: The *Savoy* had published "The Idiots"; the *Cornhill Magazine* "The Lagoon"; *Cosmopolis* "An Outpost of Progress." This forty-year-old writer impressed the not very numerous readers of these youthful magazines as a remarkable beginner.

Scarcely had "An Outpost of Progress" appeared than Conrad

[5] Cf. M. Valéry Larbaud's remarkable study of Henley in *Ce Vice Impuni, la Lecture . . . Domaine anglais,* pp. 116–54.

[6] The "Preface" did not appear in the first edition of the French translation of *The Nigger of the Narcissus,* but was included in the reissue.

received an enthusiastic letter from a reader who wanted to meet him. This was by no means a nobody, but R. B. Cunninghame Graham, a descendant of one of the best Scottish families, who, after ten years or so of adventurous life on the South American continent, had returned to Scotland to be elected Labour M.P. for a Glasgow constituency. More recently he had been exploring unpacified Morocco and had just returned from captivity in Moorish hands. The generous, picturesque personality of this man, known to all his friends as "Don Roberto," could not fail to appeal to Conrad. Soon after their first meeting, late in 1897, he told his friend Sanderson about it in these words:

> I went up to town at the beginning of this month to dine with Cunninghame Graham on his return from the captivity among the Moors. We had exchanged 4 or 5 letters before. He is a most interesting man, not at all bigoted in his social-istic-republican ideas, which I treated to his face with a philo-sophic contempt. We got on very well. Of course, as is often the case, the groundwork of his ideas is, I may say, intensely aristocratic. We talked in two languages. I like him,—and I verily believe he likes me.[7]

He did, indeed, like him. Cunninghame Graham, who was later to achieve some renown as the author of several volumes of short stories, remained one of Conrad's most constant and affectionate friends to the very last.

The Nigger of the Narcissus earned for his author another delight-ful friendship. The story had still not quite finished running in the *New Review* when one of the assistants of the publisher Heinemann informed Conrad that Stephen Crane, who had just arrived in England, had expressed a vehement wish to meet him. This young American writer of twenty-four had recently made a stir with the publication, at the end of 1895, of a remarkable war book, *The Red Badge of Courage,* which Conrad had just read with great sympathy.

Stephen Crane had been enchanted with *The Nigger of the Narcissus.* The author could not help being pleased by the appreci-ation of this exceptionally gifted young man. From their meeting

[7] Letter of December 26, 1897.

sprang a close friendship, which was prematurely interrupted by Crane's death before the age of thirty, on June 5, 1900.

While his own work was making unusual friends for him, Joseph Conrad was himself acting as patron of a young writer who was to have a particularly brilliant career. He passed on to Edward Garnett the manuscript of a volume of short stories entitled *From the Four Corners* and signed John Saint-John. This was the first book—and the short-lived pseudonym—of John Galsworthy.

The Nigger of the Narcissus was originally supposed to be a fairly brief tale, intended to fill out a collection of Conrad's earliest short stories, but it developed into a separate book which appeared at the end of 1897. At first it did not have much success with the general public, but sailors were very interested in it, and some writers immediately expressed their enthusiasm for the qualities of vision and style of one of the most authentic and powerful sea stories in English literature. We may mention, among others, this note made in his *Diary* on December 6, 1897 by Arnold Bennett, who was then on the threshold of his career:

> This afternoon, reading in the *New Review* . . . the conclusion of Joseph Conrad's superb book, *The Nigger of the Narcissus,* I had a mind to go on at once with my Staffordshire novel, treating it in the Conrad manner, which after all is my own, on a grander scale.

The Nigger of the Narcissus barely finished, Conrad went back to his memories of Malaya and, taking up again the theme of remorse which he had already used in "The Lagoon," though this time in a less pathetic and more highly developed form, wrote "Karain," a story which marked the beginning of his association with *Blackwood's Magazine*. The financial and moral support of this widely read magazine was a very precious help to him in subsequent years.

During this same year, 1897, in another story, "The Return," he tried his hand at a kind of writing that reflected the very temporary influence of Meredith and Henry James and revealed almost nothing of his own personality.

In this way he completed the number of short stories needed

for the collection *Tales of Unrest* and went back to the *Rescuer* after an interruption of over a year.

A few weeks later, on January 15, 1898, the writer experienced a quite different emotion: the birth of a son; but neither these new family ties nor this series of publications succeeded in binding him once and for all to the land or in silencing the call of old Ocean, so dear to him for many years. A fortnight after the birth of his son he wrote to Cunninghame Graham: "Wouldn't I jump at a command, if some literary shipowner suddenly offered it to me!"

This was more than an idle notion, a vague desire, a passing longing, for six months later he wrote again: "Cunninghame Graham got into his head to get me the command of a steamer or ship," and shortly afterward he went to Glasgow to see some shipowners. Mrs. Conrad has said in her memoirs that at this time she calmly reckoned with having to leave, with her baby, at a moment's notice aboard her husband's ship.

> Now some shadow of possibility to go to sea has been thus presented to me I am almost frantic with the longing to get away [he wrote].[8]

All this time this desire was growing in him he still felt obliged, before he sailed, to finish that interminable *Rescuer,* promised to an American publisher who had already given him more than one advance on it. The day after his trip to Scotland he wrote to Garnett:

> My impression is that a command will come out of it sooner or later—most likely later, when the pressing need is past and I have found my way on shore.[9]

At this point, Cunninghame Graham, who, through his influence with Scottish shipowners, had tried to arrange Conrad's return to sea, had to go back to Morocco. Not a single offer reached the former captain from Glasgow and at last he resigned himself to his new vocation, making no more attempts from now on to go back to the old one.

[8] Letter of July 19, 1898 to R. B. Cunninghame Graham.
[9] Letter of September 29, 1898.

In February, 1898, Stephen Crane had invited the Conrads to spend ten days in a country house at Ravensbrook in Surrey, where he was living. Conrad accepted. "I feel that if there is no break I will go crazy or go out altogether," he wrote to Garnett. For the last eighteen months, except for a few visits with Sanderson, Galsworthy, Garnett, or Cunninghame Graham, he had had no opportunity to exchange ideas, discuss methods, or reinforce his creative instinct. Introspective as he was, immersed in memories and long solitary meditations, he nevertheless took an active pleasure in conversation and had inherited a sociable temperament. He was encouraged by the sympathy his early books had won for him among colleagues, but an exchange of correspondence did not satisfy him: he needed direct human contact. In this new life he missed the team spirit he had known and appreciated for so long on board ship. He readily accepted the invitation of Stephen Crane, whose house was crowded just then with a group of more or less sought-after journalists of varying talents and a few young writers. There he met a very gifted young man who was profoundly convinced of his own merits. Ford Madox Hueffer. Being related to several outstanding figures among the Pre-Raphaelites, treated by the writers and painters of this group as a spoiled child, tending, through a sort of Germanic romanticism, to take his conception of people, of things and of himself for reality, and, in addition, showing a passionate and sincere interest in literature, Ford Madox Hueffer attached himself to Conrad, did him a few favors, played up to him, and some years later on one occasion even became his collaborator.

Their close relationship began in 1899, cooled by the end of 1902 and was broken around 1910. After the novelist's death, Ford Madox Hueffer (later Ford Madox Ford) felt no compunction in hinting that Conrad owed all his talent and a great part of his fame to him, that he had been his master and had inspired the best of his work. These claims of a pathological liar are hardly worth refuting: facts suffice. Even before Hueffer had crossed the horizon of Conrad's life the latter had written *The Nigger of the Narcissus* and "Youth"—proof enough that he no longer needed anyone else's help to discover and express himself.

So he had gone back once more to that interminable *Rescuer* but he could not manage to get out of the impasse in which he felt himself trapped. His irritability was so great that he was seized by violent new attacks of gout. He was constantly forced to take to his bed; his funds were running out; he did not know where to turn. He would send to his faithful Garnett the pages he had just written—painfully, in fury and despair. "Writing is as difficult as ever. . . . A ridiculously small quantity of the *Rescue* has been done. I am horribly sick of life."

Having such difficulty in finishing off the composition of this *Rescue* and knowing quite well that even if he made good progress it would still take him several months, he was compelled by the necessity of earning some money immediately to heed Edward Garnett's urging to write short stories. Through Cunninghame Graham's influence, he also tried—in vain—to come to an agreement with the *Saturday Review* of which Frank Harris was then editor. On the other hand, the indignation aroused in him by a derogatory article, published in London, on Alphonse Daudet, who had just died, led to his collaboration on a new magazine, *The Outlook*. However, he contributed only two articles to it, one on Alphonse Daudet, the other, entitled "Sea Stories," on Marryat and Fenimore Cooper. A third dealing with Kipling never appeared, for unknown reasons. He was even less interested than usual in literary criticism at this time, because he was overflowing with plots for stories. He told Garnett that he had four stories in his head: "Jim," "Youth," "Dynamite," "A Sailor." And in the space of a few days, in May and June, 1898, he wrote one of his masterpieces, "Youth," and began what he expected to be a fairly short story and what was to become one of his longest and most famous novels: *Lord Jim.* But reluctantly he has to keep his mind from straying; *The Rescue* weighs on him as a necessity, a threat, and a reproach. Yet again he goes back to work on it, but with no pleasure any more.

"The work itself is only like throwing words into a bottomless hole," he writes. And again, to Edward Garnett, on March 29, 1898:

> I sit down religiously every morning, I sit down for eight hours every day—and the sitting down is all. In the course of that working day of 8 hours I write 3 sentences which I erase

before leaving the table in despair. . . . I ask myself some-times whether I am bewitched, whether I am the victim of an evil eye? But there is no "jettatura" in England—is there? I assure you—speaking soberly and on my word of honour—that sometimes it takes all my resolution and power of self control to refrain from butting my head against the wall. . . . After such crises of despair I doze for hours still half conscious that there is that story that I am unable to write. Then I wake up, try again—and at last go to bed completely done-up. So the days pass and nothing is done. At night I sleep. In the morning I get up with the horror of that power-lessness I must face through a day of vain efforts. . . .

I seem to have lost all *sense* of style and yet I am haunted, mercilessly haunted by the *necessity* of style. And that story I can't write weaves itself into all I see, into all I speak, into all I think, into the lines of every book I try to read. . . . You know how bad it is when one *feels* one's liver, or lungs. Well, I feel my brain. I am distinctly conscious of the con-tents of my head. My story is there in a fluid—in an evading shape. I can't get hold of it. It is all there—to bursting, yet I can't get hold of it no more than you can grasp a handful of water.

Most of the summer went by in this way, and Conrad, who had a habit of blaming the place where he was living for his irritability, began to show a deep dislike for Ivy Walls. Ford Madox Hueffer then suggested that he should rent an old farmhouse at Stanford, near Hythe in southwest Kent, which he had lived in himself and which was furnished with pieces of furniture that had belonged to various members of the Rossetti family and to the painter Ford Madox Brown. Conrad liked it all at first sight—the appearance of this house with its roof of old tiles, its setting, the Kent landscape, amid which he was to live, in various places, till his dying day, and he hoped it would bring about a revival of his creative imagina-tion. This hope was almost immediately realized. He went to live there at the beginning of autumn, and the Pent Farm period was to be the most productive of the writer's whole life.

This spot, which seemed so remote, was actually, thanks to a

temporary set of circumstances, at the very heart of English literary
life of that period. Situated above the Stour valley, about three miles
from the sea, at the base of the little point on the English coast
in the neighborhood of the Cinque Ports, between Hastings and
Dover, Pent Farm was not far from either Brede Place, where
Stephen Crane had settled, or Rye, where Henry James lived, and
a few miles from Winchelsea where Ford Madox Hueffer made
long stays. H. G. Wells lived at Sandgate, and through Cunninghame Graham Conrad had met that remarkable writer and striking personality, W. H. Hudson, who had a house at that time at
New Romney, not far from Sandgate. When we add that John
Galsworthy often came to Pent Farm, that H. G. Wells brought
with him George Bernard Shaw, then at the dawn of his fame,
and the naturalistic novelist George Gissing, then at the close of
his career, that Edward Garnett came from time to time to see the
man whose first literary steps he had guided and encouraged, it
will be readily understood that, for all his apparent isolation, the
author of *The Nigger of the Narcissus* was never at any time in
his life in such constant contact with first-class writers. The following extract from a letter in Polish to his cousin, Madame Zagórska,
written at the end of 1898, will give, better than any commentary, an
impression of his life and state of mind at this period:

As you will see, we have come to live here: this is also
quite a small farmhouse but much more convenient and—
what is important—situated on higher ground. I couldn't
work any more in the other house. Here it is going better,
although I haven't anything to boast about yet. We are only
five kilometers from the sea. The railway station is only three
kilometers away and Canterbury only one and a half. From
my window I can see the farm buildings and if I lean out
and look to the right I see the valley of the Stour, which rises,
so to speak, behind the third hedge from the farmyard. Behind the house lie the Kentish Downs which slope zigzag
down to the sea, like the battlements of a fortress.

A very lonely and rather narrow road, along which, it is
whispered, old Lord Roxby (who died eighty years ago)
sometimes rides at night in a four-in-hand which he drives

himself. The odd thing, however, is that he has no head. Why he should leave his head at home when he goes driving, no one can explain. But I must confess that in the two months we have lived here we have not yet heard the sound of wheels, and, although I sometimes go far a walk along this road around midnight, I have still not seen the four-in-hand.

On the other side of the little garden lie quiet meadows and wasteland, crisscrossed by hedges, with here and there an oak or a cluster of young ash trees. Three little villages nestle among the hills and you can see nothing but their church steeples. The coloring of the country shows yellow and pale brown tints among which can be discerned in the distance emerald-green meadows. And you don't hear a sound except the panting and sniffing of the London-Dover express trains.

We live like a family of hermits. From time to time some pious pilgrim *appartenant à la grande fraternité des lettres* comes to pay a visit to the celebrated Joseph Conrad and seek his blessing. Sometimes he gets it, sometimes not, for the hermit is stern and dyspeptic and *n'entend pas la plaisanterie en matière d'art*. In any case the pilgrim gets a decent dinner and a Spartan bed, and goes on his way. I am even expecting one today—the author of *Jocelyn* [John Galsworthy] which he dedicated to me. The book is not outstanding, but the man is very charming and likable, and rich. *Que diable fait-il dans cette galère,* in which we sail along, using our pens for oars, on an ocean of ink, *pour n'arriver nulle part, hélas!*

My wife is dreaming of a visit to Poland, which for her means a visit to you. And I have the same dream too. *Pourquoi pas?* It doesn't cost anything to travel in our thoughts among those we love. It doesn't cost anything—except a little heartache when we find out how far the dream is from the reality.[10]

Even if Poland did not appear in his works, she still had her place, growing more secret as it grew more profound, in his dreams and in his heart. As we have just seen, he corresponded with his

10 Letter of December 18, 1898.

Zagórski cousins in his native tongue; they sent him news of the family and the nation; but it was surely not through them that he learned of a controversy in which, through no fault of his own, he found himself involved—a controversy which affected him deeply and which is probably echoed, though thematically transposed, in one of his books. Joseph Conrad Korzeniowski's literary debut had not gone entirely unnoticed in Poland. In November, 1896, on the publication of his second novel, the Warsaw *Literary Review* (*Przeglad Literacki*) had reported the success achieved by this Pole in England, and at the same time, on November 16, 1896, Joseph Conrad wrote to Edward Garnett: "They have heard of me in Poland through Chicago . . . and think of trying for translations of *A.F.* and *Outcast.*" Early the next year the Polish translation of this second novel was serialized in the *Warsaw Weekly Review of Fashion and Fiction* under the title *Wygnaniec* (*An Outcast*).

At the instigation of Henry James, who had informed him of the existence of this compatriot of his turned English writer, the Polish critic and philosopher, Vincent Lutoslawski, himself the author of a notable work on Plato—also in English—had paid a very hurried visit to Joseph Conrad in 1897. Eighteen months later he published in *Kraj* (*The Nation*), the Polish newspaper in St. Petersburg, an article entitled: "Emigration of the Talents," in which he sustained the thesis that Poles established or naturalized abroad could serve the cause of their fatherland just as well as those who had stayed in Poland. He cited Conrad's case in support of his thesis, recalling his visit to him and his reply to the question why he had not written in Polish: "I should never have dared to foist my attempts upon the beautiful literature of Poland."

In the same issue of this paper, an editor, Thaddeus Zuk Skarzewski, had vehemently protested against Vincent Lutoslawski's argument; a month later, in the same paper, under the same heading, a woman novelist, Elise Orzeszko, attacked the argument even more violently and declared flatly that Joseph Conrad had betrayed the cause of Poland and was no better than a renegade.

This passionate controversy made quite a stir and was reported in other publications. Twelve years later Lutoslawski recalled all the excitement in a series of articles in *Iskierki Warszawski*. Elise

Orzeszko did not hesitate to write to Conrad herself informing him of these accusations. He was very upset by them and it was to their echo that he was replying, much later, when he wrote this characteristic passage in the second chapter of *A Personal Record:*

> The part of the inexplicable should be allowed for in appraising the conduct of men in a world where no explanation is final. No charge of faithlessness ought to be lightly uttered. The appearances of this perishable life are deceptive, like everything that falls under the judgment of our imperfect senses. The inner voice may remain true enough in its secret counsel. The fidelity to a special tradition may last through the events of an unrelated existence, following faithfully, too, the traced way of an inexplicable impulse.

But before that he had made another reply, a more subtle and more profound one.

The year 1898 had been devoted to the creation of two indisputable works of art, finished in June and December, which were direct echoes of his own experiences: "Youth" and "Heart of Darkness." The former narrated the exact, authentic circumstances of the wreck of the *Palestine;* the latter was nothing but a detailed account of his ill-fated Congo adventure. The events, however, were magnified by the writer's genius, illumined by flashes of ardent or somber light, and these lyrical, pathetic pages, torn from the dream journal of this mighty dreamer, attained the grandeur of eternal adventures, the majesty of classical creations.

Delivered of these personal dreams, he had tried—once more in vain—to pick up the still hanging thread of *Rescue.* Discouraged afresh at never getting done with this novel, he tried another story, the idea of which had been haunting him for a long time and which he hesitated to approach. He thought of it at first as a fairly short story, but its depth and scope were to claim him for more than a year, until mid-July, 1900. It was *Lord Jim,* one of his longest novels, the one his name is still most frequently associated with, the one that poses the most baffling and gripping problem of his whole creative output.

Once more, as in "The Lagoon" and "Karain," Joseph Conrad took as his *point de départ* the theme of remorse: this time in more detail and in circumstances closer to his own experience. This insistence is suggestive; it is natural to see in this literary obsession with remorse a projection, an echo, of a personal worry, of an anxiety, a regret, or some secret failing.

This hypothesis is supported by the fact that in *Lord Jim,* as in "Youth" and "Heart of Darkness," the autobiographical nature of which is beyond doubt, the narrator is that same Marlow whom Conrad had already made the protagonist of his own adventures and philosophy. At the same time the novelist has lent Lord Jim certain similarities to himself, even some of the circumstances of his own life. It is therefore quite legitimate to ask how much of Conrad there is in Jim and to look for a source common to both the real and the fictitious life. As we know, the *point de départ* of *Lord Jim* is the desertion of his post by a young merchant-navy officer who, yielding to the evil counsel of a shameless commander and an unscrupulous engineer, jumps into a lifeboat, leaving his ship, which is loaded with pilgrims, to go down swiftly and inevitably. The ship escapes its fate. Stripped of his rank by a maritime tribunal, Jim thinks of nothing but redeeming himself, avoiding any places where he believes or suspects that his dereliction is known, until his final redemption in death.

A personal scrutiny of all the "sea papers" relating to Joseph Conrad has convinced me that never throughout his maritime career, either as an ordinary seaman or as an officer, did he fail in his duty. That in the course of his maritime life Conrad, with his lively imagination, coming to the sea under the influence of dreams and aspirations, a foreigner among French or English crews, should more than once have dreaded being found unequal to his task is more than likely: it is almost certain. That he should have made his own apprehensions the *point de départ* of Jim's downfall is not inconceivable when we know that the story of the captain who went blind in "The End of the Tether" had its source, according to Captain Craig, in Joseph Conrad's fears for his own eyes aboard the *Vidar*.

Lord Jim is not only a development of the theme of remorse but also of the responsibility borne even by the man who believes himself free and exempt from any obligation to society, like Conrad himself. An eminent Polish woman of letters, Madame Marie

Dombrowska, penetrated the secret source of *Lord Jim* when she wrote, two years after the novelist's death:

> The feeling of responsibility is the rigorous principle that his heroes, and Conrad himself, obey. . . . The feeling of responsibility became the very atmosphere of his life; its breath pervaded his whole work. Even unconsciously Conrad puts the imprint of its sovereign force upon all his creations. . . . Something in his life posed a lasting contradiction to his instinct of fidelity and loyalty: he had abandoned his fatherland at the time of its greatest misfortunes. No doubt Conrad's ethical morality predisposed him to fidelity to rationally accepted causes rather than those bequeathed him by tradition. . . . Just like Lord Jim, Conrad could not bring to an end the dramatic episode of his youth. Nothing can end a conflict on such a plane. Poland seemed to Conrad a responsibility denied, a duty repudiated.

This mental conflict and Madame Orzeszko's vehement attack, which came shortly before he began *Lord Jim,* were without doubt the sources of this literary creation into which, as in the majority of his books, the author poured more of himself than was at first apparent.

Indeed, he wrote, shortly afterward, in December, 1903, to his compatriot, the historian Casimir Waliszewski:

> My point of view, whether on land or sea, is English, but you must not conclude from that that I have become an Englishman. By no means. The *homo duplex* has, in my case, more than one meaning. You will understand me. I won't enlarge on this subject.

And twelve years later:

> A journey into . . . the past; a fearful enough prospect for him who had not known how to preserve against his impulses the order and continuity of his life—so that at times it presented itself to his conscience as a series of betrayals.[11]

11 *Notes on Life and Letters,* "Poland Revisited," p. 149.

How sure he was this time of being able to finish his task, although *Lord Jim* had grown so much in scope, is shown by the fact that he allowed its publication to begin in the October, 1899, number of *Blackwood's Magazine,* eight months before this novel was completely finished. The period of vacillation was over. By resolutely turning his back on that interminable *Rescue,* Joseph Conrad had freed himself of all his uncertainties, and, in spite of material difficulties that continued to threaten him and painful and frequent attacks of gout, he handles his work with the same firm will and decision with which he used to handle a ship in a gale or a dead calm.

He wrote to Cunninghame Graham:

Je me suis colleté avec la mort ou peu s'en faut. However not this time yet, it seems. I've been ill since the 26th of Jan. and have only tottered downstairs yesterday.

Malaria, bronchitis and gout. In reality a breakdown. I am better, but I've no sense of *rebound,* don't you know. I remain under the shadow.

Ma pauvre femme est exténuée . . . I am afraid she'll break down next, and that would be the end of the world. I wish I could give her a change but,—*quelle misère!*

I think that tomorrow I'll be able to begin writing again. What sort of stuff it'll be, devil only knows. *Moi aussi je suis exténué. Il faut se raidir.*[12]

And five weeks later he says to Edward Garnett:

I am still at Jim. I've been beastly ill in February. . . . I am old and sick and in debt—but lately I've found I can still write—it comes! it comes!—and I am young and healthy and rich.[13]

About the time he was finishing *Lord Jim,* in April, his aunt, Madame Poradowska, whom he had not seen for several years, came to visit him. Madame Poradowska, who still lived in Brussels,

[12] Letter of February 13, 1900.
[13] Letter of March 26, 1900.

persuaded him to take his family for a few weeks to a Belgian seaside resort. After a few days in Bruges, where they joined the Hueffers, they spent the end of July and the first two weeks of August at the Grand-Hôtel de la Plage at Knocke-sur-Mer. This holiday, however, did not turn out very well. Conrad was incapable of working there and his little boy was ill almost the whole time.

The years 1901 and 1902 were spent in seclusion at Pent Farm; they were years of poverty and hard work. Joseph Conrad wrote one after another: "Typhoon," "Falk," "Amy Foster," and "The End of the Tether" and spent several months reshaping and elaborating a novel which Ford Madox Hueffer had written under the title *Seraphina* and which after considerable changes due to Conrad's collaboration was to appear over the names of both authors and to be called *Romance*.

The only distractions in this hard-working life were an occasional visit to the Hueffers at Winchelsea, to Henry James at Rye, to H. G. Wells at Sandgate; sometimes a luncheon in London with a few colleagues at the Mont Blanc Restaurant, arranged by Edward Garnett. It was an existence devoid of adventures except those he was using in his work which he generally drew from his own past.

Possibly because the Latin-American atmosphere of a large part of *Romance,* with its Cuban setting, brought back memories of his youthful voyages to the West Indies, and because of the particular appeal that everything concerning the South American continent had held for him in his childhood, the moment he had finished *Romance,* he shut himself up completely at Pent Farm from the beginning of 1903 until September 3, 1904, and plunged into his vastest, most powerful, most minutely thought-out novel, *Nostromo,* in which, with nothing to go on but some reading and a few glimpses of scenery in 1875, he managed to create the authentic atmosphere of a South American republic with all its ventures, rivalries, passions, exaltations, and disappointments.

An overwhelming task, of which he wrote four years later, in *A Personal Record:*

All I know, is that, for twenty months, neglecting the common joys of life that fall to the lot of the humblest on this earth, I had, like the prophet of old, "wrestled with the Lord"

for my creation, for the headlands of the coast, for the darkness of the Placid Gulf, the light on the snows, the clouds on
the sky, and for the breath of life that had to be blown into
the shapes of men and women, of Latin and Saxon, of Jew
and Gentile. These are, perhaps, strong words, but it is difficult to characterize otherwise the intimacy and the strain of
a creative effort in which mind and will and conscience are
engaged to the full, hour after hour, day after day, away from
the world, and to the exclusion of all that makes life really
lovable and gentle—something for which a material parallel
can only be found in the everlasting sombre stress of the west-
ward winter passage round Cape Horn. For that too is the
wrestling of men with the might of their Creator, in a great
isolation from the world, without the amenities and consola-
tions of life, a lonely struggle under a sense of over-matched
littleness, for no reward that could be adequate, but for the
mere winning of a longitude. . . .

. . . I suppose I slept, and ate the food put before me, and
talked connectedly to my household on suitable occasions.
But I had never been aware of the even flow of daily life,
made easy and noiseless for me by a silent, watchful, tireless
affection. Indeed, it seemed to me that I had been sitting at
that table surrounded by the litter of a desperate fray for
days and nights on end. It seemed so, because of the intense
weariness of which that interruption had made me aware—
the awful disenchantment of a mind realising suddenly the
futility of an enormous task, joined to a bodily fatigue such
as no ordinary amount of fairly heavy physical labour could
ever account for. I have carried bags of wheat on my back,
bent almost double under a ship's deck-beams, from six in the
morning till six in the evening (with an hour and a half off
for meals), so I ought to know.

But what Conrad forgets to mention in this passage from his
memoirs is that during this same period a bank which had advanced
him a little money failed, that his wife suffered a bad fall in London as a result of which she remained a semi-invalid for the rest of
her life and had to undergo a series of operations, that he himself

was incessantly tortured and often incapacitated by gout (five attacks in eleven months in 1903) and that nevertheless, while writing *Nostromo* during the day, he still found time and strength in the night hours to dictate to Ford Madox Hueffer some of the pieces for the collection that was to become *The Mirror of the Sea,* that lyrical summing up of his experiences at sea, and in addition to write some excellent pages on Maupassant as a preface to a selection of his stories to be published in English.

XII

Under Western Eyes
(1905-1914)

There must be a wonderful soothing
power in mere words since so many
men have used them for self-com-
munion.

Under Western Eyes

THE COMPLETION OF *Nostromo* had exhausted the writer's strength;
he finished with his literary problems only to find them replaced
by serious concern over the health of his wife, who had to undergo
a painful operation on her knee. As soon as she could be moved
at all they decided to go to the Mediterranean in search of rest and
a more clement winter. Capri was their choice and on January 15,
1905, accompanied by a nurse and their little boy, they embarked
for the Continent. The night before they left, Conrad wrote to
H. G. Wells:

A mad extravagant thing to do, but if I bring a book back
from Capri it will be some justification. Jessie must have some
change and I myself feel at the end of my tether.

They left Paris after one night at the Hôtel de Saint-Petersbourg.
They were in a hurry to reach their destination, but bad weather
kept them several days in Naples before the sea was calm enough

for the invalid to risk the passage. We get an idea of the situation and of Joseph Conrad's state of mind from a letter he sent to his friend John Galsworthy as soon as he landed in Capri:

> I had foreseen everything in planning that voyage but that, and the delay of all these days in the hotel has utterly ruined me. In fact to be able to get over to Capri, I had to leave 150 frcs. unpaid on my bill and am beginning life in charge of a party of four with 30 frcs. in my pocket.
> The nervous irritation of these days in Naples prevented me from doing anything. I got 1000 words of a political article written (and that's all) during the voyage. . . . I think we will be very comfortable here. But the whole expedition is a mad thing really, for it rests upon what I am not certain of—my power to produce some sixty thousand words in 4 months. I feel sick with apprehension at times.[1]

As it turned out, they spent four months at the Villa di Maria in Capri, though the weather was poor most of the time. Conrad suffered by turns from bronchitis, influenza, and a persistent insomnia, and the only literary profit the holiday showed was one article which he had begun during the journey.

No sooner had he set foot on the Continent than he rediscovered the phantoms of his youth. It was the time when Europe was beginning to be alarmed at the German Kaiser's loudmouthed agitations, the time when Russia was suffering her first reverses in the war with Japan. The Pole lying dormant in Conrad's heart and mind once more came face to face with the enemies of his country. Ever since leaving Paris he had had in mind an article intended to enlighten English readers about the European situation and the precarious nature of the concord of Europe. This he did with an outspokenness with regard to Russia which must have astonished many contemporary readers, voicing views on Germany which the two ensuing wars have shown to be nothing short of prophetic. This essay, "Autocracy and War," exceptional as it is in Conrad's work, shows that if he had up to then held himself aloof from political controversy, it was by no means for lack of interest. *"Le prussianisme, violà l'ennemi!"* was the conclusion of his article.

[1] Letter of January 21, 1905.

The calm poetic shores of the Bay of Naples had certainly not bestowed on him the carefree peacefulness that lures so many tourists; they had only strengthened his feelings of attachment to the West and his anxieties about the dangers threatening it.

As soon as he had settled down in Capri he began to plan a novel with a Mediterranean setting. He thought he had found a subject in the struggle between the British and the French for Capri in 1808. He even began research on this but gave it up before he had really got started.

Apart from a meeting in Capri with a charming Polish aristocrat, Count Sigismond Szembek, whose family had been connected with the Korzeniowskis and the Bobrowskis, this Italian holiday was enlivened only by the company of the Scottish writer Norman Douglas; a visit (which annoyed Conrad) from Frank Harris and Austin Harrison; the pleasure of seeing the Galsworthys once or twice at Amalfi, and an excursion to Pompeii. Szembek and Conrad soon began to see each other almost every day, reminiscing together about their homeland and their memories of an unhappy past. It was Count Szembek, too, who told him about a misadventure he had recently suffered in Naples, which, with minor modifications, inspired Conrad's story "Il Conde."

Obviously, just looking at the Mediterranean for four months had not satisfied this former sailor. He wanted to get closer to its charm, recapture sensations now a quarter of a century old, and, in search of his past, he decided to go from Naples to Marseilles by freighter.

We have no record of the novelist's feelings during this passage, in the course of which he spent hour after hour on deck, despite bad weather, but we can imagine the flood of memories surging through his mind when he saw again the harbor of Marseilles, city of his first loves and of his initiation into the mysteries of the sea, which he had left in secret, so to speak, some thirty years ago to plunge into the unknown.

Their stay at the Hôtel de Genève in Marseilles was brief, although Aunt Marguerite Poradowska was there to welcome the travelers. The weather was appalling. Conrad was in a hurry to get back to work and seems to have missed a meeting he had been looking forward to with a young French writer who had recently requested the honor of translating *The Nigger of the Narcissus.*

This writer was Robert d'Humières, who was not to realize his ambition until four years later but who was Conrad's earliest admirer in France.

Many factors were responsible for his quick return to England: his inability to work in Capri; the news that through the influence of Edmund Gosse and the artist William Rothenstein, the Prime Minister, Mr. Balfour, had decided to award him a civil-list pension in view of the quality of his work and his need for money; the fact that the Stage Society proposed to produce the one-act play *One Day More,* which he had dramatized from his story "Tomorrow." By the end of May he had resumed the routine of life at Pent Farm.

The one-act play was produced in London on June 25 and the two following nights by a non-commercial company. It had a *succès d'estime* to which the author was quite reconciled, as the following extract from a letter to John Galsworthy shows:

> As to the success of my thing, I can't say anything. I've heard that some papers praised it and some ran it down. On Tuesday when we went (like the imbeciles we are) there was some clapping but obviously the very smart audience did not catch on. And no wonder! On the other hand the celebrated "man of the hour," G. B. Shaw, was ecstatic and enthusiastic. "Dramatist," says he. With three plays of his own running simultaneously at the height of the season he is entitled to speak. Of course, I don't think I am a dramatist. But I believe I've 3 or even 5 acts somewhere in me. At any rate the reception of the play was not such as to encourage me to sacrifice six months to the stage. Besides I haven't the six months to throw away.[2]

He still had to write the last two chapters of *The Mirror of the Sea,* the last of which was a tribute to the Mediterranean and at the same time a fragment of his memoirs. This collection of experiences and impressions was finished by early autumn. Almost immediately he started a novel, *The Secret Agent,* about a group of anarchists in London. He owed his knowledge of the details of this back-

[2] Letter of June 30, 1905.

ground to a friend and regarded it, in his own words, as "a sustained effort in ironical treatment of a melodramatic subject."

His stay in Capri seems to have renewed his feeling of kinship with the Continent. Before the winter was over he was already anxious to leave England again in search of a better climate. This time he chose France and they spent two months in Montpellier.

This stay was entirely successful. The Languedoc climate was very beneficial to him; he liked the town and the people and he was glad to be back in the French atmosphere he had once been so familiar with. Looking down from the windows of the Hôtel Riche et Continental, where they were staying, he was delighted by the life and color of the Place de la Comédie. Sometimes he listened to conversations in the Café Riche, tinged with the attractive accent of the Midi to which he had grown accustomed in his youth. In Montpellier he corrected the final proofs of *The Mirror of the Sea* and wrote the major part of *The Secret Agent*. He left with the firm intention of coming back the following winter. In August, in the London house lent to them by John Galsworthy, the novelist's second son, John Alexander, was born.

The Mirror of the Sea appeared in October and brought tributes—not very numerous but unusually warm—not only from sailors but also from writers; foremost among them, this time, was Rudyard Kipling, who sent Conrad the following letter:

Oct. 9, 1906

Dear Conrad,

What a book—*The Mirror of the Sea!* I took it up as soon as it arrived and sailed along with it until I went to bed. Certainly I recognized the description of the winds, which I consider almost as splendid as the description of the darkness in "Typhoon," but I have read and re-read it all and I thank you sincerely and gratefully. This ought to make an even more vivid impression on someone who has sailed in sailing ships than on me, and that's saying a lot.

"Kipling sends me an enthusiastic little note. The Age of Miracles is setting in! . . . The End of the World is at hand," said Conrad in a letter to Galsworthy.

This book's lack of success when it first appeared was the reason for a rather odd statement made by Conrad two years later in a letter to Major Ernest Dawson:

> I don't think of the sea now. No one cares about it really, or I would have had as much success here as Loti in France.[3]

Before the year was out, the family was back in the Hôtel Riche in Montpellier, having fled, as Conrad wrote, "in a sort of panic before the menaces of the winter."

At first the novelist found there everything he was looking for. The weather that winter was particularly mild; he made trips with his family to Palavas, Maguelonne, and into the foothills. Again he let himself fall under the spell of the town and the café conversations, in which he was soon taking part; he made friends with an artillery officer with whom he had frequent talks on military subjects familiar to him through family tradition and through stories told to him in childhood.

These conversations gave rise almost on the spot to the story entitled "The Duel," which vividly narrates an episode in the wars of the First Empire. "I tried to put into it a little of the military spirit of the time. I have two of Napoleon's officers among my ancestors: my maternal great-uncle and my paternal grandfather. So it is a family affair, so to speak," he wrote to a French friend about this story, which is outstanding in his work for the gay spirit that pervades it from beginning to end and for its happy ending. Another result of these military conversations was the idea for a novel describing the state of anxious alertness and suspense that hung over the western part of the Mediterranean during Napoleon's exile on the Isle of Elba. Conrad even did some background research in the Montpellier library for this novel, the theme of which he carried with him for sixteen years, beginning to write it on the eve of his death and never finishing it.

In Montpellier he had become so acclimatized to French life that he corrected and even partly rewrote a French translation of "Karain." He reread Daudet, Maupassant, and Anatole France, took an interest in local life and thought of staying on until the beginning of summer. The memory of a shy and frightened young

[3] Letter of June 25, 1908.

girl musician glimpsed among the members of the little orchestra in the Café Riche was later to inspire one of his most pathetic feminine characters, Lena, the heroine of *Victory*. However, he was not just taking a holiday in this French atmosphere in which he felt so much at home; he was still conscious of being an English writer and during this period he wrote the first chapters of a novel which was, he knew, to be a long one and which he called *Chance*.

This hard-working peace was suddenly shattered. The novelist's two children fell ill and both almost died. He himself was grievously plagued by gout. His letters between the end of February and June, 1907, tell of the renewed agony in which he lived, being unable to postpone the correction of *The Secret Agent* and the continuation of *Chance*. March and April were nothing but a continuous nightmare.

As soon as the children had halfway recovered, it was decided, on Dr. Grasset's advice, that the whole family should go to Switzerland. Thus in mid-May, after a few days at the Hôtel de la Poste in Geneva, Conrad found himself back for the fourth time in the Pension de la Roseraie at Champel, hoping the hydropathic sanatorium would do his children as much good as it had done him in years past.

Their convalescence took almost three months. They stayed at Champel until the middle of August. The novelist's state of anxiety and irritability during this period was responsible for the unfavorable light in which he painted Geneva the following year.

He was approaching fifty; his fame was still very limited. Even if the majority of critics and writers was well aware of the exceptional qualities of personality, the power of his vision, and the originality of his style, his reputation with the general public had hardly increased in the twelve years since he had published *Almayer's Folly*. The material remuneration of work which often exhausted him was mediocre. Four or five years earlier, however, he had had the good luck to meet a man who had an unshakable faith in the merits and future of the author of *Lord Jim* and who had taken it upon himself to secure for him not only profitable outlets in England and the United States but also the material tranquillity necessary for the composition of work which by its very nature could neither be hurried nor become immediately popular. The admiration, helpfulness, business sense, and money of J. B. Pinker had already enabled Conrad to finish *Nostromo* in comparative peace. In the writer's letters to his friend and business manager we can follow the labors, doubts, and exasperations of the one, the reassuring confidence of the other. Thanks to Pinker's ever-present and unfailing support, Conrad's confidence in his own powers grew stronger.

From the Hôtel de la Roseraie in Champel, on July 30, 1907, in the course of a letter to Pinker, he wrote this:

> I think I can safely say that the *Secret Agent* is *not* the sort of novel to make what comes after more difficult to place. Neither will it, I fancy, knock my prices down. *Chance* itself will be altogether different in tone and treatment of course, but it will be salable I believe. By the end of September you will have a really considerable lot of it to show. Of course it will not be on popular lines. Nothing of mine can be, I fear. But even Meredith ended by getting his sales. Now, I haven't Meredith's delicacy, and that's a point in my favour. I reckon I may make certain of the support of the Press for the next few years. The young men who are coming in to write criticisms are in my favour so far. At least all of whom I've heard are. I don't get in the way of established reputations. One may read everybody and yet in the end want to read me—for a change if for nothing else. For I don't resemble anybody; and yet I am not specialized enough to call up imitators as to matter or style. There is nothing in me but a turn of mind which, whether valuable or worthless, cannot be imitated.

Completely devoid of any literary vanity, Conrad nevertheless had a very exact sense of his own value, and neither anxiety nor illness could break his courage.

This trip to the Continent had in the end left too many unhappy memories behind for him to think of repeating it; besides, like many former sailors, he was inclined to stay put. "No more trips abroad!" he wrote in the same letter to J. B. Pinker, "I am sick of them." And in fact he was not to leave Great Britain again for the next seven years. Yet he was bound to the Continent by old or recent links and for some time it was the Continent alone that inspired his thoughts.

The Pent Farm period was over. On his return from Geneva, Conrad, who was inclined to take violent dislikes to houses, decided that he could not work there any longer and wanted to be nearer London. In September, 1907, the whole family went to live at Someries, near Luton in Bedfordshire, about forty minutes from London by train. He did not stay there long and less than a year later moved to Aldington in Kent, the county to which he was to remain faithful for the rest of his life. Hardly had he settled at Someries than a violent attack of gout—the result of overwork and worry—made it quite impossible for him to work or even sleep at all for nearly two months. He tried—"convulsively" as he said himself—to get on with *Chance* but he was overcome by weariness and, putting this book aside, he wrote, in the next two years, three books totally different in character but all relying on the Continent for inspiration and setting: the brief story called "Il Conde," which was nothing but the adventure Count Szembek had met with in Naples; a novel with the preliminary title of *Razumov*, afterward called *Under Western Eyes*, first suggested by an anecdote told him in 1895 by a chance acquaintance in Geneva and recalled to his memory by his recent visit to that city, and finally a volume of reminiscences [4] in which Poland and France played a major role and in which he tried to narrate the circumstances of his first contact with the sea and also with the art of writing.

In *Under Western Eyes* his aim was to "capture the very soul of things Russian." The title makes it clear that "things Russian" were for him not Western but "foreign," but the circumstances of his birth, childhood, and early youth had made him painfully familiar with them. As a Pole whose life had been tainted by Russian tyranny, it was harder for him than for anyone else to depict the characters and scenes of this novel without giving way to any secret rancor. He managed it at the cost of tremendous mental tension, maintaining the impartiality and generosity of opinion which are the essential hallmarks of Conrad's whole work. No book gave him more trouble or demanded more painstaking care. He spent close to two years on it, two years harassed by material

---

[4] *Some Reminiscences,* later to become *A Personal Record.* (Tr.)

worry and attacks of gout. Early in 1908 he wrote to John Galsworthy:

> Ah! my dear, you don't know what inspiration-killing
> anxiety it is to think: "Is it salable?" There's nothing more
> cruel than to be caught between one's impulse, one's act,
> and that question, which for me simply is a question of life
> and death. There are moments when the mere fear sweeps
> my head clean of every thought. It is agonizing—no less.
> And, . . . you know, . . . that pressure grows from day to
> day instead of getting less.[5]

Later that year, writing to the poet Arthur Symons, he said in
his own favor:

> One thing I am certain of is that I have approached the
> object of my task, things human, in a spirit of piety. The
> earth is a temple where there is going on a mystery play,
> childish and poignant, ridiculous and awful enough, in all
> conscience. Once in I've tried to behave decently. I have not
> degraded any quasi-religious sentiment by tears and groans;
> and if I have been amused or indignant, I've neither grinned
> nor gnashed my teeth. In other words, I've tried to write with
> dignity, not out of regard for myself, but for the sake of the
> spectacle, the play with an obscure beginning and an unfath-
> omable *dénouement*.[6]

During this same year, 1908, Ford Madox Hueffer decided to
start a literary monthly, *The English Review,* the first number of
which appeared in October. Pressed by Hueffer to collaborate,
Conrad interrupted his work on *Under Western Eyes* and dictated
some chapters of his memoirs, depicting his family, his distant
homeland, his sad childhood, his early aspirations, his sea training,
his meeting with Almayer, and the incomprehensible, irresistible
impulse that had compelled him to write. Set down with an emotion
veiled in humility, a fatalism tinged with irony, these memoirs
constituted a very delicate and profound tribute to those who had

[5] Letter of January 6, 1908.
[6] Letter of August 29, 1908.

played a part in the formation of his character and in guiding the course of his life.

At the end of 1909 he summed up his situation and state of mind as follows, in a letter to John Galsworthy:

> I sit 12 hours at the table, sleep six, and worry the rest of the time, feeling age creeping on and looking at those I love. For two years I haven't seen a picture, heard a note of music, had a moment of ease in human intercourse—not really.[7]

A great part of that year had been spent in interminable exhausting attacks of gout; these had even forced him to abandon the publication of his *Reminiscences,* which he had originally intended to expand considerably.

In July, 1909, he had just written the last few lines of the *Reminiscences,* when the mail brought him a long six-page letter signed with an unknown name. A certain Carlos M. Marris, master mariner, wished first to express, on behalf of himself and his comrades in the merchant navy, their admiration and gratitude for that incomparable collection of maritime impressions and sea lore, *The Mirror of the Sea.* He went on to say that in Malaya he had known nearly all the characters the author had introduced into his books and that he, like them, had participated in plenty of adventures. Moreover, he had commanded the very ship, the *Vidar,* in which Joseph Conrad, as first mate, had got to know Almayer.

In 1909 Joseph Conrad was no longer by any means unknown, but his reputation was only just beginning to extend beyond a restricted circle of readers. To be sure, he had already received flattering, encouraging, interesting letters from readers, writers, and sailors, but in the twenty years since he had ceased to roam the Malay Archipelago this was the first time any voice had reminded him, not only of its familiar images, but of the very thought of people he believed had vanished from the world for ever. He had been so convinced that they would never hear of his books that he had even kept their real names: Almayer, Lingard, Babalatchi, Abdullah. This unexpected letter was like a message from these ghosts.

[7] Letter of December 22, 1909.

During the preceding months, while he was writing *Under Western Eyes* and *Some Reminiscences,* Joseph Conrad had plunged again and again into the secret places of his strange past—a past incomprehensible and mysterious to his English audience and usually painful to himself.

Captain Marris, back in England for a few months, came to visit the novelist, who wrote to his friend J. B. Pinker shortly afterward:

> I had a visit from a man out of the Malay Seas. It was like the raising of a lot of dead—dead to me, because most of them live out there and even read my books and wonder who the devil has been around taking notes.[8]

Captain Marris's visit made such a deep impression on him that Conrad could not even wait to finish *Under Western Eyes.* Two months before he completed it, he wrote in less than two weeks one of the most perfect of his short stories, "The Secret Sharer." The next year two more remarkable stories, "A Smile of Fortune" and "Freya of the Seven Isles," together with "The Secret Sharer," made up *'Twixt Land and Sea,* a collection inspired by this passing visitor and dedicated to that messenger from the past, glimpsed for a moment only to slip back immediately into the night.

In November, 1909, writing to the artist William Rothenstein, he recapitulated his literary situation in these words:

> The fourteenth year of my writing life draws to an end, and when I look at the result I am appalled. I speak from a worldly point of view, but then we live in the world and its weights and measures impose themselves upon our judgment,—yes, even upon our feelings. One needn't be particularly vile and base to suffer a little from that truth. And there are just 14 published volumes. Not a great tale. But you know as well as anybody that of these years a full third must be taken off for illness alone,—not speaking of other pieces of bad luck. So I don't think I've been indolent or even unduly slow, taking into consideration the nature of my work. I mention this so that some day you should, at need, defend my memory: for I am pretty certain of coming in for some hard

sayings,—unless indeed no one ever says anything,—which is quite possible, too.[9]

And a few days later in a letter to John Galsworthy he added this melancholy reflection:

I wish sometimes I had remained at sea, which, had I honestly stuck to it, would no doubt be rolling now over my head.

Nineteen hundred and ten to 1914 was a period of great loneliness. As soon as he had finished *Under Western Eyes,* he was seriously ill for weeks. Incapable of any work at all, he began to loathe the Aldington house—which was in any case not very comfortable. He could not rest until they had found another, also in Kent, not far from Ashford. There, at Capel House, he lived an utterly secluded life. For months he did not even go up to London, saw almost no one. His only link with the world was his letters, few in number and limited to a handful of loyal friends, in which he appeared in his usual light: affectionate, generous, encouraging to his colleagues and hesitant about his own work.

This was also the period when he was—if we may use the expression—farthest from himself, when his work drew least obviously upon his memories or experiences. Neither *Chance* nor *Victory* contains any personal allusions that are not entirely superficial. With his fiftieth year he seems to have attained a sort of self-detachment coinciding with a richness of technique, the power and scope of which are exemplified in these two novels.

In a life and career full of strange circumstances, it is worth noting that *Chance,* the novel which shows the greatest complexity of technique—an extraordinary virtuosity, one might say—and which contains the greatest number of ideas and points of view, as seen through the character of Marlow, was the one that came most easily to the author. This painstaking writer, always worrying about expression if not about the plan, took barely ten months to write it.

By another strange chance this was also the novel that determined his fame. It was high time: he had been writing for fifteen years—

[9] Letter of November 15, 1909.

admirable pages, admirable books, which had not succeeded in pleasing, or even reaching, the general public. Even the excellent J. B. Pinker himself, appalled at the advances that had mounted up over six or seven years, found himself forced to refuse any further ones. The writer's health seems to have been worse than ever during this period. Four or five times he had to give up work on *Victory,* which took him nearly two years to write, for he had to interrupt it again in order to finish several short stories.

Even some of his friends—his best friends among them—did not seem to understand his deepest feelings and his artistic impartiality. Edward Garnett thought he had detected hatred in *Under Western Eyes* and Conrad felt obliged to write him the following reply— with a warmth he rarely showed when dealing with a friend:

> You are so russianised my dear that you don't know the truth when you see it—unless it smells of cabbage-soup when it at once secures your profoundest respect. I suppose one must make allowances for your position of Russian Ambassador to the Republic of Letters. Official pronouncements ought to be taken with a grain of salt and that is how I shall take your article in the *Nation* which I hope to see tomorrow. . . .
>
> But it is hard after lavishing a "wealth of tenderness" on Tekla and Sophia, to be charged with the rather low trick of putting one's hate into a novel. If you seriously think that I have done that then my dear fellow let me tell you that you don't know what the accent of hate is. Is it possible that you haven't seen that in this book I am concerned with nothing but ideas, to the exclusion of everything else, with no arrière pensée of any kind. Or are you like the Italians (and most women), incapable of conceiving that anybody ever should speak with perfect detachment, without some subtle hidden purpose, for the sake of what is said, with no desire of gratifying some small personal spite—or vanity.
>
> As to discussing Russia, it's the most chimeric of enterprises, since it is there for anyone to look at. "La Russie c'est le néant" Prince Bismarck said in 1864—and forthwith pro-

ceeded to prove it by 20 years of the most contemptuous policy towards that "Great Power." C'est le néant. Anybody with eyes can see it.

And anyhow if hatred there were it would be too big a thing to be put into a 6/-novel. This too might have occurred to you, if you had condescended to look beyond the literary horizon where all things sacred and profane are turned into copy.[10]

But his reputation was growing by degrees. In the United States his books, published some years before, were beginning to arouse enthusiasm. Conrad, no stranger to irony, declared himself very interested to find himself discovered by his own publisher after ten years. He was receiving inquiries about a complete edition of his works. The New York *Herald* had just bought and serialized *Chance*. During this period *The Nigger of the Narcissus* appeared in French, quickly followed by *The Secret Agent*. "You cannot imagine how touched I am at the idea of being read in French by Frenchmen," he wrote to H. D. Davray. One of his contemporary readers wrote to a friend:

> Have you been reading J. Conrad's novel *The Secret Agent* in *Le Temps*? It contains an absolutely delightful set of scoundrels, and the ending is really sublime. It is described in the most calm and detached way and it is only after thinking about it that you say to yourself: "But these people are monsters!"

This reader was none other than Claude Debussy.[11] The French writers André Gide, Valery Larbaud, Gilbert de Voisins, St. Léger-Léger, came to see him. His works were translated into Swedish, Danish, German. His name was being heard more and more frequently in Italy and Spain. For the first time in many years he had no material worries. J. B. Pinker's advances were repaid.

Sixteen years previously, in October, 1897, Conrad had written

---

[10] Letter of October 20, 1911.
[11] Letter to Jacques Durand, July 8, 1910.

(in French) to a Polish friend of his childhood, the sister of his friends the Taubes of Cracow, now Baroness Jeanne de Brunnow, who, after seeing one of his books, had asked if he remembered her:

> I have a certain—literary—reputation, but the future is anything but certain, for I am not a *popular* author and probably never shall be. That does not disturb me, for it was never my ambition to write for the all-powerful masses. I have no liking for democracy—and democracy has no liking for me. I have come to be appreciated by a few chosen minds and I have no doubt that I can sell well enough—on a limited scale, of course—to earn my living. I have no dreams of making a fortune—and anyhow you don't find fortunes in inkwells. But I admit that I dream of peace, of a little fame, and of being able to devote the rest of my life to the service of art, free from material worries. And there, Madame, you have the secret of my life.

He was approaching sixty before he was at last able to achieve the goal he had set himself.

This English writer of Polish birth, whose literary talents had been shaped by France and whose noble strength and melancholy generosity typified the spirit of the West, did achieve the reputation he had dreamed of—and also European fame.

XIII

Poland Revisited

(1914)

And you may take my word for it . . .
that in the course of my navigations on
the earthly globe, I never departed in
mind or heart from my native country.

Letter to Casimir Waliszewski,
Nov. 15, 1903.

WHILE THE WRITER Joseph Conrad Korzeniowski was still almost
unknown to the general public even in England, Poland, as we
have seen, was concerned about him in various ways. Even in
France the first individuals to take notice of his name and work
were Poles. As early as 1903, Teodor de Wyzewa, who edited the
"Literature Abroad" column in the *Revue des Deux Mondes,* had
mentioned him one day to Casimir Waliszewski, another Pole,
who had become the French historian of czarist Russia. That
same year, at the end of October, Casimir Waliszewski had made
a study of several of Conrad's books and had entered into correspondence with him. He had received letters from Conrad, some in
French, some in Polish, all friendly in tone, and shortly afterward,
in January and February, 1904, he published an article in French
in the *Revue des Revues* and in Polish in the Saint Petersburg *Kraj*
(the paper in which Conrad had been so violently attacked eight

years previously), under the title "A Case of Naturalization: Joseph Conrad," containing a discerning analysis of *The Nigger of the Narcissus* and "Typhoon" and penetrating insights into *Lord Jim* and some of the short stories. This was the earliest study of Conrad in France.

From time to time a letter was sent off to his homeland or received from there—from his Zagórska cousin, his friend the Baroness of Brunnow, or Count Szembek. From time to time a compatriot would propose to visit him, though the visit did not always materialize. In 1912 Arnold Bennett had met a young Polish writer and journalist, Joseph Retinger, introduced by friends of his in Paris, and put him in touch with Conrad. The young man admired him intensely and became devoted to him.

Poland was not unaware of the growing reputation of this prodigal son. In the first weeks of 1914 one of the editors of *Tygodnik Illustrowany,* Warsaw's biggest illustrated paper, came to Capel House to interview Conrad. He was received with unusual cordiality and the conversation proved far more interesting than the general run of such interviews, as the resulting article, which appeared in Warsaw on April 8, 1914, shows. This remains an extraordinarily significant document.

In it Conrad's first thought had been to pay homage to the culture of Poland, which had enriched his whole youth, and to express the sincere admiration he still held for the great poets who had been the spokesmen of the oppressed nation: Adam Mickiewicz, whose *Pan Tadeusz* he had often read aloud to his father (though he preferred *Konrad Wallenrod* and *Grazina*), and Slowacki. Over the years he had come to recognize Slowacki's superiority to Mickiewicz. "That man is the soul of all Poland," he told his interviewer.

In the course of this interview he quoted authors and works which seemed to be just as fresh in his memory as when he had left Poland, forty years earlier. He referred to people of minor importance, among others the poet and geographer Vincent Pol, who quite often used to come to see Apollo Korzeniowski and whose face with its big white drooping mustache he still remembered. Toward the end of his talk with this journalist, Marius Dambrowski, he added:

In commenting on my works, the English critics always say that they find in them things that are incomprehensible, unfathomable. Only you people can fathom the unfathomable, comprehend the incomprehensible, for that is the Polish part of me.

At this same period Joseph Retinger, the other Pole, was visiting the novelist frequently and pressing him to go to Poland, where relatives, friends, and unknown admirers would be so glad to see him. Conrad was deaf to his proposals. More than once he had been tempted to undertake the journey, but each time the importance and difficulty of his work, his always precarious health, his dislike of traveling, had outweighed his dreams. What could he hope to find in his native country? Phantoms and graves! But his wife and children joined in the pleas of his young compatriot: they had a great desire to get to know that country, which seemed to them far away and so mysterious. He was still hesitating.

How many years had passed since December, 1896, when he wrote to his Zagórski cousins:

I had intended to come to the country for the holidays— and by "the country" I mean yours. It was an uncertain, timid plan, although my desire was intense. I didn't tell you, hardly even let myself think about it. Still, the disappointment is cruel. There will be no holidays for me this year: I console myself with the thought that there is next year— and will be other years—and sometimes desires are realized —(not often).

Those desires had not been realized. At the end of June, 1914, however, having written the last lines of his novel *Victory,* he finally yielded to his family's entreaties and his own wishes, so long denied. The whole family, accompanied by Joseph Retinger, agreed to go and visit the latter's mother-in-law, only about sixteen miles from Cracow but in Russian Poland.

Despite the alarming rumors that were already spreading across Europe, the little group of travelers embarked for Hamburg on Saturday, July, 26, 1914, at Harwich, with the intention of proceeding to Cracow via Berlin.

As Joseph Conrad wrote the following year:

> I was pleased with the idea of showing my companions
> what Polish country life was like; to visit the town where
> I was at school before the boys by my side should grow too
> old, and gaining an individual past of their own, should
> lose their unsophisticated interest in mine. . . . I trusted to
> the fresh receptivity of these young beings in whom, unless
> Heredity is an empty word, there should have been a fibre
> which would answer to the sight, to the atmosphere, to the
> memories of that corner of the earth where my own boyhood
> had received its earliest independent impressions.[1]

The crossing of the North Sea and the journey across Germany
were uneventful. The North Sea had been the scene of several of
his sea memories, but he had almost no associations with Germany.
He had only traveled across this country twice and his aversion for
its inhabitants in general killed any curiosity he might have about
them. Even in his youth he had averted his eyes from Germany
as from a threatening phantom and during this journey no mur-
mur of war pierced his deliberate abstraction.

They arrived in Cracow late at night, but when he had eaten a
hasty supper he could no longer resist the call of his memories. He
hurried out into the street with his elder boy: he felt simultaneously
a violent desire and a strong reluctance to see again this city he had
left forty years ago. And now, after so many voyages and adventures all over the wide world, he was amazed to be able to find
his way so easily in the town of his childhood. Little or nothing
seemed changed, for all the years that had gone by.

> To our right the unequal massive towers of St. Mary's
> Church soared aloft into the ethereal radiance of the air, very
> black on their shaded sides, glowing with a soft phosphores-
> cent sheen on the others. In the distance the Florian Gate,
> thick and squat under its pointed roof, barred the street with
> the square shoulders of the old city wall. In the narrow,
> brilliantly pale vista of bluish flagstones and silvery fronts of
> houses, its black archway stood out small and very distinct.[2]

[1] *Notes on Life and Letters*, "Poland Revisited."
[2] Ibid.

In this "coldly illuminated and dumb emptiness," the former master mariner of the British merchant navy, the English novelist with the European reputation saw again the little boy of eleven going to his preparatory school in Florian Street. He saw the apartment in Poselska Street; his father's last days; he saw himself walking in the funeral procession, dumfounded and almost emotionless, on a beautiful May afternoon. It seemed to him that he was about to become the helpless prey of the shadows he had called up. "Let's go back to the hotel," he said to his son. "It's getting late." And that night his mind was invaded not by the idea of a possible war but by a flood of memories.

The next two days he spent wandering about Cracow. His visit had aroused interest and curiosity. Friends and half-forgotten relatives wanted to meet them and vied with one another in belittling their fears of imminent war. No one in Cracow believed in war, although the Austrian Army had been partly mobilized. Crossing Silesia, the travelers had noticed that the bridges were under military guard. "Austria will back down" was the conviction of the best-informed people.

On July 30 in the early afternoon Joseph Conrad took his son to see the university and signed the visitors' book in the Jagellon Library. The librarian, though not related to him, shared his name, Joseph Korzeniowski, and informed him that the library owned the greater part of Apollo Korzeniowski's manuscripts and various letters to intimate friends written about 1860. Joseph Conrad leafed through them quickly, not without emotion, and accepted the librarian's offer to have them copied during the vacation.

In the range of the deserted vaulted rooms lined with books, full of august memories, and in the passionless silence of all this enshrined wisdom, we walked here and there talking of the past, the great historical past in which lived the inextinguishable spark of national life; and all around us the centuries-old buildings lay still and empty, composing themselves to rest after a year of work on the minds of another generation.

No echo of the German ultimatum to Russia penetrated that academical peace. But the news had come. When we stepped into the street out of the deserted main quadrangle,

we three, I imagine, were the only people in town who did
not know of it.[3]

And yet, in spite of everything, they still believed in peace. According to plan, Conrad and his family drove out about ten miles from
the city to visit an old school friend of his who had done brilliantly
in school and at the university and had since then acquired a
world-wide reputation "as the producer of a wonderful kind of
beetroot seed."

As they were having tea in the garden, looking down the gentle
slope of the land at the view of the city in the distance, the possibility of war faded from their minds. Conrad was back in his
native atmosphere. Suddenly their hostess came out with a telegram
in her hand. "General mobilisation," she said calmly. They had to
rush back to town. As they passed through the villages they saw
horses already assembled in the squares and guarded by soldiers,
groups of peasants silently watching officers with notebooks in their
hands, checking off requisitions; women crying on the doorsteps of
their homes.

At last they reached Cracow, and in *Notes on Life and Letters*
Conrad has recorded an impression of their first evening there after
mobilization:

> The shops and the gateways of the houses were of course
> closed, but all through the dark hours the town hummed with
> voices; the echoes of distant shouts entered the open windows
> of our bedroom. Groups of men talking noisily walked in the
> middle of the roadway escorted by distressed woman; men
> of all callings and of all classes going to report themselves
> at the fortress. Now and then a military car tooting furiously
> would whisk through the streets empty of wheeled traffic,
> like an intensely black shadow under the great flood of
> electric lights on the grey pavement.
>
> But what produced the greatest impression on my mind was
> a gathering at night in the coffee-room of my hotel of a few
> men of mark whom I was asked to join. The shutters were
> up. For some reason or other the electric light was not
> switched on, and the big room was lit up only by a few tall

candles, just enough for us to see each other's faces by. I saw in those faces the awful desolation of men whose country, torn in three, found itself engaged in the contest with no will of its own and not even the power to assert itself at the cost of life. All the past was gone, and there was no future, whatever happened; no road which did not seem to lead to moral annihilation.

After forty years of absence he found himself back in his childhood city at one of the most tragic moments in the history of his homeland.

The only thing left to do in the circumstances was to get his family out of the way of possible shells as quickly as possible. They could not get through to Vienna. He decided to leave immediately for Zakopane, a health resort in the Polish Carpathians, about a hundred miles away. After an eleven-hour train journey they found a temporary refuge in the Villa Konstantinowka, where his cousin, Madame Charles Zagórska, and her two daughters were living.

As he had written a few days earlier to John Galsworthy from Cracow, having a crippled wife and a feverish child, he preferred to be stranded in Poland where he had friends, in a place remote from any military operations, rather than try to get through and find himself caught in some small German town in the midst of the armies.

Refugees in large numbers were already crowding into Zakopane. Without being sure that the letter would ever reach him, he wrote to J. B. Pinker on August 8:

> You have no idea of the state of affairs here. Here we are a score of refugees of various nationalities (with a good many children) cut off from all news and expecting to have a very hungry time of it before long.

At the same time he asked the American ambassador in London, Mr. Walter Page (who had lately been his publisher in New York), to get in touch with his colleague in Vienna on his behalf. Before long their situation was further complicated by the declaration of war between Austria and Britain.

There they were, with no resources, no money, no warm clothes, no reliable news about the events swamping Europe. Fortunately his whole family was included in the affection extended to this former Pole. "The Poles' natural generosity found an opportunity to express itself." Madame Zagórska and her two daughters were connected with many distinguished people, and during the two months of his enforced stay in Zakopane Joseph Conrad made several interesting acquaintances, among others Stefan Zeromski, whom he had been wanting to meet.

Two months had passed and the refugees were beginning to lose patience: their hope of getting out of this country was diminishing every day in spite of renewed efforts by friends in Cracow and Vienna. At last they received permission to go to Vienna—nothing but a few words scribbled on the card of an officer, a friend of theirs from Cracow. Once there, they would put themselves in the hands of the ambassador of the United States, who would try to get them through to Italy.

Their farewells were tinged with emotion. Shortly before their departure the Villa Konstantinowka was invaded by a swarm of new friends who wanted to show their sympathy and admiration for the son of the former political prisoner, for this man who, of a different country and a different language, was still one of them by race and tradition.

On October 7, in a blizzard, crammed somehow into an open carriage, the travelers reached a little station. A train already over-flowing with wounded soldiers took eighteen hours to bring them to Cracow, which had changed completely in two months. The approaches to the station were barricaded with barbed wire; an uninterrupted stream of sick and wounded men passed through the refreshment room. Conrad and his family had to wait eleven hours for the train to Vienna, where they arrived without too many tribulations, though only after spending a whole day on a journey which normally took five hours.

As soon as they reached Vienna the novelist was bedridden for five days with a violent attack of gout, while Ambassador Frederick Penfield made every possible effort to get them to Italy. It was October 20 before they reached Milan via Carmona.

Barely a fortnight after they left Vienna the ambassador of the United States was ordered by the Austro-Hungarian government

not under any circumstances to permit the departure of Joseph
Conrad and his family until the end of hostilities.

In Milan, where they spent a few days at the Palace Hotel, they
were at last able to hear some accurate news of the war, to send
for money, to breathe more freely, and to look around for a way
of getting to England. Less than a week later they embarked at
Genoa in a Dutch ship returning to Rotterdam from Java and
calling at London. On November 3, 1914, they landed at Tilbury
on the Thames.

Of this return voyage there remains only this impression, Joseph
Conrad's conclusions to his notes on *Poland Revisited,* written some
months later:

> On that sea-route I might have picked up a memory at
> every mile if the past had not been eclipsed by the tremendous
> actuality. We saw the signs of it in the emptiness of the
> Mediterranean, the aspect of Gibraltar, the misty glimpse in
> the Bay of Biscay of an outward-bound convoy of transports,
> in the presence of British submarines in the Channel. In-
> numerable drifters flying the Naval flag dotted the narrow
> waters and two Naval officers coming on board off the
> South Foreland, piloted the ship through the Downs.
>
> The Downs! There they were, thick with the memories of
> my sea-life. But what were to me now the futilities of an
> individual past? As our ship's head swung into the estuary
> of the Thames, a deep, yet faint, concussion passed through
> the air, a shock rather than a sound, which missing my ear
> found its way straight into my heart. Turning instinctively to
> look at my boys, I happened to meet my wife's eyes. She also
> had felt profoundly, coming from far away across the grey
> distances of the sea, the faint boom of the big guns at work
> on the coast of Flanders—shaping the future.

XIV

Last Days

(1915-1924)

Nobody can say with what thoughts, with what regrets, with what words on their lips they died. But there is something fine in the sudden passing away of these hearts from the extremity of struggle and stress and tremendous uproar,—from the vast unrestful rage of the surface to the profound peace of the depths, sleeping untroubled since the beginning of ages.

The Mirror of the Sea

DURING THE PASSAGE from Genoa to London in this Dutch ship, his feelings for the sea and the particular anxieties involved in wartime navigation, combined perhaps with memories of his early years, kept Joseph Conrad on deck hour after hour. On debarking, the gout which had incapacitated him in Vienna began to torment him again. Back at Capel House, he was not able to stand on his feet for two weeks and was overcome by an insuperable apathy. His mind strayed back and forth over recent tragic impressions of his unfortunate homeland, the prospect of his seventeen-year-old son's enlisting immediately, the dangers threatening all the moral values he held dear, and the futility which, it seemed to him, must forever mark his work.

Yet inertia and discouragement were so foreign to his nature: his nerves and imagination were in such dire need of the concentration and discipline of literary work, that he set to again. The artistic detachment which had characterized his work of recent years now gave way to a new period of introspection. First he wanted to record a few impressions and memories of the visit to Poland, so brusquely interrupted. Then, after finishing this forty-page essay, he spent almost the whole of 1915 recalling in a fairly short story, *The Shadow-Line,* the circumstances that led up to his first command, at one of the most uncertain moments of his life, when chance had played a master role.

In the meantime his elder son had enlisted and was about to be commissioned second lieutenant in a heavy-artillery unit of the British Army. He was not yet eighteen, and for almost three years his father's thoughts were constantly straying toward the plains of Flanders or Picardy. Conrad's thoughts were with French friends engaged in the struggle, too, as is shown by this passage from a letter written in French early in 1915 to Mr. Jean Schlumberger:

> I, who saw the disastrous shadow of '70 fall upon the world, am happy to have lived long enough to see the soul of France affirm its high valor. For it has done so! The moral ascendency is established. No one here doubts it. There remains only the triumph of arms in which I wish you your share of the soldier's glory and the peace of mind of the righteous.
>
> Yours, in unshakable confidence in the future . . .

His son was now on the Armentières front. The father tried his best to hide his anxiety but he spent long hours at his desk with nothing to show for it. Often, incapable of writing, he was forced to dictate. About the middle of 1916, trying to make the best of a bad job, he said to André Gide:

> My health is very bad. Gout in all four paws at present. Just now my left wrist is swollen and it is all I can do to drag myself across the room with the help of two sticks. It is disgusting. My thoughts are lame too and get nowhere. The one thing that survives in me at full strength is unshakable con-

fidence in the future, the profound conviction that the shadow of Germanism is going to vanish from this earth, on which I have roamed so much.

The work he was engaged in did not satisfy him. He was distressed at not being able to contribute to the war effort. Just then the Admiralty, anxious to see the press do justice to the stupendous achievement of the British Navy, invited him to visit several ports to get an idea of the role played by the officers and men of the Volunteer Reserve, that is, the merchant-navy personnel who had been so close to his heart for forty years. In this way he visited Liverpool and Edinburgh, where, despite his precarious health and his sixty years, he quickly seized an opportunity that presented itself. "Now I have the prospect of being allowed to proceed to sea for a fortnight or so in a special service ship," he wrote to a friend on October 15, 1916, "I feel twenty years younger."

He went to the little port of Granton, near Edinburgh, to interview the commodore, Admiral Sir James Startin, who immediately gave instructions that this visitor was to be shown all methods of defense and attack against submarines. Captain Sutherland was charged with this and told Joseph Conrad that he had just been given the command of an armed brigantine submarine chaser. A brigantine—in these days of dreadnoughts and destroyers! When he heard that, Conrad's old master mariner's heart skipped a beat and he wanted to go aboard without delay. In vain they suggested a steamer engaged in a less exhausting service. He would not budge. In the end the Admiralty gave permission, and in St. Andrew's Bay Conrad boarded H. M. S. *Ready,* which had come from Dundee and which at his suggestion was baptized *Freya.* He did fourteen days' patrol duty in quite bad weather in the North Sea in this little sailing ship camouflaged to look like a Norwegian freighter with a deckload of timber. The life, in which he found an echo of the past, was stimulating; the contact with officers and men of the merchant marine awoke memories of his youth and revived his pride in having been one of them. But his health was no longer good enough. He had to go back to his desk. As he was to say the following year:

> With my uncertain health I feel that it's hardly worth while, for the infinitesimal use I may be, to throw away the chance

of doing my own work—such as it is. And I also feel very
wretched about it.[1]

During 1917, growing ever more anxious about his son and suffering from particularly poor health, he spent months in semi-idleness
broken only by the task of writing, for a de luxe edition of his
Complete Works, an Author's Note to each of his books, intended
to specify the events and impressions that had given rise to their
creation.

The Shadow-Line had appeared in March of that year, an occasion
which prompted Joseph Conrad to write to Sir Sidney Colvin, the
friend and biographer of R. L. Stevenson, this extremely important
statement, which applies to his whole work:

> Perhaps you won't find it presumption if, after 22 years of
> work, I may say that I have not been very well understood.
> I have been called a writer of the sea, of the tropics, a descrip-
> tive writer, a romantic writer—and also a realist. But as a mat-
> ter of fact all my concern has been with the "ideal" value of
> things, events, and people. That and nothing else. The humor-
> ous, the pathetic, the passionate, the sentimental *aspects* came
> in of themselves——*mais en vérité c'est les valeurs idéales des
> faits et gestes humains qui se sont imposés à mon activité
> artistique.*
>
> Whatever dramatic and narrative gifts I may have are al-
> ways, instinctively, used with that object—to get at, to bring
> forth *les valeurs idéales.*[2]

Everything was tending to make him look back at the past: inactivity; these prefaces to the books that had been the landmarks of his
last twenty-two years; the war, in which his deepest feelings were
involved. It was impossible for him to be self-detached any longer so
he decided to go to work on a subject which he had often thought
about, which he had had in mind for forty years, but which a sort
of modesty had caused him to keep private: his first experiences with
the sea and with love—the carefree enchanted days of Marseilles.
These he turned into the "story between two notes" called *The*

[1] Letter to J. B. Pinker, undated (1917).
[2] Letter of March 18, 1917.

Arrow of Gold, in which he proposed to depict the twofold passion of a young boy, casting himself back into his own state of innocence and ignorance of the world and of life at the time when he himself had lived through the very events that happen to his hero, and completely disregarding all he had learned from later experience.

From September, 1917, to June, 1918, in seclusion at Capel House, he continued to fan these glowing embers, distracted by many fears for his son's fate. "My heart is like lead," he wrote to a friend.

The armistice came and put an end to his agony but did not interrupt his train of thought. Almost as though he were haunted by the idea of his approaching end and wanted to set himself straight with the future, leaving behind no unfinished work, he had no sooner completed *The Arrow of Gold* and most of the Author's Notes than he returned to *Rescue,* put aside twenty years ago—the book which had caused him so much trouble and discouragement and which he had finally given up in despair. This time he finished it easily within a few months. Almost without effort he found the transition and development that had so long eluded him—the movement, the stress, the whole course of the book—so successfully that there is no perceptible break between the first part, which he left unchanged, and the second, which was added so much later. The reason for this was that throughout all these years Joseph Conrad had hardly changed at all; his temperament, convictions, artistic goals, were firmly determined even before he began to write. He had had almost nothing left to learn while he was writing: one might almost say that his life was over the moment he actually began to write. Moreover, no one realized better than he did himself the fundamental constancy and unity of his work. At the time when he was finishing *The Arrow of Gold* he made this statement to a stranger who had written to him:

Some critics have found fault with me for not being constantly myself. But they are wrong. I am always myself. I am a man of formed character. Certain conclusions remain immovably fixed in my mind, but I am no slave to prejudices and formulas, and I shall never be. My attitude to subjects and expressions, the angles of vision, my methods of composition will, within limits, be always changing—not because I am unstable or unprincipled but because I am free. Or perhaps it may be more exact to say, because I am always trying for freedom—within my limits.

. . . A work of art is very seldom limited to one exclusive meaning and not necessarily tending to a definite conclusion. And this for the reason that the nearer it approaches art, the more it acquires a symbolic character. This statement may surprise you, who may imagine that I am alluding to the Symbolist School of poets or prose writers. Theirs, however, is only a literary proceeding against which I have nothing to say. I am concerned here with something much larger.

. . . All the great creations of literature have been symbolic, and in that way have gained in complexity, in power, in depth and in beauty. I don't think you will quarrel with me on the ground of lack of precision; for as to precision of images and analysis my artistic conscience is at rest. I have given there all the truth that is in me; and all that the critics may say can make my honesty neither more nor less. But as to "final effect" my conscience has nothing to do with that. It is the critics' affair. . . .[3]

Without any delay or hesitation he finished *Rescue* in one continuous process; even the necessity of moving house again did not interrupt him. He wrote the end of this book in a temporary residence, not even waiting to settle down at Bishopsbourne, near Canterbury, where he was to spend the last six years of his life. Yet his determination to bring this long-foundering ship safely into harbor was not due to the advent of peace and had nothing at all to do with the wave of optimism that swept Britain after the armistice. He did not believe that lasting peace was just around the corner. Early in 1919, just after the opening of the Peace Conference, he wrote to Sir Hugh Clifford, an important officer in the British Colonial Service and his friend for many years:

I have been a prey to gout for many days and the state of public affairs does not help recovery in any great degree. True, the war is over, but in the success of our arms I never had a

[3] Letter to Barrett H. Clark, May 4, 1918.

doubt. The future, however, is obscure enough and I cannot defend myself from discontent and anxiety. It may be more instinctive than rational, but yet it cannot be denied that there is something ill-omened in the atmosphere in which the peace and reconstruction problems are being tackled. The intervention of the United States was a great piece of luck for the Western Powers, but luck too has got to be paid for. The assistance came late but the full price will have to be paid for it nevertheless.

Of course my concern is for England, which engages all my affections and all my thoughts. I look at all the problems and incertitudes of the day from that point of view and no other. As to Poland, I have never had any illusions and I must render the Poles the justice to say that they too had very few. The Polish question has been buried so long that its very political importance is not seen yet. In this war it had not been of episodic importance. If the Alliances had been differently combined the Western Powers would have delivered Poland to the German learned pig with as little compunction as they were ready to give it up to the Russian mangy dog. It is a great relief to my feelings to think than no single life has been lost on any of the fronts for the sake of Poland. The load of obligation would have been too great; and certainly, it is better to die than to live under a charge of moral bankruptcy, which would have been unfailingly made before many years. The only justification for the reëstablishment of Poland is political necessity, but that has never been very clearly seen except by a superior mind here and there, both in France and England. Nothing serious or effective will be done. Poland will have to pay the price of some pretty ugly compromise, as you will see. The mangy Russian dog having gone mad is now being invited to sit at the Conference table, on British initiative! The thing is inconceivable, but there it is. One asks oneself whether this is idealism, stupidity or hypocrisy? I do not know who are the individuals immediately responsible, but I hope they will get bitten. The whole paltry transaction of conciliating mere crime for fear of obscure political consequences makes one sick. In a class contest there is no room for conciliation. The attacked class cannot save itself by throwing honesty, dignity and convictions overboard. The issue is simply life and death, and if anything can save the situation it is only ruthless courage. And even then I am not certain. One may just as well defy an earthquake.[4]

At this point a new occupation came along to take his mind off his thoughts. An admirer of his work, Mr. Macdonald Hastings, had had the idea of making a play of *Victory;* this he submitted to the author, who suggested a few changes and who, as a result of this dramatization, began to look at some of his work in a new light. The first performance took place at the Globe Theatre in London in March and the play ran until the middle of June. Its gratifying reception was probably partly responsible for Conrad's decision, six months later, to turn *The Secret Agent* into a four-act play himself and to dramatize one of his short stories, "Because of the Dollars," which became the two-act play *Laughing Ann.*

Two years were spent on these dramatic adaptations and on revising the text of all his books ready for the publication of his *Complete Works.* But these tasks, with which he tried to fight his lassitude, were not so satisfying as a job of a completely new kind, a memorandum he wrote at the request of the Ocean Steamship Company of Liverpool to a committee appointed to study plans for a large sailing ship in which to train future officers of the merchant navy. This revival in the prestige of sail, this recognition of its classic usefulness in the training of seamen, the fact that his fame as an author had not completely eclipsed his standing as a former captain, meant a great deal to him and he devoted himself wholeheartedly to the job.

These were paltry tasks for such a mighty dreamer, but his mind was not idle, his creative spirit was as strong as ever. Having put his whole past in order, he was seized with a new interest in a book that had occurred to him twelve years earlier, in Montpellier, of which he had said to André Gide in a letter in French:

I am going to set to work to deal with Napoleon's influence on the western Mediterranean: two volumes with notes, ap-

[4] Letter of January 25, 1919.

pendices, and statistical tables. And this is to be a novel. I
have an idea I shall never finish it. This notion is not unwelcome to me. There will always be idiots to say: he aimed so
high that it killed him. A fine epitaph!

This Napoleonic novel had lodged itself firmly in his mind, and
since Mrs. Conrad, who had undergone a long series of operations
on her leg, was in need of a warmer winter climate than that of
England, Corsica seemed the natural solution. In fact, Joseph Conrad's intention to visit this island was of very long standing. Mrs.
Conrad has reported that he told her about it as early as 1896 in
Brittany and even lent her two books in English dealing with Corsica, *The Corsican Brothers* and *Barnes of New York*. At that time
he was probably less influenced by Napoleonic associations than by
the memory of Dominic Cervoni and his talks of his native island.
"I didn't go to Corsica for the sake of any novel," he was to write
shortly afterward. To see the Mediterranean again was to look back
upon his own past. Since 1919 Joseph Conrad seems to have been
doing nothing else.

They decided on a three weeks' visit to Ajaccio, traveling through
France by car by easy stages. Two days at the outset were devoted
to visiting, with their older son, the battlefields of the B.E.F. around
Armentières; then the novelist and his wife, assisted by a nurse, went
to Marseilles, via Rouen, Orléans, Moulins, Roanne, and Lyons, arriving there on January 30, 1921, a week after leaving London. From
Marseilles the novelist wrote to his friend J. B. Pinker:

> We arrived here at 5:30 after some more adventures but
> this time amongst the foothills, where I lost the way trying
> for a short cut. But we found a magnificent sunset over these
> wild and barren peaks. Then night set in and we had to lower
> the car as it were foot by foot under an amazingly starry sky,
> creeping down in perfect solitude into a sort of purple-black
> abyss which was in fact, the Valley of the Rhone. Eventually
> we reached Montélimar at about 8 o'clock . . . Great fun . . .[5]

During the first few days of February they settled down in the
Grand Hôtel d'Ajaccio, where they stayed for the whole of the

[5] Letter of January 30, 1921.

two months they spent in Corsica, except for brief excursions. Immediately he arrived, Conrad hastened to acquaint his friend J. B. Pinker's son of his slightly ironic impressions:

> The weather is bad—and no mistake. Cold. Wet . . . A lot of rather smart people are staying in this beastly hotel. Amongst others Col. Hunter, the distinguished polo player with a delicate wife and two stylish girls, of whom one is his step-daughter. Also Capt. Abercrombie, the great authority on Corsica, of which he is supposed to know more than any other man; history, topography, customs, habits . . . shooting, fishing, climbing—and everything else you can think of. I haven't cross-examined him yet. There are also a few mature wandering women and a small proportion of (rather better class) frumps. An atmosphere of intense good form pervades the place. Low tones—polite smiles—kind inquiries—small groups.
> The exploring of Corsica will be no small undertaking—I can see. The confounded island is bigger than one thought, and wilder too.[6]

A month later he remarked sadly to Edward Garnett:

> I am neither the better nor the worse for being here—in health, that is. I would perhaps have done some work if I had stayed at home. But God only knows! Head empty.[7]

His friend Pinker had come with his family to join them. The company of this sharer of his dark days and artisan of his material success played its part in making his stay in Corsica pleasant and in somewhat allaying the irritability which idleness inevitably aggravated. Yet the thought of the novel on which he was not working was always with him, as can be seen from the list of books he borrowed for rainy days from the Ajaccio library. These were: Gourgaud's *Sainte-Hélène;* Stendhal's *Napoléon;* Pellet's *Napoléon à l'île d'Elbe;* Gruyer's *Napoléon, roi de l'île d'Elbe,* which he must have read already in Montpellier in 1907; Rapp's *Mémoires;* Lanzac de Laborie's *Paris sous Napoléon*—nothing but documentary reading

---

[6] Letter of February 5, 1921.
[7] Letter of March 18, 1921.

for the novel he had begun during the preceding autumn and for which he had borrowed a few salient points from a work in French, the Memoirs of the Comtesse de Boigne.

Conrad liked to wander about the harbor of Ajaccio. He had struck up an acquaintanceship with the skipper of a little sailing ship and used to have long conversations with him. Whether he was reliving in this way the old days of the *Tremolino* or preparing for those of Attilio in *Suspense,* there is no doubt that Dominic's radiant spirit permeated his thoughts. But he could not get rid of an anxiety with no apparent cause, an almost continual uneasiness. In a letter in French he admitted to the present author:

> Well! I am nervous, exasperated, bored and so on. . . . We haven't made any excursions. It is quite cold in the afternoons. The hotel is beastly. The Corsicans are charming (I mean the ordinary people) but the mountains get on my nerves with their roads which wind and wind endlessly over precipices. It makes one want to howl.

Toward the end of their stay they spent a few days in Bastia. Conrad had thought of going to the Isle of Elba and then to Sicily but gave it up and decided to shorten the journey. At the very beginning of April they set off home, made the crossing from Ajaccio to Nice, spent a night at Toulon, the approaches to which were soon afterward to give him the setting for *The Rover,* and soon reached the north, stopping only for a few hours in Marseilles and one night in Avignon. On April 10 he was back at Bishopsbourne, determined to go on with his novel of Napoleon.

He tried—with no success—to "get his teeth into this novel," as he put it. To take his mind off it he translated into English a Polish play, *The Book of Job* by Bruno Winaver. In June he wrote to Edward Lancelot Sanderson:

> My work is in arrears. My spirits not exalted. My body full of twinges. I am tired of thinking. I mean thinking on purpose and away from reality—as a daily task.

The whole summer long he grappled desperately with this book. The bad old days of *The Rescue* seemed to have come back. Shut up for hours at a time in his "torture chamber," he managed only a few pages of this book every day—and he was not pleased with those. Faced with his inability to finish *Suspense* within the time he had allowed himself, he gave in to his publishers' urgings to put together a collection of short stories which had appeared at various times in magazines. He was short of one story to complete the volume.

It was to be a hundred-page story, but as had happened before with *Lord Jim,* it grew in the process of being written and proved to be more full-bodied than the author had at first thought. The story became a full-length novel. This was *The Rover,* the result of eight months' work almost without a break despite circumstances that were often discouraging. First and foremost of these circumstances—and one that affected him deeply—was the unexpected death in New York, in February, 1922, of his friend and literary agent, J. B. Pinker, who had been his intimate friend for twenty years, whose devotion to all his interests and affection for himself and his family had been the greatest moral and material support of his literary life.

It is impossible to doubt that in selecting for *The Rover* a French setting and characters, Conrad was influenced by his recent stay in Corsica. For almost three months he had lived in a French atmosphere, had had new opportunities to speak the language. Moreover, for a whole year his thoughts had been incessantly turning toward that part of Europe that lies between the coast of Provence, Corsica, the island of Elba and the Gulf of Genoa. *The Rover* was the offshoot of *Suspense,* as "Karain" was of *The Rescue* and "Gaspar Ruiz" of *Nostromo.*

A keen interest in Franco-British naval rivalry came quite naturally to this former seaman of both countries. This was the implicit subject of his new book and it gave him an opportunity to pay a restrained but heartfelt tribute to these two navies and two countries which held a special place in his heart.

The year before, on seeing Marseilles again and the coast of Provence and the Gulf of Lions—the whole arena of his earliest adventures as a young man and a young sailor—a flood of memories must have engulfed his heart, making him realize how far away were those days of carefree ardor. Nearly fifty years had passed, fifty years of exhausting work, material difficulties, dangerous voyages, disappointing expeditions, solitary interludes, and struggles of all kinds. Now he was seized by a tremendous physical and moral weariness. The uselessness of fighting back overwhelmed him from time to time, strengthening his innate melancholy. Sometimes he would speak of death with great serenity, as of a secret desire. Unique in all his books, the chief character of *The Rover* emerged as a seaman *who desires peace,* who is tired of the sea. The personal association is clearly revealed in a letter he wrote to John Galsworthy about this novel the following year. *"I have wanted for a long time to do a seaman's 'return' (before my own departure)."* This was the state of mind that gave birth to a book whose hero was, after all, a new incarnation of Dominic Cervoni, his former mentor.

After finishing *The Rescue,* he had had quite a bad time in one way or another. The postwar reaction, new anxieties about his wife's health, a growing and exaggerated feeling that his powers were failing—all these had combined to fill him with a sort of uncertainty, a persistent lassitude, which he was constantly struggling against. To one of his French translators, Philippe Neel, he wrote:

> I don't know what's the matter with me. Since I finished my novel *The Rover* in July I haven't done a line worth anything. There I am, wavering, heading nowhere, like a ship deserted by its company, with all its yards slack.

He was working without any inspiration. Tired of struggling with *Suspense,* he thought briefly of dramatizing *The Arrow of Gold,* but the poor reception of the dramatic version of *The Secret Agent,* the first performance of which had been given at the Ambassadors Theatre in London on November 3, 1922, did not offer him much encouragement, as he wrote to the same correspondent in France:

> My play has failed. It was put to death by the press with all imaginable reverence and respect but with a ruthlessness that was really like Ancient Rome.

The year 1923 began better. He had gone back to his novel of Napoleon with some enthusiasm when the prospect of a trip to the United States in the near future again interrupted him. In March he wrote a long introduction to an American biography of Stephen Crane. On April 20 he embarked at Glasgow for New York in the

Tuscania, commanded at the time by Captain David Bone, brother of his friend, the engraver Muirhead Bone. In this way he made his first crossing—as a passenger—of the Atlantic, one of the few oceans he had not become acquainted with during his life at sea.

For many years his New York publisher, F. N. Doubleday, had been asking Conrad to come to his country, where his readers and admirers had been steadily increasing. He was urged to lecture or give informal talks but had been evading this for a long time. The idea of the trip was distasteful to him; lecturing was out of the question because of the very strong foreign accent which he had never been able to get rid of and which, on the contrary, even seemed to get worse with age. He confided to an American friend:

> I will disclose to you that this really is the sorrow of my life;
> for if it were not for that shrinking I would love nothing bet-
> ter than to give readings from my works, for I know I can read
> expressively and dramatically and with good effect. . . .[8]

But he decided to go, after all, on condition that the trip be confined to a simple personal visit to his publisher.

No sooner had the news of his visit been made public than he was swamped with invitations: requests to preside at luncheons, dinners, all kinds of functions. On his arrival in New York he was assailed by journalists wanting interviews, authors desiring advice about their books, sending him theater tickets, and demanding to know his opinion of their plays. He was urged to preside at a poetry contest for a sonnet on the sea. Young girls wrote to him hysterically from California; Harvard students and West Point cadets wanted to see him, a stenographer offered his services for the duration of his visit. Of course there were thousands of requests for autographs too, not to mention a few cranks, among them a man apparently quite sane, who claimed, in beautifully fine handwriting, to have discovered "planetary breathing."

Nevertheless his stay in the United States, which lasted six weeks, was on the whole relatively calm. His publisher kept a strict eye on him to prevent all unnecessary strain. A luncheon with Colonel House, at which he met Paderewski and had quite a long private

[8] Letter to Elbridge L. Adams, November 20, 1922.

conversation with him about Poland, and a lecture next day, May
10, at the house of Mrs. Arthur Curtiss James of New York, were
almost the only exceptions to the quiet life he led. He gave his own
account of this unique lecture in a letter in French:

> On Thursday evening I talked and read a few extracts from
> *Victory* to a very brilliant audience in Mrs. Curtiss James'
> drawing room. More than two hundred people—the very top
> of the basket of fashionable and literary circles. There was
> fighting for invitations, I am told. Well, my dear, with almost
> no preparation it was a success. Laughs; snuffling into hand-
> kerchiefs (at Lena's death); an ovation. I closed the book at
> a quarter to eleven and there was a moment of silence before
> the storm—which quite carried me away myself. Supper at
> midnight. My reception in the press has been excellent. As
> cordial as can be—in the American way, of course. The jour-
> nalists like me—that's a fact. Enormous number of letters every
> day.

From May 15 to 24 he made an automobile trip to Boston and the
surrounding country. On June 2 he embarked at New York in the
Majestic and landed at Southampton six days later. For the first time
in his life he had had some firsthand experience of big liners. For
all the special courtesy extended to him on board, which he had
appreciated, his master mariner's soul had found little pleasure in
this kind of navigation. A few days after his return he said to the
present writer: "Those are not ships, my dear! They're locomotives."

Almost immediately he went back to his solitary hard-working life
at Bishopsbourne, with a new determination to get on with *Suspense*.
He interrupted this task only to write a few pages in memory of one
of his ships, the *Torrens,* and a remarkable essay on "Geography
and Several Explorers."

In mid-September he went to Le Havre via Southampton, together
with his wife and second son, to arrange for the boy to spend a year
with a family there in order to learn French. During this visit he
went to Cuverville in the hope—which was not realized—of meeting
André Gide. On September 15 he left Le Havre for Southampton.
This was to be his last crossing.

He went back to work, but gout interrupted him with renewed violence. In February he wrote to John Galsworthy:

> Your news that you have finished a novel brings me a bit of comfort. So there are novels that *can* be finished—then why not mine? [9]

About the same time he said to another correspondent:

> I have tackled the novel today. What a lot of work there is to do yet! However, I feel not so very much disgusted. [10]

His confidence was shaken and in spite of his courageous nature his fears were growing. In April he said to J. M. Dent, his publisher:

> I have nothing very comforting to tell you. I have had some very bad days recently in one way or another but I am living in hope of a speedy recovery. It ought to come, unless this series of ups and downs ends for good. But I have no reason to think it will.

At the beginning of the same year, 1924, he had heard that the daughter of one of his second cousins had come to London from Poland to learn English, accompanied by another young Polish girl. Early in March these two girls began to spend every weekend at Bishopsbourne, and by a strange twist of circumstances Joseph Conrad thus had regular opportunities to speak his native language— something that had almost constantly been denied him, except for three months in 1914, for fifty years.

On June 11 the Polish minister in London, Mr. Skirmunt, who had long been desirous of expressing the admiration in which this great English writer was held in his native country, gave a luncheon in his honor attended by the whole staff of the Legation. This was Conrad's last visit to London.

The great writer's wife has told us that at this time Joseph Conrad repeatedly expressed a wish to end his days in Poland. The present author remembers conversations of the same period in which the

[9] Letter of February 22, 1924.
[10] Letter to Richard Curle, February 1, 1924.

writer planned an extended stay in France and made inquiries about life in that country. These divergent intentions seem to have been the effect of a vague anxiety which never ceased to trouble him.

During the spring and the first few weeks of summer of that year several of his oldest friends came to see him: Edward Garnett, Cunninghame Graham, and also a certain number of his transatlantic admirers.

His health, which had been so bad for so many years, and the crushing burden of his literary creativeness had worn out his nerves Like the hero of *The Rover,* he wanted rest.

Quite recently he had broken his long-standing habit of wanting to talk far into the night with the friends who visited him for a few days or a few hours, covering a wide range of subjects and giving proof of an amazing breadth of knowledge and a constant lack of affectation.

Despite his weariness, he was as faithful as ever to his work. He was still busy with *Suspense.* "My mind is clearer than it has been for months, and it won't be long before I am back at work," he said to a friend, referring to that novel, which he had again abandoned in order to write an article entitled "Legends," which he envisaged as forming a part of another volume of sea memories, a volume in which he hoped to re-create some of the men he had sailed with. He wrote a few paragraphs of it that day. The next morning, Sunday, August 3, 1924, at eight-thirty in the morning, he slid to the floor from his chair. He was dead.

A worthy ending to a life dominated, despite misfortune, illness, and chance, by an unfailing and perceptive energy.

London, 1924–Paris, 1944.

Appendix

PAGE 50

The passage in which Conrad discreetly raised the veil covering his adolescent loves occurs in the first manuscript draft, entitled *The Laugh,* of what was later to become *The Arrow of Gold.* In the end the writer used only a very small portion of this draft. It is now in London, in the J. T. Wise collection in the library of the British Museum.

"A great austerity of feeling and conviction is not a very common phenomenon in youth. But that young girl seems to have been an uncommon personality, the moral centre of a group of young people on the threshold of life. Her own education appears to have been not finished at the time. But she had the power of an exalted character.

"Of that time he reminds her at great length. And no wonder. He was in love with her. But he never betrayed this sentiment to her, to anybody. He rather affected resistance to her influence. He even tried to cheat his own self in that respect.

"The secret of this resistance is that she was not his first love. That experience had come to him the year before in the late summer of his last school holiday. . . . From the nature of things first love can never be a wholly happy experience. But this man seems to have been exceptionally unlucky. His conviction is that, in colloquial phrase, he had struck something particularly wicked and even devilish. He holds that belief after thirty-five years, and positively shudders at the mere recollection. If she was really devilish, then she may count it for an amazing success. My opinion, however, is that the girl was simply very ordinarily stupid. Stupid people are very prone to turn a genuine display of sentiment into ridicule—and, women, of course, have special opportunities in this way. I imagine that at first he amused her, then he bored her (perhaps was in the way of some more serious flirtation), and discovering that she could make him suffer she let herself go to her heart's content. She amused herself again by tormenting him privately and publicly with great zest and method and finally 'executed' him in circumstances of peculiar atrocity—which don't matter here.

"Perhaps he was unduly sensitive. At any rate, he came out of it seamed, scarred, almost flayed and with a complete mistrust of himself, an abiding fear. He still thought her a superior being, but not yet a devil. That opinion came later. But he said to himself: if that's it then never, never again.

"In common parlance: once bit—twice shy. But there was something more there. He had been bitten all over as it were, enough to make him shy of expressing himself for ever.

"In the case of the other young girl (the one he is writing to after all these years) she obviously awed him a little. And yet it was she who at the last put some heart into him. It was very little that she had done. A mere pressure of the hand. But he had remembered it for five and thirty years of separation and silence."

PAGE 208

Korzeniowski

For a long time various families named Korzeniowski had existed in Poland, though they were not interrelated. As far as Conrad was concerned the sign of relationship was the name *Nalecz,* not Korzeniowski.

Joseph Korzeniowski, the Polish writer, was born in 1797 and died in 1863. Even before 1826 he had written dramas influenced by Shakespeare and Schiller and poems in which Byron's influence was obvious. Later he wrote novels and comedies which give a vivid picture of life in Warsaw and the Polish provinces.

By a strange chance, it was a son of this Joseph Korzeniowski, the Polish novelist, who, as librarian at the Jagellon University in Cracow, received Joseph Conrad in July, 1914, when he came to the library to look through the letters from his father to his friend Kaszewski, which had been deposited there.

As for English inability to pronounce or spell the name Korzeniowski, the most conclusive proof is the list of names attributed to Joseph Conrad on the certificates awarded him by the captains of the various ships in which he served.

We quote them here just as we extracted them from the original documents:

Skimmer of the Sea	Conrad Korzeniowski (in Conrad's own writing)
Duke of Sutherland	C. Kokenowski
Europa	K. Koreinowski

Loch Etive	Konrad Korzen
Palestine	C. Kerzeniowski
Riversdale	Conrad Korzeniowski
Narcissus	Conrad Korzewienski
Tilkhurst	Conrad Kokeniokth
Highland Forest	J. C. Korzeniowski
Vidar	J. C. Korzniowskir
Torrens	J. Conrad ("Korzeniowski" written in)
Torrens	F. Conrad Korzemowin
Adowa	J. Conrad

There is every reason to believe that in the only two cases where this name was correctly written in someone else's hand, Conrad had carefully spelled it out.

PAGE 211

The relevant paragraphs of the letter from Joseph Conrad to Edward Lancelot Sanderson in which he relates the circumstances of his flying visits to Paris in August, 1895, read as follows:

"I have been extremely busy and half the time in Paris. I have crossed the Channel six times (three trips) in a fortnight. I got back from my last flight on the 21st, having accomplished my purpose. As you may imagine Willems [*An Outcast of the Islands*] has been considerably neglected during that time and is not dead yet. I had, really, no time to attend to that murder. . . .

"All this came about unexpectedly . . . and in a rather curious chain of circumstances. First of all I was induced to look up and make use of my old French acquaintances for the sake of a very good fellow called Rorke . . . whom I knew some years ago and who is Hope's brother-in-law. That man owned some 150 claims on the Roodeport gold reef for the last 6 or 7 years. Of course he tried many times to sell, but during the period of depression (since 1889) nobody would look at them. Now the boom came a few months ago and a French Syndicate approached Rorke (out there in Johannesburg) and actually concluded the sale, paid £500 deposit and induced Rorke to part with documents. Then various hitches occurred. Rorke waited, paying meantime the Statutory licences,—to keep his title to the claims. For that purpose he parted with every penny he could scrape,—sold his freehold, farms, etc., etc.: and at the end of last June found himself without a penny, with his documents somewhere on the Continent of Europe,—so that he could not sell to anybody else. He wrote a despairing letter to Hope

praying to be saved. There was no time to lose. The unsophisticated
Rorke was at his last gasp. As the Syndicate was in Paris, I went over
there on the 8th and looked up people I know or used to know. They
were good enough to remember me with apparent pleasure. I enlisted
many influential and sympathetic people for my cause. Pascalis of the
Figaro,—Guesde (a deputy) and the bankers Jullien and Epstein. All
acquaintances of my young days. We found out (to my intense satisfaction) that the French Syndicate were all Germans. We sat upon
them with an order from the President from the X court and ascertained
that they have been trying to sell already to some shady people in London. The documents, reports and plans were also in London. Epstein
got very interested and proposed to come back with me. Agreed. He
snored ignobly all the way. At 8:30 in Victoria. At 10 in Hope's office.
At 3 P.M., same day, the London people (called Thompson) parted
with all the papers for the sum of £100! They had no more chance, of
course, to float a company than any crossing sweeper. As a matter of
fact they are penniless Jews. They tried to bluff and bully,—but col-
lapsed before a firm attitude. Next day Epstein, Hope and I met some
people of good standing here and before evening a Memorandum of
Association of an Anglo-French Syndicate was signed by which they
agreed to buy Rorke's claims for £8,000 cash and 25,000 shares. We
cabled Rorke the terms and he cabled consent. Meantime power of
attorney for Hope arrived from Africa. We concluded the sale. On
the 11th Aug., I was on my way back to Paris with Epstein. He snored
all the way. For two days there was much cabling and rushing about.
In my two trips I managed to get rid of £117. On the 14th (evening)
I left Paris with a check of the French Syndicate of £4,000 in my
pocket. On the 15th the English half was paid up and £8,000 less
expenses (some 370 pounds) were cabled through African Banking
Corporation to the unsophisticated Rorke,—and we all sat down and
wiped our perspiring brows.—Epstein (previously unknown to me) is
a very straightforward Jew and the French part is in very good hands.
The English undertaking is practically floated and shall be put on the
market within the next fortnight as Rorke-Roodeport Goldmine. There
are two Rhodesia directors on the board and the thing is sound. Of
course I do not make anything. My expenses are paid and I shall take
200 shares as an acknowledgement of my services. They wanted to
give me 1,000, which I declined. Yet I must say I was very smart. Nobody was more surprised than myself!

"On the 16th while I sat patting myself on the back I received a
cable from a man called Maharg—also an old acquaintance of mine,
who is now in Johannesburg. Dazzled by my success with Rorke that

fellow offered me the selling of 50 claims on the black reef next to the Minerva Mine (whose shares stand now at 20 per cent. premium). He was so certain of the value of that property that he did not want any cash for it. Was content to get paid in shares only,—but there were conditions about working capital and such like,—all calculated to guarantee the safety of future investors,—and therefore difficult to obtain from the common, garden kind of promoter. After a due amount of reflection I took the thing up. You know that I wanted funds for the base purpose of carrying on a wretched and useless existence. The thing was as honest as such things can be. In fact exceptionally so. It is a first-class property and offered cheap. I could with all due care for my honour (which is my only hereditary property) take it up. And I did so. I went over to Paris again but ultimately I have sold it here in London to people of high repute. It was exciting and interesting work and I had a glimpse into curious depths! Very curious!"

PAGE 280

French admirers of Joseph Conrad will find here some additional details on the itinerary of the automobile trip through France and Corsica made by the novelist early in 1921.

"We leave on the 23rd for Ajaccio for three months." (Letter to John Galsworthy of January 17, 1921.)

Sunday, January 23, 1921		Left London for Calais and Armentières.
"	24 "	Arrived in Rouen late in the afternoon. Dined and spent night at the Hôtel de la Poste.
"	25 "	Rouen, Louviers, Évreux, Dreux (luncheon at the Hôtel du Paradis), Chartres. At 5 o'clock breakdown on the road between Chartres and Orléans; limped into the village of Arthenay; dined and spent night there.
"	26 "	Orléans, lunched, dined and spent night at the Hôtel Moderne. Bought books at a bookshop in the rue de la République. (Letter to Madame F. Aubry, Orléans, 27.1.21. *Lettres françaises*.)

January 27, 1921   Orléans, Vierzon, Bourges (luncheon at the Hôtel de France), Moulins (dined and spent night at the Grand-Hôtel de l'Allier).

"   28   "   Moulins-Roanne (luncheon at the Hôtel du Commerce), Lyon (dined and spent night at the Hôtel Royal, place Bellecour).

"   29   "   Lyon-Montélimar. Arrived 8 P.M.

Sunday,   "   30   "   Montélimar-Avignon (luncheon). (Letter to G. Jean-Aubry, Ajaccio, 23.2.21. *Lettres françaises,* p. 163.) Arrived Marseilles at 5:30. Stayed at Splendide Hôtel, 31, boulevard d'Athènes. (Letter to J. B. Pinker, Sunday, January 30, 1921. 9 P.M. G. Jean-Aubry, *Joseph Conrad: Life & Letters*) (". . . to Marseilles. We stayed there the best part of three days . . ." Jessie Conrad, *Joseph Conrad and His Circle,* p. 226.)

February 5,   "   Ajaccio, Grand-Hôtel d'Ajaccio & Continental. (Letter to Eric Pinker dated 5.2.21. "The weather is bad . . . The exploring of Corsica will be no small undertaking. . . . The confounded island is bigger than one thought.")

"   11   "   Conrad's signature at the top of a page in the visitors' book at Napoleon's house.

"   23   "   Letter to G. Jean-Aubry.

"   26   "   Began to borrow books from the Ajaccio Library. Took out others on March 1, 9, 10, 14, and 21.

March   "   Wrote a preface for the Hugh Walpole Anthology, J. M. Dent & Sons, London, 1922.

"   18   "   Ajaccio. Letter to Edward Garnett.

"   21   "   Letter to J. B. Pinker.

April   "   Left Ajaccio for Nice. Stopped at Toulon. Avignon: visit to the Roumanille bookshop; conversation with Mme. Jules Boissière (Térèse Roumanille).

Bibliography

I *The Polish Cradle* (1857–1874)

POLISH DOCUMENTS AND WORKS

Bobrowski Document: A small handwritten notebook entitled: "For the information of my dear nephew Konrad Korzeniowski," containing a preamble dated December 1, 1869, a full account of the life of Apollo and Evelina Korzeniowska up to their deaths, and a complete statement of accounts showing credits and expenses connected with Joseph Conrad up to February 4, 1890, when the notebook was given to his nephew by Thaddeus Bobrowski.

Bobrowski Note: Manuscript page in Thaddeus Bobrowski's writing with the heading: "Information which may be useful to you."

Letter from Thaddeus Bobrowski to Jósef Konrad Korzeniowski. Nowofastov, September 20, 1869.

Letter from Kasimir Bobrowski to Jósef Konrad Korzeniowski. Loms, December 13, 1869.

Death Certificate of Apollo Korzeniowski, dated Cracow, November 9, 1872.

Baptismal Certificate of Jósef Konrad Korzeniowski, dated Cracow, May 10, 1872. (With a Russian translation of same.)

Document concerning the guardianship of Jósef Konrad Korzeniowski, Cracow, August 2, 1870.

Copy of the decision of the Cracow Municipal Council, December 28, 1872.

(All the above documents were included among the papers sent to G. Jean-Aubry by Mrs. Joseph Conrad after the writer's death.)

Fifteen letters, 1854–60, from Apollo Korzeniowski and one letter from Evelina Korzeniowska, 1857, to Jósef Ignacz Kraszewski.

Two letters from Stefan Buszczynski to Jósef Ignacz Kraszewski. Cracow, January 13, 1870 and Venice, December 7, 1880.

Fourteen letters from Apollo Korzeniowski to Kasimir Kraszewski, from January 20, 1860 to December 24, 1880.

Letter from Madame Teofila Bobrowska to Kasimir Kraszewski. Cracow, June 12, 1869.

(All these manuscript letters are in the Jagellon Library, University of Cracow, Poland.)

Korzeniowski Dossier. Dossier containing the official transcript of the interrogations of Apollo and Evelina Korzeniowska of November 27, 1861, February 26, March 13 and 14, 1862; letters of Evelina Korzeniowska to her husband; Nowofastov, May 10, 1861, Jitomir, June 9 and 19 and July 8, 1861; letter from Madame Teofila Bobrowska to her son-in-law, Jitomir, July 8, 1861; and a note from Jósef Konrad to his father of the same year. (In the National Archives of Ancient Documents, Ministry of Public Instruction & Religion, Warsaw. Notes taken in Warsaw, June 21, 1927 by the present author with the help of Professor Janosz Iwaszkiewicz and Mr. Stefan Pomoranski.)

Apolla Nalecza Korzeniowskiego. *Dla Mileko Grosza.* Pub. Josephat Chryzko, St. Petersburg, 1859. (A copy in the Polish Library in Paris bears a dedication to Caroline and Charles Poradowski "From an unknown but very devoted cousin.")

Id. "Akt Pierwsky." Pub. Igel, Lwow, 1869. Item 4 from the Theatrical Library of Lwow. (Polish Library, Paris.)

Letter from Apollo Korzeniowski (1865) to his cousins Jan and Gabriella Zagórski, quoted in Stefan Zeromski's preface to the Polish translation of *Almayer's Folly* (*Szalenstwo Almayera.* Wydawnictwo Domu Ksiazki Polskiej, Warsaw.) This letter appears in English in the March, 1927, issue of the *Fortnightly Review,* London.

Letter from Apollo Korzeniowski to Julian Bartoszewicz of June 12, 1854, quoted in an article of Kasimierz Bartoszewicz in *Nowa Reforma,* Cracow, June, 1926.

Thaddeus Bobrowski. *Memoirs.* (*Pamietniki Tadeusz Bobrowskiego.*) Lwow, 1900.

Stefan Buszczynski. *Malo znany poeta.* Cracow, 1870.

Michael Rolle. *In illo tempore.* Pub. Brody, Lwow, 1914. (cf. chapter entitled "Zapomniany Poeta" ("The Forgotten Poet") devoted to Apollo Korzeniowski, pp. 29–35.)

Estreicher. *Bibliografia polska,* Vol. II, Cracow, 1874.

Krecki. *Zbior matejatow do historji powstania,* 1863.

W. Danilewski. *Notatki,* 1908.

Korbut, Literatura polska, Vol. III, Warsaw, 1930.

Stanislaw Mleczko. "Conrad's Native Land," *Nowy Kurjer Polski,* August 29 and 31, 1936.

M. Dabrowski. "Rozmowa Z. J. Conrada." *Tydognik Illustrowany,* No. 16, April 18, 1914, p. 308. Photographs of the family contributed by Mrs. Joseph Conrad.

Jósef Ujejki. "O Konradzie Korzeniowski," *Dom Ksiazki Polskiej.* Warsaw, 1936.

RUSSIAN DOCUMENT

Passport delivered to Apollo Korzeniowski by the Ministry of the Interior of the Russian Empire, dated December 2, 1867, signed by Prince S. Galitzine with the date: Chernikov, January 5, 1868. With a German translation of same. (Found among Joseph Conrad's papers after his death.)

FRENCH DOCUMENTS AND WORKS

Joseph Conrad. Letter to Casimir Waliszewski, December 5, 1903. (*Lettres Françaises,* Gallimard, Paris, 1930.)

H. de Balzac. "Lettre sur Kiev." *Les Cahiers balzaciens.* Pub. Marcel Bouteron, Editions Lapina, Paris, 1927.

Sophie de Korwin-Pietrowska. *Balzac et le monde slave.* Librairie Champion, Paris, 1933.

Ladislas Mieckiwicz. *Souvenirs,* Vol. II (1861–72). Gebethner & Wolf, 1927. (Original in French)

G. Jean-Aubry. *Un Héros polonais de Conrad: le Prince Roman.* Pub. A. A. M. Stols, Maestricht, 1933.

ENGLISH DOCUMENTS AND WORKS

Birth Certificate of Joseph Conrad Korzeniowski. The Standard Life Insurance Co.'s Office, 83, King William Street, London. (Document, dated January 21, 1901, found among the writer's papers.)

Unfinished manuscript entitled "The Laugh," rough draft of the first chapter of *The Arrow of Gold,* manuscript of 94 pp., now in Thomas J. Wise collection, London.

Letters of Joseph Conrad to Edward Garnett of December 7, 1897, March 20, 1898, and January 20, 1900, in *Letters from Joseph Conrad, 1895 to 1924,* edited with an introduction and notes by Edward Garnett, The Nonesuch Press, London, 1928.

Letter of Joseph Conrad in *The New Republic.* New York, August 4, 1918.

Gustav Morf. *The Polish Heritage of Joseph Conrad.* Sampson Low Marston & Co. Ltd., London, 1930.

Aniela Zagórska. "Conrad's Visit to Poland." Article published in the periodical *Poland,* New York, issue of September, 1926. p. 545.

WORKS OF JOSEPH CONRAD

A Personal Record, "Author's Note" and Chapters I, II, III and V.

Notes on Life and Letters, "Poland Revisited."

Last Essays, "Geography and Some Explorers."

II *French Days* (1874–1878)

POLISH DOCUMENTS

Bobrowski Document. (See above.)

Letters from Thaddeus Bobrowski to Jósef Konrad Korzeniowski: September 27, October 14, 1876; June 22, August 8, September 14, 1877; May 28, 1878.

FRENCH DOCUMENTS AND WORKS

Note concerning the ships *Mont-Blanc* and *Saint-Antoine,* supplied by the Inscription Maritime de Marseille. January 15, 1925.

Note concerning the crew of the ship *Mont-Blanc,* supplied by the Inscription Maritime du Havre, January 20, 1925.

Note concerning the ship *Mont-Blanc,* supplied by the Inscription Maritime de Marseille, January 22, 1925.

Note concerning the ship *Mont-Blanc,* supplied by the Inscription Maritime d'Oran, January 24, 1925.

Note concerning the ship *Saint-Antoine,* supplied by the Inscription Maritime de Nantes, January 30, 1925.

Note concerning Dominic Cervoni, supplied by the Inscription Maritime de Bastia, May 13, 1925.

Sea Service Record of Dominique-André Cervoni, supplied by the Inscription Maritime de Bastia, 1925.

Documents concerning the voyages of the ships *Mont-Blanc* and *Saint-Antoine* for the years 1874, 1875, 1876, 1877, consulted in the Archives of the Inscription Maritime de Marseille in April, 1926.

Certificate awarded by C. Delestang & Son, shipowners, Marseilles, to Conrad Korzeniowski, dated April 26, 1880, with an English translation of same certified by the French Consul General in London, J. Jusserand, in the same year.

Journal du Havre for the year 1875.

Report of Captain Duteil of the *Mont-Blanc.* (*Journal du Havre,* December 23, 1875.) Marseilles *Sémaphore,* issues of April 25 and June 6, 1878.

François Prieur. "Joseph Conrad et les pilotes de Marseille." (*Le Petit Provençal,* May 15, 1925.)

Judith Gautier. *Le Second Rang du Collier.* Juven, Paris. (In Chapter III there is an allusion to Mrs. Blunt, one of the characters in *The Arrow of Gold.*)

ENGLISH DOCUMENTS AND WORKS

Map of the house in the Rue des Consuls drawn by Joseph Conrad on the back of page 49 of "The Laugh," the manuscript draft of the first chapter of *The Arrow of Gold.* (Thomas J. Wise collection, London.)

Letter from Joseph Conrad to Richard Curle dated 22.7.1923 in G. Jean-Aubry: *Joseph Conrad: Life and Letters,* Vol. II, Wm. Heinemann, London, 1927.

Letter of the chief librarian of the Lowestoft Library to G. Jean-Aubry, October 13, 1925.

WORKS OF JOSEPH CONRAD

A Personal Record, Chapters VI and VII.

The Mirror of the Sea. "The Nursery of the Craft" and "The Tremolino."

The Arrow of Gold.

Nostromo. "Author's Note."

Victory. "Author's Note."

III *Youth* (1878–1883)

POLISH DOCUMENTS

Letters from Thaddeus Bobrowski to Jósef Konrad Korzeniowski of July 8 and September 14, 1878; November 7, 1879; February 12, May 30, June 17, July 10, 1880; May 13 and 30, June 28, August 15, September 11 and 23, 1881; January 20, April 24, May 26 and August 11, 1882.

Letter from Casimir Bobrowski to Jósef Konrad Korzeniowski, April 30, 1882.

ENGLISH DOCUMENTS AND WORKS

Letters from Joseph Conrad to:

H. G. Wells, September 6, 1898.

R. B. Cunninghame Graham, February 4, 1898 (unpublished).

Joseph de Smet, January 23, 1911.

Alfred Knopf, September 5, 1913 (unpublished).

The Sydney Bulletin, March 23, 1916.

F. G. Cooper, October 12, 1921 (unpublished).

Statement of the General Register and Record Office (Shipping and Seamen). Note concerning Joseph Conrad Korzeniowski's sea service. August 7, 1925.

Further note giving ports of call during voyages referred to in preceding document, August 8, 1925.

CERTIFICATES

Skimmer of the Sea. Lowestoft, September 23, 1878.

Duke of Sutherland. London, October 10, 1879.

Europa. London, January 30, 1880.

Loch Etive. London, April 23, 1881.

Palestine. Singapore, April 3, 1883.

Personal Certificates awarded to Joseph Conrad by William Stuart, master of *Loch Etive,* April 27, 1881 and by J. Beard, master of *Palestine,* April 4, 1883.

Letter from Thomas Moxon (of Moxon & Co. Ltd., Brisbane) to Joseph Conrad, March 13, 1917, with a note concerning the burning of the cargo of the *Palestine.*

Letters of Mr. Basil Lubbock to G. Jean-Aubry, October 1 and 6, 1925.

R. L. Mégros. *Joseph Conrad's Mind and Method.* Faber & Faber, London, 1931.

WORKS OF JOSEPH CONRAD
Youth.
Notes on Life and Letters.
The Mirror of the Sea.
Chance (Part I, Chapter I).

IV *Landfalls and Departures* (1883–1887)

POLISH DOCUMENTS
Bobrowski Document.

Letters from Thaddeus Bobrowski to Jósef Konrad Korzeniowski: June 5 and 24, July 9, August 31, 1883; June 13, August 14, 1885; April 5 and 24, July 6 and 20, August 24, September 9 and 30, November 9 and 26, 1886.

Letter from Stefan Buszczynski to Jósef Konrad Korzeniowski, October 28, 1883.

Letter from Casimir Bobrowski to Jósef Konrad Korzeniowski, December 8, 1884.

ENGLISH DOCUMENTS

CERTIFICATES
Riversdale. Madras, April 17, 1884.
Narcissus. Dunkirk, October 17, 1884.
Tilkhurst. Dundee, June 17, 1886.
Certificate of Naturalization of Jósef Konrad Korzeniowski, London, August 19, 1886.
Master's Certificate. London, November 11, 1886.

Letters from Joseph Conrad to Spiridion Kliszczewski:
Singapore, September 27, 1885.
"   October 13, 1885.
Calcutta   November 25, 1885.
"   December 19, 1885.
"   January 6, 1886.
(Supplied by the recipient. These letters appear in *Joseph Conrad: Life and Letters* by G. Jean-Aubry. Vol. I, pp. 79–86.)
Letters from Spiridion Kliszczewski to G. Jean-Aubry, December, 1924 and May 20, 1925.

Works of Joseph Conrad
The Nigger of the Narcissus.
The Mirror of the Sea. Chapter I.

French Documents
Note of the Inscription Maritime de Dunkerque concerning the discharge of the *Narcissus,* March 3, 1925.
G. Jean-Aubry. "Un récent entretien avec Joseph Conrad." *Les Nouvelles Littéraires,* issue of August 9, 1924.

V   *Meeting Almayer*

Polish Documents
Letters from Thaddeus Bobrowski to Jósef Konrad Korzeniowski: April 17, August 20 and September 18, 1887.

English Documents

Certificates
Highland Forest. Samarang, July 1, 1887.
Vidar. Singapore, January 4, 1888.

Letter of Joseph Conrad to J. M. Dent, March 27, 1917.
Letter of J. C. Niven (former chief engineer of the *Vidar*) to G. Jean-Aubry, September 17, 1925.
Conversation with Captain David Craig of the *Vidar,* October 13, 1924.
Note of Captain David Craig, December, 1924.

Works of Joseph Conrad
The Mirror of the Sea. "The Weight of the Burden."
A Personal Record. Chapter IV.
Almayer's Folly

An Outcast of the Islands.
The End of the Tether.

VI *First Command* (1888)

POLISH DOCUMENTS
Letters from Thaddeus Bobrowski to Jósef Konrad Korzeniowski: January 13, March 19 and May 22, 1888.

ENGLISH DOCUMENTS
Memorandum from Mr. Henry Ellis, Master Attendant at Singapore, January 19, 1888.
Letter from William Willis, doctor of the British Legation in Siam, February, 1888.
Letter from Messrs. Henry Simpson & Sons, shipowners, Port Adelaide, Australia, April 5, 1888.
Charts of the Gulf of Siam and the Torres Strait showing the course set by Captain Joseph Conrad Korzeniowski in February, 1888, and September, 1889. (These documents were found among Joseph Conrad's papers after his death.)

WORKS OF JOSEPH CONRAD
The Shadow-Line.
Falk.
The Mirror of the Sea. "In Captivity" and "Emblems of Hope."
Last Essays. "Geography and Some Explorers."

VII *The Pearl of the Ocean* (1888)

POLISH DOCUMENTS
Letters from Thaddeus Bobrowski to Jósef Konrad Korzeniowski: September 24, 1888 and January 3, 1889.

FRENCH DOCUMENTS AND WORKS
Letters from M. Auguste Esnouf (Savinien Mérédac) of Curepipe, Mauritius, to G. Jean-Aubry: February 28, June 28, August 4 and 22, 1931; January 10, May 12 and 26, July 14 and 31, October 29, 1932 and June 10, 1933.
Inquiry of M. Savinien Mérédac into Joseph Conrad's stay in Port Louis, Mauritius in 1888. Five pages, together with supplementary documents as follows:
    1. Letters from M. Paul Langlois to M. Esnouf, June 21, 1931.
       Letter from M. G. Garbert, ship broker, to M. Esnouf, July 6, 1931.

Letters from Mme. L—— to M. Esnouf, June 16 and July 7, 1931.

Letter from Mlle. L—— to M. Esnouf, June 20, 1931.

Letter from M. Joseph Schmidt to M. Esnouf, July 29, 1931.

2. Summary of M. Esnouf's interview with Mme. L—— on July 4, 1931 and of a second interview on July 11, 1931, with a supplementary "Note."

3. Memorandum from Messrs. Blyth Bros. & Co.

4. Letter from M. P. Emilien Pastor to M. Esnouf, July 14, 1931.

Robert Edward Hart. "Clartés anglaises—Joseph Conrad." The Port Louis *Radical,* April 25, 1931.

Savinien Mérédac. "Joseph Conrad et nous," article followed by extracts from a letter from M. Paul Langlois. *L'Essor,* periodical of the Port Louis Literary Circle, February 15, 1931.

Notice concerning Captain J. C. Korzeniowski. The Port Louis *Radical,* Tuesday, June 16, 1931.

Savinien Mérédac. "Joseph Conrad chez nous." The Port Louis *Radical,* Friday, August 7, 1931.

Photographic reproduction of a page in Joseph Conrad Korzeniowski's handwriting in an album. (Port Louis, Mauritius, 1888.)

ENGLISH DOCUMENTS AND WORKS

Letters from Messrs. Henry Simpson & Sons, shipowners, Port Adelaide, Australia, January 19, 1889 and April 2, 1889.

J. G. Sutherland. *At Sea with Joseph Conrad.* Grant Richards, London, 1922.

VIII *Heart of Darkness* (1889–1890)

RUSSIAN DOCUMENT

Official Russian Gazette, No. 49, for the year 1889, with this note in English in Conrad's handwriting: "Russian Official Gazette containing the announcement of the Senatorial Decree releasing Conrad Korzeniowski from his allegiance as Russian subject."

POLISH DOCUMENTS

Letter of Joseph Conrad to Marie Tyska, London, May 20, 1890.

Letter of Joseph Conrad to Charles Zagórski, Sierra Leone, May 22, 1890.

Letters of Joseph Conrad to Alexander Poradowski, London, January 16 and 20, 1890.

Letters from Thaddeus Bobrowski to Jósef Konrad Korzeniowski: June 24, July 22, November 9, December 27, 1890. (Apparently the letters of the year 1889 and the beginning of 1890 have been lost.)

Bobrowski Document. (See above.)

FRENCH DOCUMENTS AND WORKS

Korzeniowski Dossier in the files of the Société Anonyme Belge pour le Commerce du Haut-Congo, Brussels, containing the following items:

1. Letter from M. G. C. de Baerdemacker, ship broker, Ghent, to M. Albert Thys, Brussels, September 24, 1889.

2. Ditto: October 30, 1889.

3. Letter from Messrs. Barr, Moering & Co., London to M. Albert Thys, Brussels, October 31, 1889.

4. Letter from Messrs. Walford & Co., Antwerp, to M. Albert Thys, Brussels, November 15, 1889.

5. Letter from Messrs. Barr, Moering & Co., London, to M. G. C. de Baerdemacker, Ghent, November 19, 1889.

6. Four letters from Joseph Conrad to M. Albert Thys:
   London, November 4, 1889.
   London, November 28, 1889.
   London, December 27, 1889.
   Kazimierowka, April 11, 1890.

7. Two letters from Mme. M. Poradowska to M. Albert Thys:
   Lublin (Poland) November 29, 1890
   Ixelles (Belgium) January 6, 1891

Letters from Joseph Conrad to Mme. Poradowska:
London, February 4, 1890.
Warsaw, February 11, 1890.
Lipovetz, February 14, 1890.
Kazimierowka, March 10, 1890.
Kazimierowka, March 23, 1890.
Kazimierowka, April 14, 1890.
Teneriffe, May 15, 1890.
Libreville, June 10, 1890.
Matadi, June 18, 1890.
Kinchassa, September 26, 1890.

(These letters, and subsequent ones, of Joseph Conrad to Mme. Poradowska are today in the library of Yale University, New Haven, U.S.A. The present author had access to them in London in December, 1933, shortly before their sale. In 1940 they appeared in an English translation published by Yale University Press.) (Translator's Note: *Letters of Joseph Conrad to Marguerite Poradowska* edited Gee & Sturm, Yale University Press, New Haven, 1940.)

Notes of a conversation with Mme. Montrésor, sister-in-law of Thaddeus Bobrowski, Warsaw, June, 1927.

Record of the twenty-fifth voyage of the SS *Ville de Maceio* (May 4, 1890–August 8, 1890) supplied by the Compagnie des Chargeurs Réunis, Le Havre.

Letter from Camille Delcommune to Joseph Conrad Korzeniowski. Stanley Falls, September 6, 1890.

Note of the Société Anonyme pour le Commerce du Haut-Congo, April 15, 1925, concerning Captain Conrad Korseniowski and Georges-Antoine Klein.

Mouvement Géographique, Belgian periodical, issues of May 4, July 20, August 10, September 21, October 19, November 2, December 21, 1890; November 1 and 15, 1891.

Bulletin Officiel de l'État Indépendant du Congo, March and October, 1889 and July, 1891.

Congo Illustré, issues of December 25, 1891; January 17, May 8, July 17, 1892; February 26, August 27, 1893 and February 11, 1894.

G.-M. Alexis. *Le Congo Belge Illustré.* Dessein, Liège, 1888.

Captain Albert Thys. *Au Congo et au Kassaï.* Weissenbruch, Brussels, 1888.

Alexandre Delcommune. *Vingt Ans de Vie Africaine.* Brussels, 1922.

Camille Coquillat. *Sur le Haut-Congo.* J. Lebègue et Cie, Paris, 1888.

Map of the Lower Congo by H. Droogmans, April, 1910.

Map of the Lower Congo, Geographic Service of the Ministry for Colonies, Brussels.

Revue Encyclopédique Larousse, No. 169, 1896. Note on Mme. Marguerite Poradowska.

Letter of M. Mathieu Crickboom to G. Jean-Aubry, Brussels, June 25, 1926, concerning Alexander Poradowski.

Éventail, Brussels. Issue of October 25, 1895. Note concerning Émile Gachet.

Letters from M. L. Guebels, président du tribunal civil, Elizabethville, Belgian Congo to:
André Gide, May 3, 1925
G. Jean-Aubry, September 4 and December 8, 1925; October 14, 1926 and January 10, 1927.

G. Jean-Aubry. "Joseph Conrad au Congo." *Mercure de France,* October 15, 1925. (Fifty reprints were made of this article.)

Marguerite Poradowska:
"Yaga," *Revue des Deux Mondes,* August 1 and 15, 1887.
"Demoiselle Micia," *Revue des Deux Mondes,* December 1 and 15, 1888. January 1, 1889.
"Simple Récit," *Revue des Deux Mondes,* August 1, 1889.

ENGLISH DOCUMENTS
Two letters from the Russian Embassy in London to Messrs. Barr, Moering & Co., April 20 and 26, 1889 concerning Jósef Konrad Korzeniowski's British naturalization.

L. G. Redmond-Howard. *Sir Roger Casement: a character sketch.* Hodges, Fidgis & Co., Dublin, 1916.

Letter of John D. Gordan, Harvard University, Cambridge, Mass. to G. Jean-Aubry, November 11, 1938, concerning the manuscript of "Heart of Darkness," now in the library of Yale University, U.S.A.

WORKS OF JOSEPH CONRAD

Last Essays. "Congo Diary," pp. 238–53. (A French translation of this document figures in G. Jean-Aubry's article "Conrad au Congo." cf. above.)

Photographs of three pages of the original of "Congo Diary," now in the library of Harvard University, U.S.A.

"Heart of Darkness" (in the volume *Youth*).

A Personal Record. Chapters I and IV.

Last Essays. "Geography and Some Explorers." p. 24 ff.

IX *'Twixt Land and Sea* (1891–1894)

POLISH DOCUMENTS

Letters from Thaddeus Bobrowski to Jósef Konrad Korzeniowski: March 10 and 24, April 12, June 6 and 27, July 1 and 30, August 26, October 8, November 9, 1891; September 18, October 1 and 17, 1892; May 22, July 13, 1893.

FRENCH DOCUMENTS AND WORKS

Letters from Joseph Conrad to Mme. Poradowska:
London, February [1], [8], 17 and 27, March 12 and 30, April 14, May 1 and 10, 1891.
Geneva, La Roseraie, June 3 and 10, 1891.
London, June 22, July 2, 8, 22 and 30, August 5 and 26, September 15 and 30, October 16 and 22, November 14, 1891.
Adelaide, March 5 and April 6, 1892.
London, September 4 and 13, October 4 and 19, 1892.
Adelaide, February 4, 1893.
Capetown, May 17, 1893.
Kazimierowka, September 14, 1893.
London, November 5, 1893.
Rouen, December 6, 18, 20 and 25, 1893; January 1, [7] and 9, 1894.
London, January 20, 1894.

Letters of Mme. Poradowska to Joseph Conrad:
[Poland], June 7, 1890.
Brussels, February 4, 1891.

Marguerite Poradowska. "Popes et Popadias," *Revue des Deux Mondes,* November 15 and December 1, 1892.

Prospectus of the Hôtel-pension de la Roseraie, Champel, near Geneva.

Letter from the Doctor of the hydropathic sanatorium, Champel, November 16, 1925.

Journal de Rouen, issues of December, 1893 and January, 1894.

ENGLISH DOCUMENTS AND WORKS

CERTIFICATES

Torrens. London, September 13, 1892.

Torrens. London, July 29, 1893.

Adowa. London, January 17, 1894.

Personal certificate of Captain Cope of the *Torrens'* to Captain Korzeniowski, London, October 17, 1893.

John Galsworthy. "Reminiscences of Joseph Conrad" (*Castles in Spain and Other Screeds,* London, 1927) translated into French in the issue of the *Nouvelle Revue Française* entitled "Hommage à Joseph Conrad," October, 1924.

Conversations with John Galsworthy at Grove Lodge, Hampstead, October, 1925.

Basil Lubbock. *The Colonial Clippers.* James Brown & Son, Glasgow 1921.

WORKS OF JOSEPH CONRAD

A Personal Record. Chapter I.

Last Essays. The Torrens.

X *Within the Tides* (1894–1896)

POLISH DOCUMENTS

Letter from Thaddeus Florkowski to Joseph Conrad, February, 1894.

Letter from Stanislas Zaleski to Joseph Conrad, February, 1894.

Letter from Charles Zagórski to Joseph Conrad, March 21, 1896.

Letter from Mme. Charles Zagórska to Joseph Conrad, March 21, 1896. (All supplied by Mrs. Joseph Conrad.)

Letter from Joseph Conrad to Charles Zagórski, March 10, 1896.

Letter from Joseph Conrad to Mme. Aniela Zagórska, Ile-Grande, June 12, 1896. (Supplied by Mlle. Angèle Zagórska.)

FRENCH DOCUMENTS AND WORKS

Letters from Joseph Conrad to Mme. Poradowska:
  London, February 2 and 18; March 2, Wednesday [March]; Thursday [April], 1894.
  Elstree, April 16 and 24, undated [April].

London, May 2, undated [May], Wednesday [May], Thursday [May]; Monday [July].

Champel, August 8; Saturday [August]; September 5.

London, September 8; October 2, 4, 10 and 23; Wednesday [November], Monday [November]; Thursday [December]; Monday morning [December]; December 27, 1894. Saturday [January]; undated [March]; Friday evening [April], April 2 and 30, 1895.

Champel, May 2, 6, 12, 20, 25 and [30].

London, June 17, 1895.

Letters from the Compagnie Universelle du Canal Maritime de Suez to G. Jean-Aubrey. 1938.

A. Rivoallan. "L'alchimie de Conrad." An article on Conrad's stay in Brittany and its literary consequences. *Bulletin de France-Grande Bretagne,* thirteenth year, No. 96, May, 1930.

Letter from Charles le Goffic to G. Jean-Aubry, August 21, 1930.

ENGLISH DOCUMENTS AND WORKS

Letter from Joseph Conrad to M. Chesson, May 6, 1918.

Twenty Letters to Joseph Conrad. The First Edition Club, London, 1926.

Letters from Joseph Conrad, 1895 to 1924, edited with an Introduction and Notes by Edward Garnett. The Nonesuch Press, London, 1928.

G. Jean-Aubry. *Joseph Conrad: Life and Letters.* Wm. Heinemann, London and Doubleday-Page, New York, 1927.

"An Outcast of the Islands." Article (unsigned) by H. G. Wells in the May 16, 1896, issue of the *Saturday Review.*

Conversations with Edward Garnett over the years 1924 to 1929.

Crosby Gaige. *The Sisters.* New York, 1928.

A Conrad Memorial Library. The Collection of George T. Keating. Doubleday, Doran & Co., New York, 1929. (Letters to Fisher Unwin, Brussels, March 12, 1895; Elstree, [end of March, 1895]; Champel, Geneva, May 18, 1895.)

Jessie Conrad. *Joseph Conrad as I Knew Him.* Wm. Heinemann, London, 1926.

Jessie Conrad. *Joseph Conrad and His Circle.* Jarrolds, London, 1925.

WORKS OF JOSEPH CONRAD

A Personal Record.

An Outcast of the Islands. "Author's Note."

"The Idiots." (In the volume *Tales of Unrest.*)

Reproduction of the manuscript of *Almayer's Folly.* (Sale catalogue of the John Quinn Library, New York. The Anderson Galleries, New York, 1923.)

XI *The Weight of the Burden* (1897-1904)

POLISH DOCUMENTS AND WORKS

Przeglad Literacki (*The Literary Review*). No. 11, Cracow, November, 1896.

Tygodnik mod i powiesci. Warsaw, January 1897 et seq., *Wygnaniec,* Polish translation by M(arie) G(asiorowska) of *An Outcast of the Islands.*

Unpublished letters from Joseph Conrad to Mme. Charles Zagórska (supplied by the daughter of the recipient, Mlle. Angèle Zagórska): June 12 and December 20, 1896; December 20, 1897; January 21, February 6, April 12 and December 25, 1898; February 7, April 12 and December 25, 1899.

Vincent Lutoslawski. "The Emigration of the Talents." *Kraj,* St. Petersburg, issue of March 31, 1899.

Iskierki Warzawski, Warsaw, 1911.

Tyfiodnik Illustrowany, Warsaw, No. 1, 1925.

Elise Orzeszko. "The Emigration of the Talents." *Kraj,* St. Petersburg, No. 16, April 28, 1899.

Pier Grzegorczyk. *Ruch Literackie.* Vol. II, No. 5, p. 136. Warsaw, 1927.

Josef Ujejski. "O Konradzie Korzeniowski." (*Dom Ksiazki Polskiej*), Warsaw, 1936.

FRENCH DOCUMENTS AND WORKS

Joseph Conrad. *Lettres Françaises.* Gallimard, Paris.

Marie Dombrowska. "Le vaisseau embrasé de Lord Jim." (*La Pologne Littéraire,* No. 3, Warsaw, December 15, 1926.

Jessie Conrad. *Joseph Conrad.* Chapters III, IV, V, VI, VII. Gallimard, Paris, 1939.

Valéry Larbaud. Ce Vice impuni . . . Domaine anglais. Chapter dealing with W. E. Henley. Gallimard, Paris, 1938.

Joseph Ujejaki. *Joseph Conrad.* Translated from Polish by Pierre Duméril. Éditions Edgar Malfére, Paris, 1939.

ENGLISH DOCUMENTS AND WORKS

G. Jean-Aubry. *Joseph Conrad: Life and Letters.* Vol. I, pp. 164-339. Wm. Heinemann, London, 1927.

Letters from Joseph Conrad, 1895 to 1924, edited by Edward Garnett, pp. 45-195. The Nonesuch Press, 1928.

New Review, London. Issues of July to December, 1897.

Cornhill Magazine, London. Issue of January, 1897.

Cosmopolis, London. Issues of June and July, 1897.

Blackwood's Magazine, Edinburgh. Issue of November, 1897.

Thomas Beer. *Stephen Crane, a study in American letters.* With a preface by Joseph Conrad: Alfred A. Knopf, New York, 1923.

Arnold Bennett. *Diary.* Vol. I (1896–1910). Cassel & Co., London, 1930.

John Saint-John [John Galsworthy] *The Four Winds.* Wm. Heinemann, London.

Ford Madox Ford. *Return to Yesterday.* Victor Gollancz, London, 1931.

WORKS OF JOSEPH CONRAD
Notes on Life and Letters.
A Personal Record. Chapter V.
Romance.

XII *Under Western Eyes* (1905–1914)

ENGLISH DOCUMENTS AND WORKS
Letters from Joseph Conrad, 1895–1924, edited by Edward Garnett, pp. 199–265. The Nonesuch Press, London, 1928.

G. Jean-Aubry. *Joseph Conrad: Life and Letters.* Vol. II, pp. 1–163. Wm. Heinemann, London, 1927.

Twenty Letters to Conrad. The First Edition Club, London, 1926. (Letter from Rudyard Kipling.)

Three letters from Carlos M. Marris to Joseph Conrad: July 18 and September 6, 1909; and January 11, 1910.

Conversations with Edward Garnett over the years 1924 to 1928 and with Sir Hugh Clifford in 1925.

WORKS OF JOSEPH CONRAD
Notes on Life and Letters. "Autocracy and War."
The Secret Agent.
One Day More.
Under Western Eyes. "Author's Note."
Victory. "Author's Note."

Three handwritten notes on copies of *A Set of Six, Under Western Eyes* and *Victory* that formerly belonged to Mr. Richard Curle.

FRENCH DOCUMENTS AND WORKS
Ida R. Sée. "Joseph Conrad à Montpellier." *Le Petit Méridional,* Montpellier, September 6, 1924.

Letter from Robert d'Humières to Joseph Conrad, April 26, 1907.

Letter from Mme. Marguerite Poradowska to Joseph Conrad. April 26, 1907.

Letter from the Librarian of the City of Montpellier to G. Jean-Aubry, August 17, 1925.

XIII *Poland Revisited* (1914)

POLISH DOCUMENTS AND WORKS

Kazimir Waliszewski. "A Polish Novelist in English Literature: Joseph Conrad." *Kraj,* Nos. 3–7, St. Petersburg, January and February, 1904.

Marjan Dombrowski. "Interview with Joseph Conrad." *Tygodnik Illustrowany.* No. 16, Warsaw, April 18, 1914.

Signature: Konrad Korzeniowski in the visitors' book at the Jagellon Library, Cracow. July 30, 1914.

ENGLISH DOCUMENTS AND WORKS

Passport dated July 23, 1914, granted to "Mr. Conrad Korzeniowski, British subject, 1886, of Russian origin, travelling to Europe, accompanied by his wife, Mrs. Jessie Conrad and his children: Borys (age 16) and John (age 7) Korzeniowski. [Signed] Konrad Korzeniowski."

Passport of the U.S. Embassy, Vienna, dated August 24, 1914.

Letters from Joseph Conrad to:

John Galsworthy, Grand–Hôtel, Cracow, August 1, and Capel House, November 15, 1914.

J. B. Pinker, Villa Konstantinowka, Zakopane (Galicia), August 8 and September 15, 1914 and Palace Hotel, Milan, October 20, 1914.

Aniela Zagórska. "Conrad's Visit to Poland." *Poland,* New York, issue of September, 1926.

Letter from Frederick C. Penfield, U.S. Ambassador, Vienna, to F. M. Doubleday of Doubleday, Page & Co., publishers, New York, December 9, 1914.

G. Jean-Aubry. *Joseph Conrad: Life and Letters,* Vol. II, pp. 7–8 and 158–62. Wm. Heinemann, London, 1927.

WORKS OF JOSEPH CONRAD

Notes on Life and Letters. "Poland Revisited" and "First News."

FRENCH DOCUMENTS AND WORKS

Casimir Waliszewski. "Un Cas de Naturalisation Littéraire: Joseph Conrad." *Revue des Revues,* December 1903, pp. 734–48.

Letters from Joseph Conrad to Casimir Waliszewski (1903–04) in *Lettres Françaises,* p. 52 ff. Gallimard, Paris, 1930.

ITALIAN DOCUMENT

Visa of the Italian Embassy, Vienna, October 18, 1914.

XIV   *Last Days* (1915–1924)

ENGLISH DOCUMENTS AND WORKS

Letter from Vice Admiral Harry G. Stileman to Joseph Conrad, Liverpool, September 27, 1916.

Letter from Admiral Sir Douglas Brownrigg to Joseph Conrad, October 13, 1916.

J. G. Sutherland. *At Sea with Joseph Conrad*. Grant Richards, London, 1922. (With a preface by Joseph Conrad.)

Letters from Joseph Conrad, 1895 to 1924 edited by Edward Garnett, pp. 266–335. The Nonesuch Press, London, 1928.

G. Jean-Aubry. *Joseph Conrad: Life and Letters*. Vol. II, pp. 164–348. Wm. Heinemann, London, 1927.

A collection of approximately one hundred letters sent to Joseph Conrad by various American individuals during his stay in New York. (1923)

R. B. Cunninghame Graham. "Inveni Portam—Joseph Conrad." Article published in the *Saturday Review* of August 16, 1924 and reissued as a pamphlet under the same title (one hundred and fifty-seven copies) by the Rowfant Club, Cleveland, 1924.

Richard Curle. *Joseph Conrad's Last Day*. A thirty-page pamphlet (one hundred copies) privately printed. London, 1924.

Letters of Joseph Conrad to Marguerite Poradowska, Yale University Press, 1940. Letter of December 30, 1920 in an English translation.

FRENCH DOCUMENTS AND WORKS

Joseph Conrad. *Lettres Françaises*. Gallimard, Paris, 1930.

Special issue of the *Nouvelle Revue Française* devoted to Joseph Conrad, October, 1924.

INDEX

(The names preceded by an asterisk are characters in Conrad's writings.)